D0900234

Beyond the
Tenure Track

COMMUNITY COLLEGE OF
ALLEGHENY COUNTY

PE
64
.P48
A3
1991

Beyond the Tenure Track

Fifteen Months in the Life
of an English Professor

James Phelan

OHIO STATE UNIVERSITY PRESS ▪ *Columbus*

Copyright © 1991 by the Ohio State University Press.
All rights reserved.

Library of Congress Cataloging-in-Publication Data

Phelan, James, 1951–
    Beyond the tenure track : fifteen months in the life of an English
professor / James Phelan.
        p. cm.
    ISBN 0–8142–0535–6
    ISBN 0–8142–0546–1 (pbk.)
    1. Phelan, James, 1951– —Diaries. 2. English teachers—United
States—Diaries. 3. College teachers—United States—Diaries.
4. English philology—Study and teaching (Higher)—Ohio—Columbus—
History—20th century. 5. Ohio State University—Faculty—Diaries.
I. Title.
PE64.P48A3 1991
807.1'1'092—dc20
[B]   90–41403
                                                                            CIP

The paper in this book meets the guidelines for permanence and durability of
the Committee on Production Guidelines for Book Longevity of the Council on
Library Resources. ∞

Printed in the U.S.A.

9 8 7 6 5 4 3 2 1

for Betty

Contents

Preface

In a sense, this book exists because I was one of those weird people who always liked school, liked it so much that the idea of never leaving it soon became very appealing. By the time I was in fourth or fifth grade, I began to imagine myself as a teacher, to guess how the process of my education looked from my teachers' viewpoints, to think how I'd conduct that process if I were in charge. As I progressed through grammar school, high school, college, and graduate school, my desire to become a teacher remained constant, even as the form of the desire altered. The stage I was in became the stage at which I wanted to teach. Now, twelve years beyond the Ph.D., securely tenured in the English department at Ohio State University, I am used to the idea that with no new formal stages to experience, no meta-Ph.D.s to pursue, I occupy a place I set out to reach a long time ago. This book, a journal that I kept over the fifteen-month period from January 1987 to March 1988, is an attempt to convey the quality and texture of life in that place: its ups, downs, and level places; its satisfactions, frustrations, and routines; its successes, disappointments, and standoffs. As I advanced in writing the journal, I realized that I was invested not only in explaining my version of academic life to a hypothetical audience of the curious ("What's it like being an English professor?") and the noncomprehending ("So you only teach eight hours a week? Must be nice") but also in assessing it myself. Now that I've gotten what I've wanted, what do I make of it?

Like any journal, this one is selective, and the title of the book suggests some of the principles of my selection. The emphasis is on the events of my work life, but I could not fully describe life beyond the tenure track if I talked only about courses, students, colleagues, committees, and research. Because my "living with tenure" has been influenced—in more ways than I can record—by my marriage to Betty Menaghan, an associate professor in OSU's sociology department, I have included some parts of the narrative of our life together. My work life has also been significantly influenced by our two children, Katie and Michael (aged seven and four in January of '87), and I have therefore tried to give some sense of them and their interactions with Betty and me as well. Finally, my living with tenure has been affected by my career as an aging jock, and I have included some of my experiences in that line. The entries themselves range from discussions of somewhat esoteric debates in contemporary critical theory to accounts of academic bureaucracy, and from vignettes about life in the two-career family to reports about road races I have run. But the center of the book is my work as a university professor.

In January 1987, I was fifteen months into a twenty-seven month stint of working without a quarter off (though I did not have to teach every one of those nine quarters), and I anticipated carrying the journal through until December 1987 when I would enter a wonderful region called ON LEAVE. But as anyone who stays with the journal into the fall of 1987 will see, some events demanded to be followed into the early months of 1988. Despite being constrained in this way by the narrative of my life, the book is only partly a narrative. Each of its five sections tries to capture the changing rhythm of my work and my feelings about its progress, but the journal's development certainly does not follow the trajectory of a novelistic plot. Instead, like much other journal writing, it is frequently digressive upon the incident, as incidents provoke reflections that transform the mode of the book from narrative to essay and then back again. The book does not seek to advance any grand thesis, but it does push several small ones. It is not an exposé of what is wrong with the academy, but it does occasionally criticize and occasionally honor the institutional structures of the academic life. The book decidedly does not aspire to do a kiss-and-tell job on the English department—or any other person or unit—at OSU, but necessarily talks about my colleagues and especially about my students. (I have used the real names of my colleagues, but have changed the names of my students except where they gave me permission not to or where they were performing publicly.)

In recounting the experiences and thoughts of someone-in-the-midst-of-things, the journal describes some general conditions of academic life in America these days—or perhaps better, what part of the academy looks like from a particular vantage point within it. At the same time, of course, my experiences in the academy influence the way I look at other parts of my life. Although I do not claim to speak for anybody other than myself, and although I am acutely aware that all the events I recount here could—and no doubt would—be given a different significance if narrated by someone else, I assume that I am not unique, that my experiences have been partially shaped by institutional and cultural forces and conditions that also partially shape the lives of other academics. Although this is a personal book, I assume that many of its readers will find some of its territory more familiar than foreign.

Acknowledgments

A *book* (as someone famous should have once said) is not made by weirdness alone, and I would like to thank several people who have been crucial to the making and shaping of this one. Without the support of two people at the Ohio State University Press, I'd still be planning to write *Beyond the Tenure Track*—someday. Peter Givler, director of the press, responded with enthusiastic encouragement to my first entry and general plan, thereby licensing me to believe that what I had to say might be of interest to someone besides my mother. Alex Holzman, assistant director, responded with generosity and good advice to the installments I periodically submitted, enabling me to quiet my recurring doubts enough to keep writing.

Besides Peter and Alex, many readers helped me discover the statue inside the large slab of rock I initially quarried. My colleagues Murray Beja, Julian Markels, and Jim Battersby helped me to chip the incidental away from the (more) essential and to distinguish between some felicitous and infelicitous uses of my hammer and chisel. A reader for the press, Francis Russell Hart, provided the most extraordinary report I've ever seen. His long and perceptive disquisition on journal writing, this journal, the profession of English studies, and many, many of my entries was a very useful guide to my decisions about where else to place the chisel and how hard to swing the hammer. My friend Jamie Barlowe-Kayes offered even more valuable and extensive advice. Her insightful questions and comments led me to look at the events I report and the way I report them from many different angles, a process of envisioning that enabled me to understand more fully the implications of many entries and to develop the principles underlying the book's final shape.

At every stage of the writing—from the initial concept to early efforts to evolving understanding to final revisions—I have also been influenced by advice and feedback from my best friend, partner, and spouse. But

even more important for the book's existence is the life I have with Betty
Menaghan, the larger sustaining context in which my work and hers are
carried out. In recognition of that context and with gratitude for all that
we have shared in our life together—before tenure and after—I dedicate
this book to Betty.

Juggling—and Wobbling

Sunday, 4 January 1987

End of Christmas break. Tomorrow morning the quarter and its round of classes, meetings, student conferences, papers to read and write start up again. As I think about reengaging, I'm also resolving to carry out my oft-deferred plan of keeping this journal, making a record of what that engagement is like, voicing the thoughts playing in my head as I go about my work. Some of these thoughts have recurred frequently since September when Betty's tenure became official.

Two tenured jobs at the same university: the long climb that Betty and I began in graduate school almost fifteen years ago, when we had not read any guidebooks and were blissfully ignorant of the path, has led us, if not to a Summit of Academe, at least to a place where we can catch our breath and contemplate the prospect before us. It's a nice view. Though the horizon isn't cloudless and the terrain's not postcard-perfect, most of what we see from here looks good.

We've had a typically varied path up—in some places it's been very smooth, in others rough, and we've done our share of running, walking, dawdling, crawling, and resting. At times—especially after the arrival of Katie and Michael—we've felt that all we were really doing was juggling in place. But I suppose the broad outline of our story is not all that different from the stories of other people getting established in academia or in other professional pursuits: starting out with more ideals than knowledge, learning how things actually work, integrating the knowledge with the ideals, worrying about whether one is able to make the grade, bitching about the whole process of certification and evaluation, questioning whether it's worth succeeding, and then, after an apprenticeship of several years and with some combination of ability, hard work, and good fortune, making it. "When the gods want to punish us, they answer our prayers," Oscar Wilde said. What do the gods have in mind for us?

So far it doesn't seem that they're after punishment, but perhaps that's because the place we're in isn't exactly the place we prayed to reach. When we left Boston for graduate school at the University of Chicago in the fall of 1972, neither Betty nor I would have said that our ideal job would be at a huge university in the Midwest—a small liberal arts college in New England was more what we born-and-bred Easterners had in mind. Now here we are in Columbus, decidedly not an Eastern city, teaching English and sociology on the second largest campus in the country, a place where football is king and "Buckeye" is a term referring not to a vision problem but to a loyal Ohioan and a loyal Ohio Stater—it is, improbably enough, a term of honor. And our departments—especially Betty's—are not the models of collegial intellectual inquiry that we had prayed to find. Yet on the whole, we like it here.

After ten years, we are finally beginning to think of Columbus as our permanent home. Given that we moved around a lot during our first seven years of marriage, and given our feelings about Ohio State and Columbus, we have until recently been inclined to think of our residence here as provisional and tentative. We weren't sure if they would keep us, weren't sure how much we wanted to stay. But lately "Columbus, Ohio" seems less an answer to a question in a geography quiz on state capitals and more like a plausible, if not entirely natural, answer to the question "Where do you live?" I still can't call myself a Buckeye, and I feel awkward referring to the football team in the first person plural, but the bicoastal arrogance that we ourselves once viewed the place with now seems silly (in memory) and obnoxious (when expressed by one of our East or West Coast relatives and friends).

As I think more specifically about my status as a tenured academic, I am reminded of a scene in the movie version of *The Right Stuff*—a rather ordinary scene that nevertheless affected me very much. Gordo Cooper, played by Dennis Quaid, is driving cross-country to Edwards Air Force Base with his wife sitting beside him and his two sons in the back. The sun is shining, the top on the convertible is down, and Gordo's spirits are high. He talks with his wife about their move to Edwards as the beginning of their way up the Air Force ladder and cajoles her into sharing his optimism, his confidence, his high spirits. The scene ends with his getting her to ask, "Who's the best test pilot you ever saw?" and his answering, with a Cheshire Cat grin on his face, "You're looking at him." The scene is referred to several times later in the movie, most notably at the end, when a reporter asks Gordo the same question. He starts to answer, "Chuck Yeager" (everybody's example of the pilot with the right stuff) but then gets interrupted and changes his mind. The reporters applaud wildly when he says, "You're looking at him," and the audience gets the point about how the Mercury program and its attendant media attention have transformed the test-pilot subculture.

Yet the real power of the early scene for me is the way it captures a moment in a life very different from mine. Watching it, I was pierced with a pang of—well, what? Envy? Desire? Loss? Regret? Probably some mixture of these. It hit me that since entering graduate school, I've never felt that full of confidence, chutzpah, and high spirits about my career, and at thirty-five I know I'll never feel that way. I am not Gordo Cooper nor was meant to be, but I believe there's more than a personality difference involved.

When at the age of twenty-one I started graduate school at Chicago, I wasn't really ready for it. Like many of my classmates and many of the students I now see at OSU, I spent a good part of the first year trying to figure out what the professional study of literature was all about. The process was complicated by a fierce, though often friendly, competition among our large class for admission to the Ph.D. program. I got off to a lousy start my first quarter and so felt that my doubts about my ability were confirmed by the external evidence of my grades. During all our time at Chicago I never got completely over that quarter. We went to New Jersey that Christmas and returned in time for winter quarter. As we drove back into the city, I had a physical reaction that recurred every time we came back to Hyde Park after more than two days away. As we approached the Chicago Skyway, I felt a tightening in my neck muscles that gradually increased as we got closer to the university; it seemed that some heavy object was hovering over me, making me stiffen and huddle against myself. No chutzpah in my ride to the training grounds.

I did eventually feel competent as a graduate student—and eventually confident enough in my ability to have only minimal tenure anxiety—but I've never had the kind of omnipotent feeling that Quaid conveys. I have had euphoric moments. I walked on air for a week after getting this job at OSU. My heart often filled with joy during my first quarter of teaching. I've felt wonderfully complimented by people I respect. But a key ingredient in all that euphoria has been gratitude: thank God, they hired me; thank God, I'm doing what I've dreamed of doing; thank God, he's a generous man. Getting tenure in my case did not produce that euphoria, perhaps because I felt it was something I had earned rather than something I'd been given. And though there was something very satisfying about finally having tenure, it certainly didn't give me Gordo's cockiness. But it has made me able to do what I could not do as a graduate student or even as an assistant professor: drive into Chicago without feeling my neck muscles involuntarily tighten.

Monday, 5 *January* 1987

Back to work; a hectic day, though no one thing was especially demanding. It took me over two hours to sort through all the mail that had accumulated in my mailbox over the break. And I didn't read it all. The phone rang constantly, as grad school applicants and current students wanted to talk with the director of graduate studies about the status of their applications or the reasons why they thought one requirement or another should be waived. I had many short visits with colleagues and students, and somewhere in there the first meeting of my critical writing class. I'm surprisingly tired.

Actually, today was the kind of day I would have welcomed when I first came here and wanted to feel a part of the place. When I arrived in the fall of 1977 as a twenty-six-year-old assistant professor, I desperately wanted to connect with colleagues and especially students, to fill—or at least play—the role of the faculty member whose office hours would be crowded with interested, eager students. That first quarter I had two courses, one at eight, the other at twelve, Monday to Thursday, and since I wasn't going anywhere anyway, I held office hours between nine and twelve. I used to sit there, working at this and that, waiting and hoping that some one or other of my students would come in and talk. They usually didn't. Around the middle of the quarter I required them to come for conferences—as much for my own sake as theirs—and in a few cases we got beyond the main agenda of discussing their papers or exams. But even among that small group, very few came back. As I remember that quarter, I smile at my own eagerness and naïveté: I was teaching sophomore-level courses that most of the students took to fulfill a requirement. Most had little or no interest in me beyond how I might work them, grade them, and entertain them on their way to checking off that requirement.

I think too that I waited so eagerly because it was a lonely quarter for me: Betty and I had just begun a year of commuting between here and Washington, D.C.; my new colleagues, though generally warm and friendly, had their own workloads and pressures to deal with. My life was focused very intently on those two classes and the students in them. I dedicated most of my waking hours to planning for and assessing those two forty-eight minute sessions a day. Although I think that in many ways I'm a better teacher now than I was ten years ago, I know I'd be better yet if I could still bring that same intensity of interest, concern, and hope to all my classes.

Wednesday, 7 January 1987

This week marks the beginning of my eleventh year of teaching at OSU. I'm not sure I could easily tally up what I've learned about this sometimes simple and rewarding, sometimes complex and frustrating activity, but I do feel more aware, more respectful of its difficulty than I did when I began. Should anyone expect to be able to teach students how to write well in ten weeks? Can one expect to teach a new group of students about the rewards of the life of the mind every quarter? Should anyone believe that as a thesis adviser he or she can give the proper balance of guidance and freedom and then go on to judge a student's work with the proper balance of sympathy and rigor? For each student? Can one do that while remembering that in addition to the life of the mind students writing theses also live very acutely the life of the emotions?

I've been worrying these questions about thesis advising as I've taken on more M.A. and Ph.D. students and especially as I've been replaying in my head what happened with my most recent M.A. candidate. Lee finished a worthwhile thesis in September, but the process was far from pleasant for either of us. Last July a colleague and I decided at her oral exam that the thesis was not acceptable. After the three of us had our session and my colleague and I had expressed what we thought was wrong and how she ought to revise, Lee and I talked briefly.

"Why didn't you call me?" she asked, referring to our agreement that if I thought the thesis wasn't passable, I'd tell her and we wouldn't go through with the examination.

I had an answer for that one, but then she asked,

"So from here on I can work with you more closely? I don't have to worry about bothering you too much?"

These questions hurt. With them, Lee had in effect shifted some of the burden—and pain—of her failure to me. Well, I suppose that's why God gives graduate students advisers. And I trust He knows that I don't really begrudge her the impulse and the attempt to share her misery.

But I couldn't think of that right away. She made me feel that I had indeed let her down, that I had not done an adequate job, had shirked my responsibilities, and had betrayed her. Not a feeling that one likes wallowing in. With distance, I see more clearly that I have not done as well by Lee as I should have, but I also think the history of her thesis reveals something about the complexities of advising and being advised.

After starting off in one direction and hitting a dead end, Lee proposed doing something on a particular linguistic effect that she had noticed in just a few pieces of literature. She wanted to identify a particular kind of image, one that could be expressed only verbally, and not photographically or cinematographically. I thought she had a worthwhile case to make, even if she couldn't find many examples of the effect. I told her to read Longinus on the sublime and think of her project as parallel: they were both trying to define an effect wherever it might be found. I also recommended that she start reading poetry and looking for cases. She was, I thought, pretty well set. Then the rest of life, hers and mine, intervened.

She began to take courses in science with the idea that she would learn enough to become a science writer. As she explained to me, it was important for her to do well in those courses to prove to herself that she could think as a scientist, and to do well required that she devote almost all her time to studying her chemistry. Though I wanted her to finish, I respected her feelings and didn't push her to work on the thesis. By last winter, however, I was telling her that she ought just to write what she could, to get the thing under way. For one reason and another, she never went very far with it until last spring, when she gave me a small piece of the introduction. Her focus was shifting from her special image to poetry that employed the findings of contemporary science, but she had not yet gotten down to cases. I was still operating with the assumption that what she most needed to do was write out her ideas, so I encouraged her to go ahead with what she had, and I suggested that she bring some poems into the discussion right from the outset.

More time goes by and now it's summer quarter and she has to finish before her support as a teaching associate runs out. Furthermore, she has to finish in July because her second reader, Jim Battersby, is going to be away for the month of August. About two weeks before her deadline, she gives me another small piece. It sounds O.K., though I still don't have a clear sense of the whole project. Then she wants to move the final exam up a week so she can take a trip to Vermont with a friend. Thinking that the extra incentive will be good for her, I agree. But that means Jim and I won't get a full version of the first draft until two days before the oral. I'm to call her if it's not good enough to defend. Busy with other obligations, I don't get very far with it that day, and having to teach the next, I don't finish it until the night before the exam.

The draft's weak. She's written a polemic against poets who an-thropomorphize nature and for the incorporation of the findings of science into poetry. She has adopted the zeal and tunnel vision of a convert to a narrow-minded religious sect. Her work, for example, shows no awareness of how anthropomorphizing nature can serve ends that have little to do with getting nature right.

Still, there are some good readings of individual poems. Let's go ahead with the oral. Though Jim finds the thesis even weaker than I, Lee says enough good things about her material that we decide that the thesis is salvageable. At the same time, we all know that the dredging will not be easy. And there Lee stands, let down, disappointed, and feeling betrayed.

How should I have handled it differently? From my perspective, the key problem turned out to be that I didn't have enough time between getting the draft and conducting the oral. From Lee's, it is that she didn't get clear signals about the problems in the early parts she sent me. In retrospect, I can see that I should have insisted on reading the whole first draft before allowing her to schedule the oral. But I trusted her, had confidence in her ability. And I'm sure she trusted me to give her the feedback on the early parts that would let her know whether she was on the right track. She probably thinks I made a mistake in letting her schedule the oral—or at least in not calling it off. It seems that we trusted each other too much.

Thursday, 8 *January* 1987

With such a disruptive middle, I suppose I should not have expected the story of Lee's thesis to end smoothly—but I did and it didn't.

After Lee returns from Vermont, we meet and discuss the plan for revision. What was clear to me is not clear to her: she needs to drop the polemic, with its unjustified privileging of the scientific view, and explore instead how some twentieth-century poets have incorporated the findings of science into their poems. The thesis can take its shape from Lee's identification of some general strategies of that incorporation, and it can derive its force from her analysis of individual works. In the course of our discussion, she says several things that reveal her misunderstanding of what Jim and I tried to explain, but eventually we work through those issues and develop a plan and a timetable for revision. She'll aim for the end of August. If she can't do it by then, she can turn everything in by the last day of summer quarter break and graduate in the fall without having to register.

When she doesn't do much in August and drags her feet in the first week of September, I am not sympathetic to her problems—I think that she is just procrastinating and I'm more pained—but I try to be supportive. I appeal to her as one runner to another: you're at the twenty-mile mark in the marathon, you just need to push for the last 10K. Finally, in the last week before the deadline, she gets done, turning it in piece by piece. It's a lot better, clearly acceptable. She is focused on the poems, has worthwhile things to say about them, and in so doing teaches me something. If she had turned this in last July, there'd have been no problem. Still, part of me would like her to revise even this version. But I know that she doesn't have the time.

Then with less than forty-eight hours left, she begins a computer nightmare. First she loses a good part of her document, then she can't get it to print right. It's easy to be sympathetic to that, but I'm still muttering to myself, Why did it take you so damn long to be at this stage? With great persistence at the end and one last extension from the graduate school, Lee gets done. I'm pleased, but I also feel that something has been spoiled in the process: she has sunk in my estimation, and I suspect that I have sunk in hers.

The story has an epilogue. In November I asked Lee for the copy of the final version that she had promised me. She balked, confessing that she hated it—even calling it shit. She especially didn't want to give a copy to Jim, who has never seen the final version. More pain here: I approved it, after all—if she hates it, what does she think of my judgment? After a long talk in which I argued that she owed Jim a copy, since he trusted us enough to sign the approval form without seeing the revisions, she agreed to give us both copies. They've never come. Instead, she gave me a long note explaining why she is uncomfortable with the work she did. She felt forced to give up a position that she believed in—the validity of the scientific perspective that she was privileging in the first draft.

I think she is still confused about what she was claiming there and about how the revisions affect the force of her claims, but I now have a better understanding of why it took her so long to move from the oral to the final version. I also can see, and perhaps this is the chief lesson for me, that I was blind to a good part of what she was thinking and feeling then, that I should not have grown impatient with her for dragging her feet so much as I should have started questioning my own understanding of where she was. At the same time, seeing what I do now leads to other disappointments and self-questioning. I thought I had explained well what the problems were, what she had to give up and what she didn't in her claims about the Truth of Science. She was quick to admit that she didn't want to be in the position of saying that poetry should always follow science. So what does she think she has now claimed? Did I do a lousy job explaining it? Or is this confusion a sign of Lee's weakness as a conceptual thinker? Neither of these hypotheses is especially welcome.

One telling thing Lee did say in our last talk should probably stand as the last word on the disappointment of the whole experience. She chose Jim and me to be her readers because she thought if she did something that satisfied us, she would feel that she had really done something worthwhile. Now here she is with a thesis that we've approved and that she wants to forget.

Friday, 9 January 1987

End of the first week. Today I had the first meeting of Introduction to Graduate Study, the second half of a required M.A. course. The first half introduces students to the department and gives them some basic bibliographical skills. This half focuses on the skills needed to deal with criticism: how to read it, how to evaluate it, how to think about the relations among the multiple discourses that characterize it. We'll look at three essays in practical criticism of the same text, *Wuthering Heights*, and we'll read some theory. The students will write papers analyzing and evaluating critical arguments. Most students aren't used to thinking about criticism the way the course asks them to do. My challenge is to get them used to such thought; my fond hope is to get them to like it.

For today's session, I distributed the first pages of three articles from a recent issue of PMLA, the journal of the Modern Language Association, and asked the students if they could infer some of the assumptions underlying the way the critics set up their arguments. The primary moral I wanted to draw is that all our critical practices imply theoretical assumptions of one kind or another. The secondary moral I was after is that contemporary critics don't share a single set of assumptions but operate from disparate first principles.

I was pleased with the way the whole thing went. Many different students talked, yet I thought that the discussion stayed on track and that our move from examples to morals was warranted by what the students came up with. Their comments spurred my engagement with the issues, and I felt very involved both with what was being said and with the whole process of its development. Had it been my first time teaching the course, I would have let myself give in to the feeling that it was an overwhelming success. Experience tells me, however, that some students find it easy to get lost in a discussion like today's and that some find it hard to generate any enthusiasm for the abstract thinking involved in such a discussion. So I'm just cautiously optimistic.

I hate to admit it, but I'm also tired from the session: maintaining a clear discussion with a class of fifty for two and a half hours can be hard work. But when it goes well, it's great fun. I can draw energy from the students and then give some back to them, so that we're finally building on each other and reaching places where our thoughts have never been before. And because this building comes out of the process of mutual exchange, agreement, and disagreement, the students are also learning about the pleasures of a commitment to the life of the mind. Of course, there are more frustrating and only moderately successful days than euphoric ones, but those days when everything clicks can sustain me through many a more ordinary one.

Sunday, 11 January 1987

Although critical writing and Intro to Grad Study are very different courses, my general strategy is similar for each. I like to work by induction, to let the general conclusions I want to reach emerge out of our common exploration of numerous particulars. In the grad course, I'm going to be offering a method of reading criticism that I will outline in advance but whose power will be manifested (or not) by the effectiveness with which we use it in discussing our particular readings. Furthermore, our conclusions about the relations of different critical schools to each other should emerge from what we discover as we work through and then reflect on the individual essays that we take up. Generally, it is the process of reasoning that we began employing in our discussion yesterday that I want the students to experience and make their own.

In critical writing, induction works somewhat differently. This week we focused on the nature of interpretation as I gave the students the beginning and middle of a narrative that they helped me finish. We then interpreted it together. Next we'll look at some of the elements of fiction as we read and discuss some short stories and finally Orwell's *1984*. By then, the students should have some deeper understanding of both fiction and interpretation. The course will then try to complicate that understanding through study of a play, Arthur Miller's *Death of a Salesman*. Finally, we'll turn to poetry to complete the picture. We'll work together on building some sense of what a whole paper is, then move back and forth between looking at such parts as sentence style and paragraph development and the idea of building a paper as a whole. They're going to submit three drafts of a paper on *1984*, as well as four other papers, each of which is supposed to go through at least two drafts before I see it. Lots of opportunity for inductive learning there. And at the end I'll try to get them to reflect on some of the relations between what they do when they read and what they do when they write.

I'm not sure how much progress we made in there this week. They seemed to be paying close attention, but they weren't very talkative. Next week I'll get their papers and have a better fix on where we are. Meanwhile, I'll work on getting them to open up more in class.

Monday, 12 January 1987

Before I had tenure, I used to say that an assistant professor's work is never done. I meant not only that assistant professors live with the feeling that no matter what they've done they could always do more, but also that with tenure one's sense of time would change. An assistant professor on the tenure track starts with an apparently wide expanse of time that narrows a little with each passing day until the day five years later of Up or Out. An associate professor faces an expanse whose boundaries are not visible—they can coincide with one's life. In such a temporal territory, the concept of *finishing* one's work—especially one's research—takes on a whole different meaning. This difference has something to do with why I finished my first book two years after I began as an assistant professor, and why, six years after the publication of that book, I am still working on the second.

But after my promotion I learned that there was more to the feeling of time than that. One of the dimensions of living with tenure that I was unprepared for is the amount and variety of work that comes with the territory. An associate professor's work is never done: he or she never feels fully on top of all the tasks that come with rank. The letter of congratulations President Jennings sends when your tenure becomes official does not actually arrive accompanied by a stack of file folders, each packed with time-consuming jobs, but certain jobs fall only to the tenured. Last year, for example, I was the coordinator for the College of Humanities' annual conference in large part because some untenured professors in another department had convinced the dean that the college should sponsor a conference on critical theory. The dean and these colleagues agreed that the person in charge of running the conference ought to have tenure. Selective Service, OSU-style, came knocking at my door. Similarly, I would not have been asked to become director of graduate studies if I had not had tenure.

Tenured women are called on even more. The university's way of making amends for having so few is to overwork the ones they do have. Just this year Betty has become director of the Sociology Research Laboratory and has been appointed chair of the interim faculty committee on selective admissions. The appointment is a compliment. The switch from open to selective admissions should have significant consequences for the nature of undergraduate education here, and the faculty committee formulating the standards and policies of the new admissions system will have a tremendous influence on what happens in the next few years. To be chair is to have a lot of responsibility. It is also to take on a very time-consuming job. The committee meets three days a week for two hours at a stretch, and Betty devotes countless other hours to meeting with university officials and to preparing for the committee's sessions.

In taking on these new jobs, tenured faculty often find it difficult to continue some old ones. Finding the necessary large blocks of time to devote to research can become especially difficult. You can easily feel that you're banging your head against the rewards system and its very clear messages. You are what you publish. Your best friend is your c.v.

Research. No area of academic endeavor contributes as much to the standing afforded a college and its departments by other areas in the University and by the academic community. . . . Promotion to the rank of Professor will be considered only for those who have fulfilled the promise of their earlier work. Verifiable national or international reputation in a specific field is essential to promotion to full rank.

Thus read the official promotion and tenure guidelines of the College of Humanities. All kinds of real and symbolic capital—salary increases, respect from one's colleagues, clout with the central administration, recognition by the national scholarly community—depend on publication.

Most people who get tenure these days have internalized the drive to publish. With some, the activity of pursuing the answer to a tough question has become a reward in itself, an activity that both justifies and perpetuates one's participation in the life of the mind. With others, the desire for achievement and recognition gets internalized, and research becomes the means to satisfy that desire. With most, including me, some combination of these motives fuels the work. Living with tenure for me has meant living with some frustration about not satisfying the internalized drive more fully. I never thought it would take me so long to write a second book. Sometimes, though, I try to reason away that frustration. I do committee work and other kinds of "service" because I believe that faculty should take responsibility for what happens in their departments and in their university. I spend a lot of time parenting because I want to. I've chosen to stay in shape, to continue my life as an amateur athlete, because I came to realize that being an athlete of some kind was an important part of my identity. These reminders help not because they dissipate the frustration but because they allow me to see it as inevitable. To eliminate the frustration I'd have to undo some of my choices—and I'd make them all again in a minute; indeed, I make them all again almost every day. And accepting the frustration as an inevitable byproduct of my choices doesn't exactly mitigate its force—I still feel it—but the acceptance does sometimes help me refrain from taking the frustration out on children, students, teammates or other innocent bystanders.

Tuesday, 13 *January* 1987

Last quarter when I was working as grad chair but not teaching I made some good progress on my book. In these first ten days of the new quarter I haven't gotten back to it yet, and I'm not sure when I'll be able to.

A study of character and narrative progression, it's designed in part to complement my first book on style in the novel and in part to rethink some of my training at Chicago and my consequent assumptions about the nature of the novel. Until November, I conceived the project as one that would introduce a way of thinking about character and develop that way as I examined the relation between character and progression. Character, I would argue, has three components: the mimetic—characters are like people; the thematic—characters are vehicles for carrying general ideas; and the synthetic—characters are artificial constructs that play specific roles in the artifice of a whole novel. Progression is the mechanism controlling the relations among the components in different narratives. Once I established this general framework, I would devote the rest of the book to exploring the different kinds of relations among the components and the different kinds of progression that produce those relations. My working title was "Character, Progression, and the Craft of Narrative."

But after doing the introduction and revising the first chapter on *Pride and Prejudice* and *1984*, I realized that I could connect those central concerns with other issues in current debates about narrative and its interpretation. Thus, in addition to the exploration of character and progression in different narratives, each chapter will also take up a more general interpretive issue that can be usefully examined in light of those narratives. For example, the chapter on Orwell and Austen discusses character and progression in connection with a larger debate about the importance of identifying central themes in interpretation. In the third chapter, on Henry James's "The Beast in the Jungle" and John Fowles's *The French Lieutenant's Woman*, I reexamine and refine my conclusions by comparing them with a recent account advanced by Robert Scholes of how thematizing should move toward greater and greater generality. My plan for the next chapter—the one I'm not getting to these days—is to turn from the relations between the mimetic and thematic components of character to those between the thematic and synthetic relations and to test my approach to narrative progression against a psychoanalytically based account of narrative dynamics offered by Peter Brooks. My test case there will be Dickens's *Great Expectations*. And so on for later chapters. My new working title is "Character, Progression, and the Interpretation of Narrative."

The new conception increases the book's ambitions, even as it will situate it more firmly in contemporary critical discourse about narrative. If I can execute the conception successfully, I should have a better chance of having my voice heard in that discourse than under the original conception. There are of course no guarantees of that, as I learned from my first book. In elaborating its own theory of language in fiction, that book explicitly and extensively took on five other theories about language in literature, three of them very current, a fourth still very influential and found in the major book on style in the novel done to that date, and a fifth that was closest to my own. Although the book's method is one of its features I like most, its quiet reception made me think that in approaching this book, where the theories of character are still very much being worked out, I should just build my own theory by working closely with the novels I chose to discuss.

The conception I now have will put the methodology somewhere between that of the first book and that of my original idea for this one. I won't be consistently taking up competing theories of character and progression but will build my own theory as I move among a variety of problems in the interpretation of narrative. Sometimes I will bring in the work of other critics as a way to sharpen my own thinking about character or progression, sometimes as a way to raise problems that the developing theory will then solve. This method is more loosey-goosey than the first one, but it will enable the book to be more wide-ranging in its concerns. Now all I have to do is write the damn thing.

Wednesday, 14 *January* 1987

More thoughts on how time feels in this territory of multiple demands and sometimes flexible deadlines. When I began graduate school, I thought that I could be happy living and working in three roles: as a husband, a student, and an athlete. My life would revolve around living with Betty, reading and writing, and playing basketball. Everything else— what I owned, what I wore, where I lived—was largely extraneous. Since then my life has evolved into something rather more complicated than that, a situation that sometimes pleases, sometimes distresses me. I'm not just a student, but also a teacher and a committee member and a colleague. The reading and writing I do is not always the reading and writing I would choose. I still play ball and run, but these activities have a diminished importance in my life. I am not just a husband but also a father. And I'm an unhandy homeowner.

Of these changes, fatherhood is far and away the greatest. The job of being provider, friend, adviser, disciplinarian, model, playmate, teacher to these two people whose existence we are responsible for is demanding, frustrating, rewarding, amazing. Katie is a bright, easy-going, eager-to-please seven-year-old who is also quiet, shy, and in some ways already very private. Michael is a lively, rambunctious four-year-old who wears his mercurial emotions on his sleeve. Both of them, like their parents, are strong-willed. Katie reminds me of what I was like as a child, and while I take pleasure in that thought, it also worries me some. Not because I was unhappy, but because I was so shy and reserved that I found myself uncomfortable much of the time. I also worry that her reserve will keep us from staying good friends, that as she grows older she will share less and less of herself with me. In his extroversion, Michael is like Betty without her good sense. His recklessness is scary at times, but his exuberance and his energy are winning. I look at him and wonder whether we can give him, whether he can acquire, the good sense he needs while retaining his zest. I look at both of them and realize that in one way it would be easy to devote most of my time to parenting.

But Betty and I have chosen not to have either one of us do that, have chosen instead to try to maintain our multiple roles. We're fortunate that OSU has a good day-care program, and that Katie's school provides after-school care. We're fortunate too in the flexibility of our schedules. But the roles sometimes impinge on each other, and we feel stretched too thin. Sometimes something has to give—and because we're both hyper-responsible types, it's not always easy to decide which role of which one of us should suffer. These are the times that distress me, and sometimes I miss the concentrated intensity of my more narrowly focused life. More generally, though, I'm pleased by the expansion of my roles because that expansion has been accompanied by an expansion of values as well.

In the best of all possible worlds and with the best of all possible characters, I suppose that I would also find substantial carryover from one role to the next, that my experience as teacher would help me as parent, that what I get out of athletics would help me as a teacher, and so on. In this world and with this character, however, I don't experience such connections. I am a splitter, not a lumper, and tend to be suspicious of the occasional analogies between roles that occur to me. When the multiple roles are not straining against each other, however, my activity in one can help me keep the others in perspective. Sometimes it's comforting to know that Katie and Michael don't care whether I am more right than Theorist X about Text Y. Sometimes it helps to achieve the mastery on the basketball court that I have failed to achieve in the classroom. Sometimes it's wonderful to take refuge from it all by being together with Betty.

Thursday, 15 January 1987

A more practical consequence of the multiple demands on my time can be found in the selections I've made for the reading lists in my two

classes. In critical writing, I'm not teaching anything I haven't read before—indeed, with the possible exception of a few lyrics later in the
quarter, I'm not teaching anything I haven't taught before. I've put one or
two new things on the syllabus in the graduate course, but everything
else I already know well.

I feel ambivalent about this situation. For many years, I varied both
the courses I taught and the texts I used in the courses I repeated, so that
I would always have a fairly healthy dose of new (or only dimly remembered) material. That procedure required me to be involved in my teaching—to be not just leading but participating in the inductive inquiry of
the course—in a way that repeating the same material does not. Because
I was still thinking through the texts I was probably more ready to learn
from my students than, despite my good intentions, I now am. I suppose
there is a certain amount of hubris in blithely assigning texts I haven't
read, but I don't usually think of it that way. I'm supposed to be flexible
and smart enough to prepare new material—and whether I prepare the
new text in the summer or in the week I'm teaching it, my activity isn't
substantially different.

The hubris manifests itself in the assumptions I make about how
much work I can balance, and the fall comes when I realize that (once
again) I've made an erroneous assumption. Faced with eighty papers to
grade during the same week that I had two new novels to work up and one
or two children who did not want to end the day before 10:30, I have in
the past firmly resolved that I'd never again put on a syllabus something I
didn't already know cold. But I'd never keep the resolution because I also
wanted to write, which meant spending summers on texts I knew, and to
expand the base of my knowledge, which meant assigning new texts in
courses. What I'm doing this quarter is bowing to exigency rather than
adopting the resolution.

My own version of the greener-grass syndrome is to think that if I were
a specialist in a historical period rather than in the novel and in critical
theory, I wouldn't feel obliged to keep moving around so much in my
reading and would feel more comfortable repeating texts in courses. For
the period specialists I'm sure the syndrome works the other way. They're
too constrained. They'd like to read more widely, but their first obligation
is to keep up with developments in their fields—and the critical books
and articles proliferate like rabbits on fertility drugs.

Although I miss the feeling of growth that used to come when I'd always be teaching new texts, I like the feeling, if not of mastery, then of being in control, that I have with my present procedure. In the critical writing class I'm still engaged enough with the texts I have chosen that I don't feel stale, and since I haven't done the graduate course in a while, even the texts I've written about feel fresh. I worry, though, that a steady diet of such selection will deaden my taste for the texts or lead me into the habit of thinking that I don't have much to learn from my students. When my term as grad chair ends I'll work on a reasonable compromise between the new and the familiar in my teaching.

Friday, 16 January 1987

Two weeks into the quarter—already. We did the first article on *Wuthering Heights* today, and I think it went well. I still want to maintain caution in my optimism, but I liked what happened. And I'm less fatigued by the class than I was last week. Guess I was out of shape.

I'm a little worried about my critical writing class, though. My most provocative questions are typically met with stony silence or with answers that deny the provocation in the question. Our common induction won't work if I'm the only one who's taking my questions as ways to start thinking about our material. (What would Socrates have done if Euthyphro never answered his questions about piety?) I'm trying to decide if the class just has a quiet personality or if I'm losing them. As I look about the room every day, I feel like I have their attention, but I'd feel better if they were setting off more sparks in each other. When I taught this course last spring, I had a group of students who liked to react to my questions and each other's answers. The induction moved along very well, and my problem was more to keep it shared, to keep everybody caught up with everybody else. I'd much rather have that problem. With a responsive group, more issues relating to both the analysis of literature and writing papers about literature get raised, and the ones brought up by the students (often only implicitly) provide opportunities to meet them where they are.

Their writing is about average so far—I don't have any superlative writers, but I also have only one who needs a lot of help. Most of them are fair-to-middling with potential to improve. My challenge is to tap their potential. My hope today is that they'll help me do that by opening up more in our discussions.

Monday, 19 January 1987

Thinking again about advising, this time trying to process an experience I had a couple months ago with a dissertation student.

"When I get my proposal back with an X through the first paragraph, and with a new version of the paragraph written on the back of the page, I assume I should use that version. When you say you're surprised I've followed your suggestions so closely, I don't know what to think. I've been feeling uncomfortable all day."

Part of the problem this time was a miscommunication: I asked my question awkwardly—perhaps just stupidly. I was nominating Jamie for a dissertation fellowship, and as part of her application she needed to submit a short statement describing her project, a study of the critical paradigms controlling the interpretation of American literature. She gave me a version of the statement, and I made some—well, actually, lots of—suggestions, including the detailed ones about the first paragraph. After she adopted the suggestions wholesale, I felt odd reading that paragraph—there was my language coming through her voice. That feeling prompted me to find out whether she had thought that I was imposing my conception of the project on her and whether she had just done what I'd suggested to keep the peace. The stupid, insensitive thing was to say that I was *surprised* she had followed my suggestions so closely. What else did I expect, especially since she was working under a deadline? I was focusing too much on how I felt reading that paragraph and not enough on how the whole thing would look from where she was standing. Once Jamie told me that my question had made her uncomfortable, we were able to clarify the situation. I explained that the question had a benevolent intention, and she explained that she did in fact find the suggestions in the spirit of her project.

So I learned again how fragile the adviser-student relationship can be. Jamie has a wonderful attitude. She is not only smart and well-informed but also extremely committed to learning more and to improving her skills. She listens as well as any student I've had, yet at the same time won't swallow something just because her adviser says she should. I like and respect her a lot, and she seems to like and respect me. Then in the course of nominating her for the fellowship, I try to be conscientiously and concretely helpful, try further to make sure that I haven't gone too far, but my execution and her own situation prevent those intentions from coming through. Jamie sees an **X** and a rewritten paragraph, and then she gets a question about how much she's paid attention to my suggestions. Of course she feels uncomfortable—and suddenly certain aspects of our relationship are in jeopardy.

Problems like this one are more likely to occur with a student like Jamie who cares so much about her work and the process of writing a dissertation. Someone who cared less could have shrugged it off— there's Phelan being weird again; the things you gotta put up with if he's your adviser, but what the hey, he's not as bad as old Hobbyhorse. Because Jamie cares so much, and because we'd already established a foundation of mutual respect, she could come to me and tell me how she felt and we could work things out.

Like any mildly self-aware person, I've had periods when I've been beset by doubts about the ultimate value of my work. Through taxes and lip service, American society creates for teachers of literature nooks of their own, then forgets or ignores them. In the alleged great scheme of things we don't figure very prominently. Perhaps even in the true grand scheme we don't rate very highly. But once you ask what does really matter in the great scheme, it's easy to dismiss all kinds of things—national politics, influence with apparently important people, and so on. What really matters, I've begun to think, is in large part what people decide matters. Communities create—or at least reaffirm—the values of their members. It's crucial that I feel some fundamental connection between me and the literature I teach and write about, but it's equally crucial to have people—students, colleagues, scholars at other schools—affirm my belief in the importance of what we do. By caring about it, by saying it is important, we help to make it so. In part we make our work matter by insisting that it does. Jamie always insists—and thus helps me believe in what I'm doing.

One of the many things you never get taught in graduate school is how to function as someone's adviser. But of course you learn a great deal by watching how your advisers function. I am frequently conscious of the influence of my dissertation director, Sheldon Sacks, when I say one thing or another to one of my students. At the same time, I am aware that in some ways I work very differently. Most of what Sacks taught me about advising is inseparable from what he taught me about critical thinking, and I try to adapt that knowledge to my own style of working with students. Sacks always emphasized the importance of defining your question. Once you had that clear, you knew what your study would have to encompass and what it could leave for some other project. He also emphasized the importance of having a genuine yet manageable question—something that you wanted to know about but didn't, something that would have some significance for other work in the field, and something that could be answered in the span of one to two years. Along with Sacks's emphasis on the question came a deep concern for method, for organization, for the parts of the argument: If this is what you want to know, then how will this procedure help you know it? When he read individual chapters, he was concerned with two questions: Are there implications of the argument that need to be developed further? Does the chapter make its appropriate contribution to the developing argument?

Shelly's direction worked very well for me. I not only learned more about the content of my dissertation as I moved through it, but I also became a better thinker and better able to understand the ins and outs of dissertation-length arguments. Because of his influence and his effort, writing my dissertation felt the way it was supposed to: an appropriate capstone to my graduate education. Perhaps even more important, Shelly showed me what it meant to care about literature, critical thinking, and teaching. He didn't talk much about the importance of caring, but he always made you feel that what you were doing mattered a lot.

The big difference between my style of working with students and his is that I'm more inclined to work closely with their writing. He would read chapters and then talk to his students about them. I read, and as I do, I write. Then I give the students my comments and invite them in to talk about the chapter and the comments. I don't know that this procedure is necessarily any better, but I'm more comfortable with it—and when I don't get carried away rewriting their prose, the students, I think, like its concreteness.

Another difference of course is that between our statures in the profession. Sacks was a full professor, one of the main intellectual presences in a very prestigious department, the founding editor of *Critical Inquiry*, a journal which immediately established itself as one of the most important outlets for critical theory on either side of the Atlantic. Although he was a warm, generous soul, he was in many ways set apart from his graduate students. Because of that distance between him and me, our relationship, until the very end of my graduate career when he began to close the distance, was largely an intellectual one. We talked almost exclusively about criticism, theory, and the novel, about ideas, arguments, and philosophies. I never learned much from him about dealing with the kind of interaction Jamie and I had, or with the more difficult ones like those I had with Lee. I don't know that I regret that; just as I am not Gordo Cooper I am also not Sheldon Sacks: his ways might not fit my personality. But another reason I regret his premature death in 1979 is that now I can't talk to him about these things. I am very aware that in this dimension of advising, I am learning as I go along. I just hope that I don't give my students too many trials by my errors.

Tuesday, 20 January 1987

Next week Betty's going to Cornell to give a lecture. The man who invited her just called to tell her to be sure to bring a c.v. Is there a hidden agenda behind their invitation to her? Does Cornell have an opening that they're considering her for? She thinks not, but I wonder. It certainly wouldn't surprise me.

This possibility of course raises lots of questions—and not just about Cornell. Would I be willing to move so she could accept such an offer? Well, it would be damn hard for me. My sense of myself is tied up with my work. But if I could have a job potentially comparable to the one I have here, I would be willing to do it. I even think that I could take such a job knowing that the other school was hiring me as a way to hire Betty, provided I felt I had accomplished enough to deserve the respect of my new colleagues. The anxiety comes from feeling that I have not accomplished enough. Betty's success becomes an impetus for me to keep working at my book.

Would I be willing to move if it meant a great opportunity for Betty and no immediate opportunity for me, as would probably happen if Cornell is interested in Betty? If the operative word in the question is "willing," then no. Would I do it reluctantly? Maybe. More telling, perhaps, is that if the situation were reversed, Betty would be more willing. Sex roles? Well, not in any easy, straightforward way. As a sociologist and a feminist, Betty is very aware of the presence and power of traditional roles and very interested in combating them. And despite my long career as a jock, male dominance has never seemed either natural or defensible to me. Betty may just be more generous on this score (though perhaps it's true that she is more generous and I more identified with my work because of the way we've been socialized in this culture). In the past, Betty has also said that she thinks she is less committed to academic life in general and sociology in particular. But I wonder if that is still true. As living with tenure has for her meant taking on her jobs as director of the Sociology Research Lab and chair of the first faculty committee on selective admissions, she has gotten more involved and more committed to the department and the university. It would be harder for her to walk away from it now than it was, say, two years ago.

When we first went job-hunting ten years ago, we did decide to put my prospects first, but the event proved more complicated than we had anticipated. I went first partly because I was further along, partly because I was less ambivalently committed to pursuing an academic career, and though we never said it openly, partly because Betty was more generous. But as I was going through the process of writing letters of application, sending dossiers to schools that requested them, hoping for interviews, and finally getting a few, Betty was offered—without applying for it—a one-year position as a visiting scientist at the National Institute of Mental Health in Bethesda. Just as my situation was becoming clearer—two of the schools I had interviewed with had sent rejection letters, and a third, I had heard through the grapevine, was going to do the same, leaving me with OSU as the only attractive option—the person who offered Betty the job became firmer about both the offer and the need for a decision.

Betty and I sat down to discuss our options. I suggested that she take her job and that I try again in the next year's market. Betty argued that if I could get a job it would be wise to take it—who knew what the next year would bring? In the middle of our conversation, the phone rang. Julian Markels, chair of the English department at OSU, was offering me the job. My pleasure and satisfaction were confounded with a strong sense that this was going to make life even harder to sort out. I even expressed some dismay at Julian's request that I accept or reject the offer in ten days. After our excitement over the offer itself died down, one of us suggested that we take both jobs. Soon that possibility became the source of the true excitement, and by the next day had become our solution as well.

Although that year of commuting was difficult, we both feel that we made the right choice. Betty's boss helped her get an adjunct appointment at OSU, and that in turn led to her successful application for a full-time position. In a sense, then, that year was an important step in our both getting established here. And although our being here now is, in a way, a consequence of our putting my career first, our decision to commute also signified our commitment to the importance of both careers. We have been able to continue that commitment so far. My question now is how we'd balance our commitment against our pleasure in having one of us presented with an opportunity for greater success.

Wednesday, 21 January 1987

Recovering from a scare: Betty had a severe reaction to her allergy shot. The serum went straight to her heart and her system went into distress. They had to give her a shot of adrenalin—fast—to get her heart functioning right again. She is okay now, though still somewhat shaken. I'm shaken, and she looks fine to me. But that's just the rub: fine one minute, in serious distress the next. You can't take anything for granted. It's all so delicate, fragile, perishable.

Thursday, 22 January 1987

"I can't think of anything I could have done at OSU that I didn't do to prepare myself for the market. And though this probably sounds too egotistical, if I don't get a job, who will?"

Anne is discouraged. After lots of positive signs about success on the job market—numerous dossier requests, eight interviews at the MLA convention—she's worried that she'll come up empty. The market is supposed to be getting better, but "better" is very much a relative term. It's still very tough, so tough that it's painful to watch people go through it.

They start out so hopeful, and they sometimes end up so disappointed, dejected, and down on themselves. They know that the market is bad, they know that an OSU Ph.D. doesn't carry the prestige of one from the Ivy League schools, or Berkeley or Chicago or Virginia, they know that more and more schools are expecting publication from graduate students. After they recite this litany for you, their voices lift with hope as they mention the schools that have openings in their fields. They have to hope. The decision to spend six years or more of one's life getting a Ph.D. in English these days is itself a great act of hope. If you didn't hope you'd never even apply for jobs.

But that hope also makes people so vulnerable. I sometimes find myself trying to protect the students from their own hopes, even as I question whether I should. At one point this fall Jamie stopped in to say that, although she wasn't very far along with her dissertation, she was thinking about applying for jobs at just three places, two where she'd always dreamed of teaching and one whose geographical location was desirable for her whole family. I said that my only concern was that she would get pulled away from the dissertation and perhaps set herself up for some disappointment that would also slow her down. After she thought further about it, she decided not to apply, though, happily, my advice was less important than her own judgment that she was not ready. As she told me about her decision and her own feelings about dealing with rejection, I felt that I had been speaking too much out of an instinct to be overprotective.

I developed the instinct, I think, from my own experience on the market and especially from watching my first dissertation student enter it. Although my experience was ultimately successful, it also let me in for a lot of rejection. Ed got one interview in two years of serious job-hunting—but, hallelujah! He got the job. Ed was an excellent student, certainly one of the half-dozen best to have gone through our program since I've been here, and he wrote what I think is a first-rate dissertation on the nonfiction novel. I said all that and more in my letter of recommendation, but he just didn't get people to interview him. Working with him on the dissertation had been rewarding for me, and it was exciting to watch his ideas develop and to anticipate that they would develop further and be published a few years down the road. Seeing him get shut out in the market with his fresh Ph.D. undermined my feelings. How could I get excited in the same way and to the same extent with the next student if the dissertation were the end of the road, not the entrance to a freeway? A dissertation that is the capstone on a graduate education and no more does have a dignity of its own, and working on one like that can be rewarding in its way. But it just doesn't measure up to the experience of watching—and helping—a student develop ideas and a voice that you believe will be heard in the larger scholarly community in the next few years.

As things were going well for Anne, I was letting myself be optimistic about her chances. But here's what happens. At one school Anne was the second choice, but the first choice accepted. At another, she was in the top three, but they have already made an offer and are waiting to hear. And similar stories at two other places. I tried to bolster her spirits: in just about every case, the schools she interviewed with indicated that they wouldn't be bringing people to campus until the end of January or the beginning of February, so there is still time. The market has opened up some, and many schools, OSU included, are not getting their first choices. If nothing comes out of this year's effort in the market, something very good should come out of next year's, and in the meantime she can work on revising the dissertation into a book.

Still I am worried. She is right. If she doesn't get a job—she's earned practically every honor we give, she's had a variety of teaching, editorial, and administrative jobs, she's had the first chapter of her dissertation accepted for publication and praised highly by anonymous reviewers— who will? Or at least who of my students will? Well, as I told Anne, let's give it time.

Friday, 23 January 1987

In six hours the graduate faculty begins an all-day meeting on a proposal for the new system of general exams. I care deeply about the outcome of the meeting: a major reason that I agreed to become graduate chair was that I believed the department should revise the way we do generals. Under the current system, students must take exams in four areas, two of which must be literature fields—either the traditional periods of literary history or a genre. The greatest virtue of this system is also its greatest vice: it's a hell of a workout for the student.

The reading lists are extensive, the anxiety levels are high, the number of students who put pressure on themselves to perform spectacularly well and then crash when they don't is large, and the recovery times are long. Qualifying exams are inevitably stressful, and in graduate programs throughout the country they are a very important rite of passage: the last exam after twenty years of schooling, the most demanding certification before being admitted to the academic guild. Even allowing for all that, my perception was that the exam had taken on too much importance in our program, that it had become the central, defining experience of graduate study for our students, when it should be another step—a significant one—toward the dissertation. I wanted to do something to streamline the exam and perhaps at the same time move people along to the dissertation more quickly—at any rate to reestablish the idea that the dissertation is more important than the generals.

My original suggestion to the committee was that we change the fourth exam. Rather than preparing a new field, students would write an essay for publication in a field of their choice. Presumably, most students would write the paper in their major field and thus would both have less material to prepare and be more likely to be working on something that could lead to a dissertation. In addition, testing the student's skill at preparing work for possible publication would add an important and useful dimension to the exam.

What we'll consider at the meeting is very different from that initial proposal, and I like it better. When I proposed the revision to our committee of faculty and graduate students, we began a series of intense debates that eventually led to what we're presenting tomorrow. Rather than four fields, the student must prepare three: one in a comprehensive period (typically a one-hundred-year stretch of British or American literature), one in what we are calling "Forms of English Studies," (poetry, drama, prose fiction, creative writing, rhetoric and composition, folklore, linguistics, film, and so on), and one in either a major author or a critical problem. The rationale behind the exam is that the student ought to know as much about the different kinds of critical activity as about the content of the field. Thus each exam requires a different kind of critical thinking.

We brought the proposal to the Graduate Studies Council at the end of last quarter, but it became clear that the suggested revision was too controversial for us to decide about it in an hour or so. It also became clear that the proposal has some strong opposition. One of my colleagues called it "appalling." Since that meeting, there has been lots of talk in the department about the proposal's pros and cons. Jamie, who is one of three grad students on the committee, surveyed other students, asking such things as whether the present system needs to be changed, whether the proposed system is an improvement, whether some specialties would be favored more than others, and so on. The responses are virtually unanimous in calling for change, but are split about whether the new system is the way to go.

I don't feel confident about what will happen tomorrow. I know I'll be disappointed if we don't pass something that alters the present system. For what it's worth, I'm predicting that the proposal won't pass as is, but some slightly amended version of it will.

Saturday, 24 January 1987

Well, I was right that the committee's proposal wouldn't pass without amendment, but I was too optimistic in thinking that the amendment would be only slight. The plan we approved is different from our present system in only one way: the student must prepare three fields instead of four. All the committee's thought and work and arguments about making the exam more coherent by having students organize their fields in three different ways went for naught. What we approved today is incoherent. It refuses to define the exam. Students must prepare one historical period, but the other two fields can be anything: two more periods, rhetoric and composition, folklore and creative writing, poetry and nineteenth-century art history, critical theory and linguistics, any one of these and one more period, and so on. It's a system which, like the proposal, does acknowledge the diversity of our students and faculty, but it is one that is indifferent to any principles other than the necessity of coverage—which will now be defined as three fields rather than four. I thought we could do better than that.

The sticking point finally—and predictably—was the major author/critical problem category. Too many people thought adopting it would mean that we'd be lowering our standards, some because they felt we wouldn't be requiring enough reading, others because they felt that the reading wouldn't be important enough, and still others for both reasons. The "compromise" proposal that we passed apparently allows the majority to feel that they were responding to some need to revise the system while also maintaining their idea of standards.

One telling feature of the meeting was our discussion and vote, after the passing of the compromise, on a motion made by one of the committee members to add our category of major author/critical problem to the list of fourteen presently acceptable fields. The motion met considerable—and to me, surprising—resistance before it passed. Once the group had gone for the historical period plus any two others, I didn't see any principled reason for opposing this category. During the wine and cheese hour at the end of the day, I asked some of the opponents of the committee's proposal what they thought about the outcome of the meeting. One said, "Well, it was the democratic process at work; everybody had to make compromises. I got some things I liked and some I didn't. I don't like the major author/critical problem category." Another, trying to make me feel better, said, "At least you can still have your students prepare the way you wanted." These comments made me remember that part of the problem with the committee's proposal came from our not trusting each other. Some faculty worried that their colleagues would be too soft about allowing minor figures to be treated as major figures (we described a major author as one who produced a "substantial body of work," but we did not want to establish a canonical list). These same people also worried that some of their colleagues would approve problems that were trivial. I wouldn't argue that these people had no grounds for their worries, but I hesitate to endorse the idea that the abuse of a thing is a strong argument against it. In any case, this realization made me wonder about what other undercurrents ran beneath the various remarks.

Despite this misgiving and despite my disappointment in the outcome, I feel all right about the *process* of the meeting. People seemed to be frank about their disagreements, but I detected little personal animosity. Probably the strongest attack on the proposal came from my good friend Jim Battersby, who asserted that it was motivated by a production-line, rush-to-dissertation and publishing mentality. In his impassioned eloquence, he even worked capitalism and stagflation into the attack. Because he was so openly impugning our motives, his speech created a potentially divisive moment. The moment was also difficult for me because on most matters I very much value Jim's opinion—and because he's been very good to me since I came here. Jim is smart, principled, and dedicated to the life of the mind. But on this one I knew we had a deep disagreement. After Jim spoke, Murray Beja, our chair, let me respond. I tried to move us away from Jim's way of talking about the proposal, first, by showing that I could laugh about the attack—"I resemble that!" (I was relieved to see that Jim laughed, too)—and second, by talking about the pedagogical principles behind the proposal. I succeeded in moving us away from Jim's attack on our motives, but obviously I didn't succeed in getting people to buy the pedagogical principles. We just couldn't get people over the quantity-coverage hump. Although I'm sure that some old scabs were rubbed off, I want to think that there was something salutary about the whole effort to come to grips with the issues our proposal raised.

Jamie, who probably ended up working harder for the proposal than anyone, takes a different view. During the wine and cheese hour, she told me she was depressed by the whole day. She came to feel that in addition to refusing to define the exam, the faculty ended up voting for the reduction in fields out of a condescension to the "poor" graduate students whom they nevertheless can't trust because, well, you know how graduate students are, always trying to make things easy on themselves. Although I don't think it was that bad, I have to admit that she has some warrant for her feelings in the remarks some people made.

In any case, I think we did succeed in one very important respect, and for this reason I'm not as discouraged as Jamie. The mountain that we ask the students to climb in doing generals has been scaled down by one-fourth. It's still formidable, but it is finally less daunting.

It has also occurred to me that if the committee had simply come forward with the proposal that we passed yesterday, it would have had as much or more trouble than the proposal we did make. I feel like I've unwittingly been involved in a negotiation like buying a new car. We went for the whole package—reduce the fields, redefine them, insist on different activities in each field (low price plus lots of options)—and got part of it (the price but not the features). The model we've bargained for is rather bland and boring for my taste, but it's an improvement over the broken-down one we were using, and if we hadn't asked for everything we probably would still be stuck with that.

Sunday, 25 January 1987

A scene from family life on this, my 36th birthday. Katie, Michael, and I drop Betty at the airport this morning so she can catch her plane to Ithaca. I have the bright idea that the three of us can go to the nearby school playground, that I can run for a half hour or so while they play, and then we can all play for a while before coming home. Both kids start out with great enthusiasm, but just six minutes into my run, Katie calls to me that she's cold and wants to go home. Trying to be flexible and under-standing, I say O.K., why don't they start home while I do another lap around the school and then catch up to them. When I get around I see that they haven't gotten very far, so I'm forced to stop—maybe this will only take a minute—and find out why. Michael doesn't want to go home. I propose that we all stay out a bit longer and run to warm up. Katie wants no part of that and finally shows me a hole in her glove that is making her finger numb. All right, let's just go home (maybe I can stay out for just a short while longer and run hard). Michael melts in tears, and I try to explain Katie's problem with no success. A new idea: let's race home; Michael and I will take one route, Katie another. Michael is cheered until in the excitement of the race he runs out of his shoe and falls on the sidewalk. The floodgates open once again. Goodbye, run, as I take up the task of comforting him with some of my birthday chocolate, which soon leads into a conflict over how much is too much. (And whose birthday is it, anyway?)

Never underestimate the difficulty of doing anything once there are three thick Micks and a generation gap involved.

Thursday, 29 January 1987

Betty liked her trip to Cornell, felt good about her lecture, and is sure that there was no hidden agenda. O.K. With that behind her, she now faces a mountain of work. Last quarter the National Institutes of Health asked her to be a reviewer of grant proposals, a duty that involves reading the proposals in advance, writing reports on them, and then going to Wash-ington for a three-day meeting to discuss them with a panel of other reviewers. Since the offer is a sign of recognition for her work and the job something useful for her own proposal writing, Betty promptly accepted. This week she's been learning what she agreed to. The pile of proposals she has had to work through is taller than Michael, and she has had to write fairly extended reports on each of twelve proposals. Meanwhile, she has been squeezing in her teaching, her meetings of the admissions committee, her supervision of the research lab, and her completion of a grant proposal that she and a colleague are submitting. Not to mention dealing with the demands of the kids ("But I want Mommy to read my bedtime story!"). Last night, after a brief nap when Michael went to bed, she got up and worked almost till dawn on the reports. Needless to say, she is exhausted tonight, but she managed to finish the reports and get them in the mail today. She's off to Washington in two weeks, before which she has countless other tasks to complete.

One difference between Betty and me is that I'm more driven. She has periods like this present one where she works long hours and remains preoccupied with that work. But then after she gets through them, she's better able to slow down, to balance the work with the other roles. As I've watched and admired her, I've come to learn the value of that balancing and have sometimes tried to be more like her. But I never really stay there: I start thinking about how much I don't know or how much I want (or sometimes need) to do, and my idea of balance becomes working more while keeping everything else going. The strains come when I can't maintain this precarious balance.

Sunday, 1 *February* 1987

Well, neither Anne nor I need despair yet. She has an offer from Cal State Northridge, and she now has campus visits scheduled to the two schools that she was most interested in going to—Louisville and Illinois. The bounce is back in her voice, the smile back on her face, the confidence back in her statements. I'm certain that she will do well with her visits, but I'm afraid to relax yet. The Northridge job doesn't sound all that desirable—it would entail a very heavy teaching load—and given the timing of her visits, she may have to turn it down before she actually has an offer from Louisville or Illinois. That she will do well doesn't mean that other candidates who will be brought in won't also do well. I'll feel a lot better when she has something firm. In the meantime, I'll put my two cents in on her preparation of her lectures. She's going to Louisville in a week and to Champaign-Urbana ten days after that.

Monday, 2 *February* 1987

Last Thursday Jamie gave a presentation about her dissertation in John Gabel's required bibliography course for first-year Ph.D. students. The idea was to give the students some sense of how what they are learning about using the resources of the library will pay off when they get to the dissertation stage, a purpose that also inevitably includes getting the students to see what doing a dissertation entails. John Gabel is an elder statesman of the department, someone who got his Ph.D. here, who has been chair, who has been on virtually every important university committee, who has been acting dean of the graduate school. He is a meticulous man, always neat, always organized, always attentive to detail—in short someone ideally suited to teaching the course. He is also one of the most widely respected members of the department, the kind of person whose opinion and judgment carry weight with the rest of us.

After Jamie's presentation, he came by my office to report that she "was wonderful. She really did you proud." In the course of this praise, he also mentioned that "she sounds so much like you it's amazing." I was very pleased for Jamie—I knew she'd take satisfaction in doing that job well, especially since she had told me the day before that she was having second thoughts about having agreed to John's request. But I felt—and still feel—very ambivalent about John's second comment, which I take as part of his whole indirect compliment to me. I like the idea that I'm a strong enough critic and teacher to influence my students, but I don't want to get into the business of remaking them in my own image. And I don't want them, especially the good, independent ones like Jamie, to be seen as people who have signed up for a Phelan makeover. When I passed on John's remarks to Jamie, I learned how extensive John perceived my influence to be. He told her she even said "O.K.?" the way I do when I'm finishing up a point. We laughed about that—"I didn't know that I said that"; "I didn't know that either of us said that"—but I think it made us both a little uneasy.

No good teacher wants to clone himself, no good student wants to be another Professor Wonderful. Yet every teacher wants to have a discernible influence on the work of her students, and every student wants to work with somebody from whom he'll learn something substantial. Sometimes the line between influence and imposition gets blurred. But these truths don't accurately reflect the process as I've experienced it. Even as I say that I don't want to clone myself, I have to acknowledge that the excitement and pleasure I derive from working closely with students often comes from watching them assimilate things I have taught them and then use that stuff in combination with their other knowledge and skills. The more they assimilate my ways of thinking and the more familiar I am—or become—with the student's material, the more the project feels like a collaboration. That feeling, I suppose, explains why I can get so tied up in a student's work and then in a student's success in the program, on the job market, and beyond. As the student is being judged, so am I.

But there's more to it than that. When the work becomes a collaboration in this way, I frequently develop a relationship with the student that becomes one kind of friendship. The friendship may be largely restricted to the work—there are lots of things about each other's lives that my advisees and I don't know. But to share the life of the mind with a student, especially when I've substantially influenced that student's conception of what the life of the mind is all about, is to enable a kind of intimacy to develop. We are sharing a very significant part of our lives. And once that happens my emotional life gets tied up with the student's. I look forward to seeing him, I want to hear what she thinks about departmental events, so-and-so's recent lecture, whatever. We're not just teacher and student, we're friends. Still, because we start out as teacher and student and remain that way until the student graduates or leaves, the friendship has some peculiar features.

We are not equals. For good or ill, I am the more powerful partner, even as the student does the far greater quantity of the work. This inequality hangs over the way the friendship might extend outside its generative intellectual world. Many topics that friends of a different sort—people who start out more as equals—would naturally talk about remain off-limits for us. Even in cases where a lot of the usual barriers get broken down, the inequality is always there coloring things. On the whole, I find these inhibitions to be a positive thing. Without some of the barriers remaining, I might be less inclined to offer necessary negative commentary, the student less inclined to learn from it. And there are some students with whom I am happy to share an intellectual friendship even as I am glad I don't share more of their lives. Nevertheless, the line between the intellectual life and the rest of life is eminently permeable, and sometimes I wonder whether the restrictions should come down.

My experience with Ronnie is a case in point. Now a first year M.A. student, Ronnie took a course from me in each of her four years as an undergraduate, and she wrote her honor's thesis under my direction. She was the star student in each of those four classes, and a lot of what she came to believe about literature and its interpretation, she learned, for better or worse, from me. In the course of those four years and twenty-five or so credit hours, we got to know each other very well. I certainly have not gotten to know any undergraduate better, and no undergraduate has gotten to know me as well as she did. We were and are very good friends. Yet if Ronnie were asked to identify the central fact of her life, she would begin to talk about something that she and I rarely discussed: she is a fundamentalist Christian. On the one hand, I feel that this silence does not limit our friendship so much as it defines its nature. We're not the kind of friends who worry about a conflict of religious belief; we are the kind who worry about the conflict of interpretations. On the other, I wonder whether the silence is simply a way to avoid a necessary discussion about the limits and extent of the reasoning skills that we both value so highly in one world. Then again I recognize that even saying that much shows how I would come out on the issue, and I'm grateful that Ronnie and I can be friends without developing a conflict over religious beliefs.

With graduate students the friendship can be even greater because they're typically closer in age to me, they share a career choice with me, and they work on theses or dissertations, which of course are more intense than anything an undergraduate does. But these differences are ones of degree, not of kind. Even though the friendship may be special, the initial teacher-student relationship is always there exerting its subtle restrictive influences. Actually, as I think further, those restrictions may be more important for my relations with graduate students, since they allow both of us to recognize from the start that holding up my end of the basic relationship may mean that at times I act more like an impersonal judge than a close friend.

One way in which the teacher-student dimension of the relationship overlaps the friend-friend dimension is that the teacher in me wants the student to identify himself with what I have taught him. I may not want clones, but I'm glad to have students who incorporate some of my ways of thinking into their work. An easy way to defend that desire is to say that it is a sign of my own belief in what I am teaching my students. It's also easy to say that the desire will become pernicious only when I demand that a student become a disciple in order to work with me. But I still worry that I may be subverting the goal of educating people to become independent scholars and thinkers. Well, I'll keep fretting about the whole problem. O.K.? Ronnie, Jamie, O.K.?

Tuesday, 3 *February* 1987

Mid-quarter crunch time. Life beyond the tenure track these days means living with fatigue, as I run from one thing to another during the day and don't get enough sleep at night. We did registration for next quarter this week, we have to read the sixty-odd applications to the program (each of which has a writing sample) and nominate the best people for fellowships in this two-week period, I have about seventy papers to grade with another seventeen coming in next week, I'm trying to revise my introduction to the volume of papers from last year's narrative conference, I need to read two chapters of Lauren's revisions so she can move along and graduate at the end of the quarter. Not to mention the normal demands of teaching, committee meetings, and the rest.

When I managed some time to get out and go for a run the other day, I was struck by how radically repositioned running had become in my life in the last two months. In November I ran the Columbus Marathon. During my training, I made sure I got out six days a week, averaged about sixty miles a week, and expended a lot of psychic energy in the whole activity—reflecting on how I felt, making plans for the next race or workout, thinking ahead to the marathon. Now I'm just happy to get out and get five miles in whenever I can. I am able to get to the gym to play basketball about twice a week—once for our intramural games—but even during some of those workouts I find myself watching the clock.

I dreamed the other night that I had decided to run another marathon on the kind of training I've been doing recently. I was apprehensive about how I'd do, but even more apprehensive about the way it conflicted with my schedule: the race was to begin at the same time that Betty and I had already agreed to go to some function at Lauren's house. In the peculiar beauty of dream logic, I was able both to warm up for the race and to be in Lauren's living room, yet I knew that I couldn't actually run the race and be there. When push came to shove, I stayed at Lauren's, though I spent my time thinking about the marathon. I won't speculate about the latent content of that dream, but its manifest content captures a lot of my feelings these days.

Thursday, 5 *February* 1987

I still haven't made any serious progress on my character book. Today, however, I agreed to follow through on a tentative offer I made in December to do a lecture in the beginning of March for the Undergraduate English Forum on *Great Expectations*. I wavered quite a bit when the student came by to check my plans; it would be a lot easier to do a piece that I've already written. But I knew that the only way I'd get into the next chapter this quarter was by promising to lecture on it. The trouble is that I have several other things coming due as well—that revised introduction to the essays from the narrative conference; a paper on A *Farewell to Arms* for a conference on Hemingway in San Diego during spring break; a paper on *Middlemarch* for this year's narrative conference at the beginning of April. The Hemingway paper already exists in an earlier incarnation, so that shouldn't be a problem, but the *Middlemarch* is still only an abstract. I am certain that I'll get something ready for all these occasions. The question will be whether quantity injures quality—or rather how serious the injury will be.

Friday, 6 *February* 1987

I remain cautiously optimistic about my graduate class. We've settled in now, have gotten used to each other, and typically make good progress in our discussions. Some people have not yet opened their mouths—easy to do with fifty people enrolled—but there is a large group willing to engage. They enter the discourse with different levels of sophistication, but that's all to the good because it helps me decide how to pitch my responses and my next questions. The course is still difficult to manage—all those voices, all those issues, so little time. The induction can get messy. I'm enjoying the challenge, even as I worry a bit about what the quiet ones are making of it all. Today we backed up from our work with *Wuthering Heights* as I gave a lecture on the history of twentieth-century criticism. In two and a half hours you're almost inevitably committed to doing more caricature than summary, but given those constraints, I thought it went off well enough. Having seen some different frameworks in our work on Brontë and having talked some about the relations among those frameworks, the students seemed very eager to learn about the larger picture.

The critical writers, my silent majority, have settled into some kind of a pattern too. They come, a few of them talk, most of them listen, some of them laugh at my jokes, they work reasonably well on their writing. How much thinking with me they're doing I'm not sure. The whole thing seems rather workmanlike—some things will get accomplished, but it's not going to be a smashing success.

Saturday, 7 *February* 1987

I frittered away this Saturday, and I'm not sure why. Work is almost always difficult to squeeze in on weekends, but today I had some time. I was tired after playing ball this morning, but not so tired that I couldn't work. Even after Betty took Katie and Michael out, I resisted the need to settle down to grading or writing, and read *Sports Illustrated* and the *New Yorker* instead. Sometimes I think I just want to assert my independence from the demands of my situation and so will ignore them as I did today. The trouble is that the demands don't shrink while they're being ignored.

Wednesday, 11 *February* 1987

Some deeply satisfying news today: Louisville has offered Anne the job. The pride and pleasure in her voice on the phone were wonderful to hear. But the first comment she made on her news says a lot about what being on the market is like: "It's such a relief." The comment was also perhaps motivated by the anxious day of waiting that she had. She knew that Louisville's committee was meeting at 2:30, but they didn't call her until 8:00. Meanwhile, she had promised Cal State Northridge that she would let them know by today whether she would accept their offer. She had to call them at about 7:30 (4:30 their time) and turn down the job, not knowing how things would turn out at Louisville or Illinois. When

Louisville called at 8:00, the committee had just finished their meeting (they were making final decisions about three positions), and the chair told Anne that they had struggled a lot over their decision for her position. When she was there last week she learned that she was one of three candidates, and that one of the others was a few years beyond his Ph.D. and publishing regularly. Anne's getting the offer over him is a very strong compliment.

Now she can go to Illinois next week with a relaxed confidence—she liked the people at Louisville and would be happy to accept their offer— and an open mind (maybe some aspects of the job will be better than at Louisville): the best conditions under which to make such a visit. Today is one of the very good days in this business.

Thursday, 12 *February* 1987

Had a revealing talk with Anne tonight. Louisville's dean called today with the official offer, which included a higher salary than Anne had expected and a stipulation that she respond by next Wednesday, the eighteenth—the day after she is to get back from Illinois. She was wondering whether she should just accept the offer and forget about going to Urbana. In fact, she seemed to hope I'd advise her to do that. I didn't, because, as I said to her, she has nothing to lose and possibly something to gain by going to Illinois—she might like it there better. And if Louisville didn't turn out well, Anne would always regret that she closed off her chances at Illinois. I suggested that she call Illinois and ask whether they could give her a decision by Wednesday, since she needed to respond to another school's offer. If they couldn't, then she should call Louisville back and see if she could have more time. Illinois could probably accommodate her request, but if not, then Louisville should give her another day or so. It's her career that's at stake, after all.

What's telling is that Anne pretty much knew what I was going to say. And she basically agreed with it. In a sense, she wasn't asking for advice so much as trying to get another voice to articulate what part of her own mind was already saying. Yet the rest of her was very attracted to the simpler solution of just saying yes to Louisville. That way the job-hunting could finally be over. Louisville was offering her an escape from one more weekend of anxious anticipation and detailed preparation followed by two more days under a microscope. It's no wonder that she was so tempted just to say yes.

That Anne would share her temptation with me—as she had shared her earlier frustration—is another sign of how the market gets to even the best students. It also gives me a glimpse of just how hard the past two months have been on her. Of all my students Anne is the most independent and the most reserved. Where others aren't shy about handing me rough drafts, Anne polishes and polishes her work before she shows it to me. Like her adviser, she likes to be—needs to feel—in control of herself and the situations in which she finds herself. Going on the market means giving up the possibility of control.

Friday, 13 *February* 1987

Betty's in Washington for her NIH reviewing. Katie, Michael, and I are muddling through. Impressively—and fortunately—our kids now take the short absences of one of us pretty much in stride. They know that they can play some angles—"Let's eat out!" (yeah, says Dad, let's); "I hope I get a nice present when Mommy comes back"—and Michael will occasionally respond to adversity by wailing "I want my Mommy," but mostly they maintain their equilibrium.

Today—or maybe Monday—is the deadline for applications for next year's freshman class. When Betty gets back she and the admissions committee will have to start looking harder at the numbers: they're supposed to get a class of 6,500 from the 14,000 or so expected applications.

Sunday, 15 *February* 1987

The graduate students did a midterm evaluation of our course on Friday. I've been right to feel cautious in my positive assessment. The course is working on the whole, but there is some dissatisfaction. Here are two especially revealing responses:

> Given the assumption that we are not supposed to know much (if anything) about critical theory when entering this course, I feel as if we actually got started only last week. I was/am not familiar with the tenets of structuralism, deconstruction, etc., and only last week did I feel that we finally got around to the "meat and potatoes" of the class. . . . While the

discussion about the articles [on *Wuthering Heights*] is good, I would like to move beyond even overstanding [evaluation] and tie the articles concretely to their particular branch of critical theory—and then show how the article evokes that particular style.

I can't imagine what might be more important than the things we're addressing in this course. That is, while there may be other considerations significant to critical theory, the essential thing nevertheless seems to be "getting at" a critic's argument. Clearly, this is no simple task, and if acquiring the skills to accomplish it takes up all our time, that's perfectly all right.

These comments represent two somewhat conflicting understandings of the purpose of the course: should it be a miniature lecture-survey in critical theory, and thus primarily concerned with imparting as much information about contemporary theory as possible in a three-hour course, or should it be primarily concerned with the students' acquisition and development of particular skills for the reading and evaluation of criticism generally? My view, and my understanding of the department's view, is the second. We require the course not because we think that theory is the one specialty that everybody ought to have but because we think that it can teach skills that will enable students to work at a more sophisticated level almost regardless of their eventual specialties. I didn't give the lecture on the schools of criticism the first week because I didn't want students to start with the idea that the goal of reading a critical article or book is to place it within some school. So I began with the session on detecting assumptions, and then we did a three-week unit in which we analyzed three different pieces of practical criticism on Brontë's novel before I did the lecture on the schools. Even though I explicitly say that the course's purposes are in the acquisition of skills as much or more than the acquisition of a body of knowledge, most of the students are very pleased to get the lecture.

As I read through the evaluations and found many students preferring the lecture to the discussions, I began to get impatient with them, even annoyed: Don't you see how much crucial learning can go on by your participating in and following the process of the discussions in which we try out ideas and through a process of weighing and sifting either confirm or revise them? Once I got beyond my defensiveness, however, I decided that it would be better to do the lecture first next time, even though I remain staunchly convinced that doing it first will not significantly alter the students' ability to analyze and evaluate the arguments of the critical essays to follow. I have become convinced, however, that it will make them feel more comfortable as they move through the course.

But I also have been thinking about why that should be. My speculative answer is that they are so accustomed to taking courses whose main purpose is the acquisition of a specifiable body of knowledge that when they face a course like this one that makes different demands on them, they almost naturally try to convert it to something they're used to. This explanation takes the onus of the problem off me (in this way I perhaps haven't gotten beyond my defensiveness), and that makes me a little suspicious of it. But in lots of other ways, I find it very attractive.

If it's right, it also makes me appreciate one of the virtues of my training at Chicago. I was continually made aware that there were scads of things I didn't know, but was also taught that it was more important for me to develop the skills for acquiring and analyzing knowledge. So I didn't worry a lot about teaching critical theory when I came here even though I had taken only one formal course in critical theory. I'd like to convey the same attitudes to my Intro to Grad Study students but so far haven't succeeded.

Tuesday, 17 *February* 1987

Anne is going to Louisville. She didn't like Illinois nearly as much, so regardless of what they tell her when they call tomorrow, she'll tell them that she's decided to take the other offer. I'm happy, Louisville is happy, and best of all Anne is happy. Illinois? In this market, they'll still do fine.

Wednesday, 18 *February* 1987

On Monday and Tuesday I had planned to visit Katie's classroom, but postponed my visit each day when we got to school and learned that Katie's regular teacher was home sick. Since Katie was excited and then let down each day, I promised I'd stay today whether she had a sub or not. I could at least get some sense of the room and of how Katie interacted with her classmates.

At 8:25, when the bell rang, she had neither her regular teacher nor a sub. The kids made their way up to the room and soon made enough noise to attract the attention of the teacher next door, who came in, saw the situation, and called the office on the intercom. At about 9 the gym teacher came up, restored some order, and started winging it. She held the fort until about 10:15, when the sub arrived and started winging it in her fashion. Though Mrs. Jones, a former regular teacher in the school, was successful in channeling the class's disparate energies into group activities, it was not a day to inspire confidence in the visiting taxpayer, not a day that would make him feel justified in deciding to move to this school system. It turns out that the office and the regular teacher had a miscommunication about her situation this week. The office expected her to call each day that she would be out; when her husband called for her yesterday, he said she'd be out until further notice. The school is now reviewing the procedures for teachers to follow in reporting their absences.

Fortunately, one of the principles of Katie's curriculum is that children work on their own. She could show me some of the projects she'd been doing and could continue a few of them. She seemed very comfortable with her work and with most of her classmates. And the work she did was fine, though I'm not sure there was enough of it. Katie, it is clear, has set herself up as Class Consultant on reading and spelling. As a result, she gets interrupted a lot and doesn't accomplish as much as she should on her own projects. I liked watching her work and enjoyed her interactions with her classmates, but I need to go back and see what it's like under better—and more typical—circumstances.

Thursday, 19 *February* 1987

I did mid-course evaluations in the critical writing course this week, and I'm surprised at how positive they are. There is some grumbling about the journal, and one person feels that we're overemphasizing writing at the expense of reading skills, but on the whole the students are praising the course. This praise doesn't have the warmth and enthusiasm that the best classes produce, but it's both fairly detailed and virtually unanimous. If I were evaluating the class I wouldn't give it such high marks.

The pull between teaching analysis and teaching writing has been stronger than usual this quarter. Although I take a rhetorical approach both to the literature and to their writing, I don't know how much they see the connections, and I worry at times that when I suspend our work on the analysis of literature to work on sentence style it will feel like two different courses to the students. But my real problem with the course remains the same: I haven't succeeded in moving them beyond their attitude of passive reception. They remain the Silent Majority, the Quiet Bunch.

A few of the students indicate that they're not used to analyzing literature in the way that I'm teaching it this quarter, so that may account for some of the silence: "I like the way your discussions test our abilities. I often find myself having a hard time understanding your arguments, but they force me to study the literature. While I don't always agree with what you say, your comments do elicit my thoughts on the subject." Would that they'd all said that. Well, I'll make another pitch about the wonderful things that can happen when you open your mouth in my class.

Beyond that I'm not sure what to do. Maybe I should just go in some day and stand there and see what happens. But I'm afraid that they'd outwait me. Besides, as the evaluations indicate, it's not yet time for desperate measures. Maybe a good pep talk will do the job.

Monday, 23 *February* 1987

We spent this weekend away from Columbus and OSU at Oglebay Park in Wheeling, West Virginia. We shared a cabin with four other families, and for the most part did no work. Instead, we played with the kids (there were eight altogether), went swimming, talked a lot with each other, and spent a large chunk of our time eating and drinking. I got out for one of my longest runs of the winter on Saturday morning, and on my shorter Sunday run I had the pleasure of watching the warm sun break out from behind the clouds and temporarily claim control of the day. It was a wonderful weekend.

It was not a complete break for me, however, since Friday made it two weeks that I've had the fifty-some papers from my graduate class and I just had to get them back. So on Saturday morning, after I ran and when everyone else headed off for the zoo and the 3-D movie, I stayed in the cabin and worked steadily at the papers for about three hours. With that start, I was able to finish them today. The striking thing—and I was conscious of it at the time—was that the three hours of grading formed

one of the pleasant features of the weekend. The sun was shining, everyone else was out doing something together, and there I was shut up in
the cabin with my burden of papers. And I liked it. I must be appropriately
batty for the profession.

The papers didn't contain any great surprises. The option that most of
them chose was to analyze the argument of a critical article and then to
assess its validity and effectiveness. Most of them did fairly well with the
first part, less well with the second. But the papers on the whole did show
that they are on the way to acquiring the skills the course is most designed to teach. And they have given me a sense of what needs to be
emphasized in the remaining weeks of the course.

Thursday, 26 *February* 1987

The condition of my office desk these days says a lot about the way I feel
my life is going. It's a mess, and I see little hope of getting it under
control until the end of the quarter. Foothills of books, memos, folders,
papers, notices, and notes to myself have sprung up at three corners,
while a three-layered mountain called a stacking tray occupies the fourth.
The terrain of this mountain is virtually indistinguishable from that of the
foothills, except that it lacks the solidity of books. Meanwhile a river of
more books, memos, folders, etc., wends its circuitous way through the
remaining territory, threatening all the time to overflow its ill-defined
banks and engulf the black boulder of the phone, which has wisely
adopted the survival strategy of ringing constantly so that I must always
be retrieving it from the encroaching river.

This topography has evolved rather quickly out of a series of utterly
mundane events. I teach my critical writing class at 2:00 every day and
have my office hours after class. In order not to stop writing altogether, I
have been trying to stay home in the mornings and work where I have a
better chance of not being interrupted. I then go into the office anywhere
from about 11:30 to 1:00 where, after a maddening hunt for a free parking
place, the following scenario typically occurs. I go to my mailbox, which I
find stuffed with memos, notices, papers, etc., and I begin to sort through
them, bringing things that can be handled by my very capable secretary,
Cartha, over to her desk, where there is also another stacking tray for me.
From that I pick up more folders, memos, notes, etc., and again try to

handle on the spot whatever I can. Nevertheless, I typically accumulate a few things to take back to my office. While I am working in the main office I often stop and chat with colleagues, or I run into students who want to know when I will be going to my office. I tell them my hours but indicate that I'm willing to see them before my class if there is time. Thus, I carry the pile of memos, notes, folders, etc., down to my office, find a place for it in the already existing ecosystem, and talk to my company. By the time he, she, or they leave, it is time for me to get ready for my class. I go off with the good intention of getting to the pile after the class. But the students line up outside the door during office hours, and the phone, threatened yet again by the new runoffs into the river, rings insistently as well. By the time the students and the phone complete their business with me, I have to go pick up the kids—or if it's Betty's day to do that, I am at last able to attend to the most pressing matters that have been waiting for me. Friday could be a day to catch up, except that my graduate class goes from 10:00 to 12:30, I have office hours before it, and on alternate weeks meeting of the Senate Steering Committee from 2:00–4:00. On weeks when I don't have Steering I try to balance the afternoon by going for a run and doing some of that work.

In the course of giving us his *Life and Opinions*, Sterne's Tristram Shandy tells us about the squeaky door hinge in the Shandy house: it just needs a little oil; his father is always remarking that he *must* fix it; and of course he never does. So they live for years with a squeaky door when a minute of attention would solve the problem. I confess that I have some Shandy door hinges—what I have come to think of as Shandies—in my life. A few characteristics distinguish a genuine Shandy from other jobs I might not do on time: (1) a Shandy is not especially difficult or time-consuming; (2) a Shandy nevertheless arouses some mild aversion in me; (3) a Shandy develops a powerful inertial force—one far greater than predicted by the laws of physics and even perhaps those of human psychology—once it is not attended to promptly.

The Evolution of a Shandy: A Case Study

Monday: My desk is getting to be a real mess. But now's not a good time to clean it. I'll do it later, if I have time—or maybe tomorrow.

Tuesday: I should clean off this desk. But I'm still behind on some of this other work. I'll take care of the desk first thing tomorrow morning: it won't take that long.

Wednesday: I know I promised myself I'd clean off this desk, but I need to go over this text before class. Anyway, a neat desk is a sign of an empty mind.

Thursday: I can't face cleaning up this mess. I'll call Betty and then go to the gym.

Friday: I'll clean my desk at the end of the quarter.

The end of the quarter: Where is that damned thing? I know it's on this desk somewhere. I've just got to find it. Maybe I will have to get serious and clean up this mess.

Friday, 27 *February* 1987

Betty and Katie are off to New Jersey for our nephew's confirmation. Michael and I will spend the weekend amusing each other. Tomorrow no doubt will be given over to cartoons and to playing with "mighty guys." Michael has a large collection of He-Man and Thundercat figures, a collection that reflects a compromise between him and his parents. We agreed that he could have the figures provided that he collected only the good guys. When we play with them, we usually conduct an imaginary battle in which the (invisible) enemy is quickly and bloodlessly routed. After the battle, the good guys all go back to the castle for tea and applesauce, and then sometimes naps. Here's to the flexible imagination of the four-year-old.

In between Michael's and my keeping each other company—or better, late at night, as, for example, right after I finish this sentence—I need to get some work done on my *Great Expectations* paper.

Saturday, 28 *February* 1987

Despite the condition of my desk, my still uncompleted Dickens paper, and my knowledge that I would be alone with Michael this weekend, I took a long lunch yesterday. A colleague, Julian Markels, and I ended up having a good talk about our research, teaching, careers, lives as jocks, the department, and a host of other things. Even as it was happening—and it felt natural—I was conscious of how rarely I've had such a talk with a colleague and of wanting it to continue. One cause of this relative lack of intimacy probably has to do with my socialization as a male. We don't let our guards down to each other and all that. Another cause surely is that I and my colleagues have let our interaction be circumscribed by the demands on our time. We talk in the halls before one of us has to go teach or get to the next meeting; we talk before or after the lecture, the committee meeting, and so on. We even schedule group discussions of common interests. We rarely schedule time to talk informally. So I find that I'm friendly with virtually all my colleagues, but close friends with very few.

A related cause here is how we spend our weekends. In graduate school, Betty and I had a fairly active social life with our peers. We spent a lot of Friday and Saturday nights going to or giving dinners for six to eight people. We've done a lot less of that here. It's a lot more effort once you have children. We're tired at the end of the week. We want to give more attention to the kids, and so on. Part of it, too, I think, is that because of our jobs, we each already have a close friend who is an academic, who understands and can share the trials, tribulations, and rewards of this business.

Still, I sometimes wonder about the fact that even considering the constraints on my friendships with students, I feel closer to many of them than to all but a few of my colleagues. I just thought of the following test: If Betty and I were to leave OSU, how many of my colleagues would I stay in touch with? Three for sure, and then possibly another three or four. If we left, how many of my current students would I stay in touch with? Probably all of them.

Monday, 2 March 1987

The department's basketball team lost by six in the finals of the faculty-staff playoffs tonight. Had the loss been three or four years ago it would have bothered me a lot more. Tonight I am just grateful that I played well enough not to feel that it was my fault we lost. Instead of replaying the game all night, I'll be able to concentrate on finishing my lecture. Better get to it.

Thursday, 5 March 1987

The lecture was hardly a triumph. I had the sense that I was saying too much too fast for the audience really to hang onto it. Still, I did manage to make some progress on the book, and that's what I most wanted. I wrote the bulk of thirty-some pages (not all of which I read) in the last week and rewrote many of them in the last two days. Had a late-night crucial discovery on Monday which led me to rework the first twenty or so pages before I could go on and finish the paper. I realized that my difference from Peter Brooks, who, like me, wants to talk about narrative dynamics, isn't just the difference between his psychoanalytical and my rhetorical approach. It's also that he sees the narrative text as essentially thematic (he emphasizes the importance of repetition) whereas I see it as both thematic and mimetic. I can claim (I think) that I can talk more adequately about "reading for the plot" than he does. One consequence of the timing of my discovery and of the direction it took me is that I feel better about the theoretical part of the paper than about the discussion of *Great Expectations*. I haven't finished working through my ideas about the novel and about the way that Wemmick's character functions. Still, I'm a lot further along than I would be if I hadn't committed myself to do the talk. The question is what kind of price I'll have to pay for having slept so little in the past week.

To paraphrase John Gabel, Lauren did herself proud in defending her dissertation today. Her committee asked her some tough questions which led her to rethink some things, but she was able to do that rethinking without getting defensive about what she had done. So rather than having the character of a defense, our meeting this morning had more the character of a conversation. Afterward Julian and Steve Fink, the other committee members, told me how well they thought it had gone and how strong they thought the dissertation had been. Steve had been on Lauren's general examination committee two or three years ago and he remarked at how much she'd progressed.

What happened, I think, is that as Lauren kept working on the dissertation, a study of what she calls "refracted discourse" in the novel—narrative passages that convey the sense of more than one consciousness being expressed (as for example in any ironic statement)—she began to understand what the whole process of writing a dissertation is all about. She began to sense what exactly her question was, and she began to think about the complicated relations between the work that she was doing in the different chapters. Once that happened, she was able to take her early first drafts and very quickly revise them into strong and clear analyses of the different novels that she was working with. Witnessing Lauren's blossoming is enough to maintain my faith in the way we do graduate education at OSU for a good long while.

Friday, 6 March 1987

Despite my pep talks, despite the icebreaker of their acting out scenes from *Death of a Salesman*, there has been no permanent change in the critical writing class. Part of the trouble is that we've now moved into our work with poetry, and as they did reveal in the one fairly lively discussion we've had recently, they're afraid of it. Here's where our inductive inquiry into fiction and drama is supposed to pay off. I want them to see that though poetry does follow different conventions it can be seen as continuous with the other genres. In one sense the direction of our induction has been from the most complicated structures to the least. Narrative fictions give us multiple characters, points of view, and scenes organized around some developing actions; drama gives us a similar multiplicity, but without the narrator it also gives us a sense of what the single voice in a particular situation can do; poetry—or at least lyric poetry—gives us that single voice for its own sake. The relative simplicity of the structure, however, is deceptive. Comprehending poetry is frequently more difficult than comprehending narrative, at least at the initial level. If they're with me this far, then we can talk about why this situation should obtain. They write it down, but I'm not sure they're convinced.

On the whole their papers are getting better. I've had them in for conferences about the second version of their *1984* papers. They are responding well to the assignment, and, I think, coming to see some things about both Orwell's narrative and the process of writing a paper that they had only dimly glimpsed on the first go-round.

I sense that some, though by no means all, of the uneasiness the graduate students expressed in their mid-quarter evaluations has dissipated. I talked again about the relation between "knowing how" and "knowing that" in the purposes of the course, and I think that the students themselves are beginning to recognize their own increased skills. We've also varied the lecture/discussion mode a few times, breaking into small groups to work for a half-hour or so on a specific question or set of questions, and the groups have taken their work seriously and caused some of the silent ones to articulate their thoughts. I feel like it's been an uphill battle to convince some of them about the value of what we've been doing, but that I've slowly been making that climb.

Sunday, 8 *March* 1987

I said a couple entries back that losing the intramural game didn't bother me the way it would have a few years ago. To explain why requires a story, one that I haven't fully put together for myself yet.

Long before I was a serious runner I was a basketball player. When I was in grammar school, I dreamed of playing in high school; when I was in high school I dreamed of playing in college; when in college I would have dreamed of playing in grad school if there were grad school teams. (Reined in by some reality principle, I never dreamed of playing in the NBA until—but that's getting ahead of the story.) Once I learned to shoot layups, I was hooked. Since then I've always gotten a little rush from watching one of my shots go through the hoop. It's like getting a small reminder that someone thinks you're special—"You love me! How amazing!"—and this reminder you have the power to evoke yourself. I have, I think, also been drawn to the game by the way it combines the necessity of teamwork with the opportunity to develop and exploit individual skills. It depends on both the predictable and the unpredictable so that it rewards both the player who masters its fundamentals and the player who is creative with them.

Playing basketball also was a way for me to establish an identity in high school and in college as well as a way to channel my competitiveness. A walk-on at Boston College, I didn't have a great career. But after riding the bench as a sophomore and a junior, I started as a senior on a .500 team, and, on the strength of my GPA more than my ppg., was named to an Academic All-American team. That last year was in many ways very satisfying. After my two years of collecting splinters, I *appreciated* starting. And after making the team as a walk-on, I felt that I had accomplished something important. Still, I wasn't entirely sorry to see that season end. Our team had, in many ways, grown further apart rather than closer over the course of our five and a half months together. We were

tired of each other, got on each other's nerves very easily. I was very glad
to win our last game and think about moving on.

When I started at Chicago, though, a funny thing happened to my
basketball career: it became more important to me than ever. I was ready
to see my senior season end in part because I fantasized that my academic life would be terrific when I wasn't giving three or more hours every day
from October 15 to March 15 to practice or games or travel. I would
imagine how wonderful it would be to have only literature courses to deal
with. When I got to Chicago and lived with those conditions, I felt that
what I really wanted to do was play basketball (when the gods want to
punish us, they answer our prayers). During my M.A. year, I played almost
every day. And having started for a Division I team just the year before, I
had a competitive advantage over the Bartlett Gym Regulars (and Irreg-
ulars) and was the unofficial rookie-of-the-year in the North Side league I
got into.

One doesn't need to be a Viennese doctor to figure out that part of my
compulsion to play that year came from my desire to possess and demonstrate a kind of mastery that I didn't feel I had in my studies. Playing
ball was also so refreshingly different. It was hot and sweaty and phys-
ically intense where school was so cerebral and frequently bloodless. It
was concentrated and compressed, offering quick resolution—"Game's
to 10; winner stays on"—where school was diluted, stretched out. I
wouldn't know if they'd decided I was Ph.D. material until well into April.

Because I liked playing ball so much and felt so unsure of whether
graduate school was for me, I tried to get a contract to play in Europe the
next year. At one point it looked like I would go to Belgium, but for
reasons I never fully understood, the contract fell through. After that the
agent who was trying to get me something and who had far more important clients (like Artis Gilmore) to worry about, stopped working on it—
though he never quite said so. I didn't give up hope until the summer,
when we were back in Boston and I had to accept the fact that it was too
late to make any plans to go to Europe in the fall. After much soul-
searching, I decided to enter the Ph.D. program. I hadn't definitely decided to commit myself to the professional study of literature, but I had
decided that I wanted to explore it further, to see if I could become good
enough at it to make it more satisfying than it was that first year. A crucial

factor in my decision was the course in the eighteenth-century novel I had taken with Sacks that spring. It gave me a glimpse of how I could connect many of the things I had always felt as a reader with what I thought of as criticism in the big time. Since my commitment was still somewhat shaky, I sometimes wonder whether going to Belgium would also have meant traveling permanently away from my Ph.D. I also wonder whether I'd have traveled away from it if I hadn't taken Shelly's course.

Though I began to feel more satisfied with graduate school once I was in the Ph.D. program, my hunger to play ball didn't abate. I would occasionally resolve to play less and study more, but I always found reasons to break these resolutions. So I went on playing often and intently—in pickup games at noon, in intramural leagues, in city leagues—for another two and a half years. Then during one intramural game I tore the ligaments in my knee and was forced to the sidelines for nine months, and after that to playing at less than full capacity for another nine. I suppose that this period of injury and convalescence could have led to my gradual withdrawal from the game, but in fact my desire to play drove me through my rehabilitation. I should lift weights to strengthen the knee once a day? O.K., I'll lift twice. And I'll work on my arms, chest, and shoulders as well as my leg. By the time my knee was fit, I was much stronger than I'd ever been, and I played with the pleasure of discovering how my newfound strength could help my game. My hunger to play, my newly acquired strength, my pleasure in playing with friends all came together and offered me much satisfaction during my last year at Chicago. At that point, Betty and I were resident heads in an undergraduate dorm, and our dorm team won the fall intramural all-comers tournament. The team I played on in the Chicago Park League won both the regular season championship and the playoffs. In the summer that same team entered one of the best leagues in the city and started beating lots of teams with much greater talent than ours.

The director of that league kept telling me that he thought I should be playing in the NBA. I regarded his talk as just the usual hyperbole. Everybody who plays any serious ball knows or has heard about hundreds of guys who allegedly were a pro team's last cut; now I could join their ranks. I knew I was too slow to cover anyone in the pros or even to bring the ball up the floor against most of the guards in the league. But then Norm said that he was going to get his friend, Ed Badger, coach of the

Bulls, to see me play. I told Norm that it was too late for me, that I was leaving Chicago to start my academic career, and that I was pretty sure I wasn't NBA material. Nevertheless, Norm did destroy the effect of the reality principle. I started dreaming about playing for the Bulls. A few weeks after our initial talk, Norm reported that Badger had been checking with other people who knew the league; the scouting report was that though I was a pro shooter, I wasn't quick enough to survive in the NBA. That sounded right—even flattering—to me. I stopped dreaming.

Then Badger did show up to see me play—the night after we had been eliminated from the playoffs, when our furious comeback fell two points short. That gave me a few days thinking about what might have been (suppose he came and I had one of my games where everything I threw up went in), but that's all. Once I learned he had come to see me play, I could have contacted him and tried out as a free agent, but despite my hunger to play that just didn't make any sense. It was August by this time and we were leaving for Columbus and Washington on September 1st. I had made a commitment to OSU. And above all, I knew that the scouting report was right. I just wasn't good enough to play in the NBA, and I didn't need to go to training camp to prove it. Still, part of me wanted to ask, where were you guys four years ago when I was floundering in the M.A. program by day and burning up the courts by night?

Once I came to Columbus, I maintained my intense desire for and satisfaction in playing for another five years, a period that included a very frustrating stretch in which I developed tendinitis in my right foot that would flare up very badly whenever I tried to play. Then I started to have knee problems again, and the league I played in with great pleasure one year became a burden the next. After Michael was born, it seemed crazy to shop around for a new league and another night out, so I dropped that part of my connection to the game. I also had to admit that I had reached a point where I wasn't going to get any better. Around this time, I started running and racing and was seduced in part by the opportunity for improvement they offered. And I was admitting to myself that if I wanted to write as well as teach and do committee work, something had to give.

Slowly, then, the hunger to pick up the charge, run the break, make the smart pass, hit the jumper has waned from my life. I still like to play, still hate to lose, still get a rush when the shot goes in, but when I'm away from the game, I don't think about it the way I used to, don't feel that itch to get out on the court and do my thing. In that sense, my own sense of myself has changed: I'm an academic who occasionally plays basketball, not a basketball player who's also an English professor. What's surprising, perhaps, is that my full acceptance of this identity has taken so long. In any case, when I think about it, I'm reminded of my age: I'm 36, not 26—or even 31.

Friday, 13 *March* 1987

The end of classes, the end of the induction. January 5th seems like a long time ago.

Not much change in the critical writing group. I tried this week to get them to see how the different pieces of the course were related to each other, to recognize not only the relation between the literary genres but also that between the composition of a literary work and the composition of a critical essay. It's worth worrying about sentence style in a critical essay for the same reason it's worth worrying about point of view in a short story. Both have important consequences for the way the reader will respond to the whole story. Heads nodded, but I wasn't sure whether our work together had actually made them *feel* the force of what I was saying or just given them enough to see that it had a kind of abstract logic.

In the graduate course, I also worked on synthesis by reviewing the variety of critical texts we had read (practical criticism, abstract theory) and the range of problems we had explored (the nature of texts, the nature of literary language, the relation of critical schools to each other, the interpretation of specific texts). But more than that, I tried to emphasize that the *way* we went at these various texts and problems was as important as the problems. If they learned some things about critical argument and literary reason in our sometimes unwieldy sessions, then the course will have prepared them properly. Their final papers will give me a good idea about that.

Monday, 16 *March* 1987

Before I finish the quarter and leave for a short vacation and then the Hemingway conference in California on the 20th, I still have a lot of grading to do and a lot of graduate committee work, including getting the T.A. offers out. I also need to finish my paper for the narrative conference in Michigan. Since I'll get back from California only a few days before I leave for Ann Arbor, I need to get the paper in the mail to my fellow panelists this week. I'm kicking myself for not having planned to do something from my book. If I'd learned anything from past experience, I'd have chosen to do part of the Dickens chapter. But I decided instead to try to write up some ideas about George Eliot's *Middlemarch* that I've been carrying around for years. Now, though, I feel that I don't have time to do Eliot justice. And my old ideas about my question—why does Eliot construct four plots rather than three or five and why does she interweave them as she does?—should be filtered through my new way of talking about progression. But my need for speed is inhibiting my efforts to do that. The paper feels like old clothes that don't quite fit anymore.

It was about three years ago that I stopped believing the pious notion that one could always make time for everything one wanted or needed to do. I began to realize instead that as a permanent consequence of the choices we've made in evolving our particular version of the two-career, two-child family, Betty and I would always have more to do than time would allow. Accepting that realization has helped me stay cool and calm most of the time, but as I've said before, there are periods when the gap between the supply of time and the demands upon it become extremely stressful and frustrating. I'm in one right now.

Betty's finish, though hectic, isn't shaping up as quite so demanding. But what's happening, of course, is that she's doing more of the preparations for our trip to California. Another consequence of our previous choices: if one of us has heavy pressure from one source, that often increases the pressure on the other from a different source.

Thursday, 19 March 1987

I need the typographical equivalent of a sigh of relief: I turned in my grades today, bringing the quarter to an official end. I'm all but finished with my *Middlemarch* paper (once more through the word processor) and tomorrow it's California, here we come.

On the whole I'm pleased with the final work turned in by both class-es. Despite my sense of struggle in our daily sessions, I can see that the critical writing course accomplished its basic objectives. The students write better than they did ten weeks ago, and they're more skilled at interpretation. The graduate students made more impressive progress. Some of the final papers displayed a kind of sophistication in under-standing and counterargument that was not at all evident in the first papers. Most showed an awareness of issues and the ins and outs of dealing with them that the group was largely innocent of back in January. I'm not sure that the means were always the best, but I'm satisfied with where most of them have ended up.

The evaluations tell their own story. Here's one from the critical writ-ing class.

> This course was definitely the most intensified writing class I have ever
> taken, which typically for me would mean that I disliked it. However, as the
> quarter went on and I felt more comfortable with my style of writing, and
> applying what we talked about in class concerning expressing oneself
> clearly, I ended up not dreading each writing assignment so much. . . . I
> feel that having completed English 302, I have a greater awareness of how
> to approach the analysis of a piece of literature, and hopefully have some
> of the writing skills necessary to express such an analysis. . . . And now
> that the Orwell paper is done, I can say that I enjoyed this course.

Several of the students commented on the lack of discussion, and some even tried to explain it. One suggested it was part of a campus-wide epidemic, another that students don't like to speak in a small class, another that I had spoken too loudly the first few days and intimidated them all. My favorite commentary, though, is this one: "You were full of ideas and enthusiasm, which was good since often times you must have felt like you were talking to tree stumps." Well, now that you mention it. . . .

Here's a not atypical one from Intro to Grad Study:

> I started out in this course with a rather skeptical attitude toward criticism
> and theory in general. In the first few weeks, I felt as if my suspicions were
> being confirmed. However, at some point, the readings, instruction, and
> class/group discussions began to become very interesting and useful. . . . I
> believe the course met its objectives for me—I can now say I have a
> greater appreciation for and comprehension of literary criticism and theory.

There were two strongly negative evaluations, but on the whole the students' comments reinforce my sense that the course worked. The evaluations are reassuring not just because of what they say but because of the attitude and feeling behind the statements. Despite their struggling, the students were engaged by this course. The evaluations for the critical writing course also reinforce my judgment of it. Though generally positive, the students have some minor complaints, but more significantly, they don't have the same degree of commitment in their statements. The course did not touch their fine-tuned spirits the way the other one touched its members.

SPRING 1987

Recovering—and Gaining Momentum

Monday, 30 March 1987

Our trip West was excellent, a very welcome break after the crazy quarter. Betty and I had some time to focus on each other and on the kids. We visited Betty's brother in Berkeley and several friends in the Bay area. Like the weather, the friendships felt warm and comfortable: it was indeed spring on the coast.

Out in Berkeley, I had two early-morning runs on the Fire Trail north of campus, a route that is simply stunning: the trail winds uphill for about three miles through an old, rich forest. Parts of it bring you along the edge of the hills so that you can look down on the forested valley in which you began. In other parts the trail opens out to display the whole panorama of San Francisco, the Bay, the bridges: nature and civilization in a seductive, illusory harmony. To run easily along that trail with its sudden breathtaking prospects, its spring morning smells, its sweet air, and even the physical challenge of its hills was wonderful therapy.

While I was soaking up all that therapy, I couldn't help but think about teaching at Berkeley as an alternate fate. A few years after my job interview there, the then-chairman told me that I was their second choice. Since things have worked out well for us at OSU, I can't have any deep regrets about what happened, and although I was disappointed in my own performance at the interview, I've seen enough now to recognize that a lot of what happened there was beyond my control. And even had I performed better, I still may not have been up to the caliber of the person they did hire. Certainly Berkeley doesn't regret their decision. The guy they hired won last year's James Russell Lowell Award, the prize given by the MLA for the best book published in a given year.

Still, being out there, thinking about being able to run on the Fire Trail all year round, and thinking about the people I know in Berkeley's English department, I started wondering about how different my life might be if I had been Berkeley's first choice. Maybe I would have been racked by tenure anxiety for seven years. Maybe Betty would never have found a job she liked. Maybe I would have felt comfortable about tenure when my book was accepted just as I did at OSU. Maybe Betty would have gotten a job she likes better. Maybe we would have spaced our kids differently. It made for some interesting speculation, however idle.

More significant, perhaps, was the reminder of how so many academics don't have much choice about some of the basic conditions of their lives—especially where to live. Certain people will decide that they won't go to a certain part of the country (Betty's brother John teased us again by saying that if he finished his dissertation, he might have to leave Berkeley for a place like Columbus), but very few—and no new Ph.D.s—have it within their power to say that they will get a job in city X or Y or Z. The school(s) in X or Y or Z have to have an opening, the opening has to be in your field, and you have to be their first choice. You're facing pretty tough odds there.

Betty and the kids headed back to Columbus last Wednesday, while I stayed on in California and went down to San Diego for the Hemingway conference. It was useful and interesting. I like Hemingway, but I dislike him too, and two days of virtually unrelieved attention to old Papa was a bit much for me. Nevertheless, I enjoyed meeting the other conferees, and the reaction to my paper on *A Farewell to Arms* taught me that things I was taking for granted need to be argued. I always assumed that Hemingway wants us to think that Frederic Henry does grow, change, and develop into a kind of tragic hero, so I was surprised when some of the aficionados there argued that he didn't. One crux is how readers take Frederic's description of the malevolent world: "If people bring so much courage to this world, the world has to kill them to break them so of course it kills them. . . . It kills the very good and the very brave and the very gentle impartially. If you are none of these it will kill you too but there will be no special hurry." I read the lines as the place where Henry articulates Hemingway's own beliefs as they're revealed in the action of the rest of the novel. Others read them as puerile, a sign of Frederic's false romanticization of his experience. What the debate allowed me to see is that as I try to develop the paper into a chapter of my book, I can link my discussion of how to assess the sexism implicit in Hemingway's portrayal of Catherine Barkley's character with a discussion of how to evaluate a "philosophical" position like this one. If we take the principles developed to assess the sexism and use them to evaluate the philosophy, what do we find?

One of the people I liked the most disagreed with me the most. Paul Smith, who gave a smart paper on what studying the manuscripts can tell us about some interpretive problems in Hemingway's short stories, argued that Frederic doesn't learn much from his whole experience. For a minute I thought he was implying that as a result the book doesn't work, and I challenged him about that. He came back by saying that I shouldn't assume that because he didn't take my view he didn't think it worked. Once we got over that rough spot we talked more amicably; he even asked for a copy of my paper.

The trouble with the conference was its timing. Now I'll have to be leaving for Ann Arbor in two days, and then three days after I return I'll have to leave again on a recruiting trip to Texas. At least I'm not teaching this quarter. But how do people who travel all the time do it?

Thursday, 2 *April* 1987

In Ann Arbor. Sleeping in a strange bed last night, I had a vivid dream of home: Betty was pregnant again; she and I were ecstatically happy about it. When I woke up and realized I'd been dreaming, I was tremendously relieved. But the dream must be a sign of my own guilt about these trips. To have another child would be to tie myself down. I certainly couldn't take three trips in three weeks. To be so happy about the condition would be to remove even the possibility of any tug away from the domestic: if the opportunity to travel arose, I wouldn't want to go. I must be very guilty.

Friday, 3 April 1987

Jamie, Anne, and I all gave our papers today. Jamie and Anne both did well, I think, and I at least survived mine. This was Jamie's first conference presentation, and she said later that she felt very nervous. I did too, just as I did last year when I watched Anne give her first paper. Last night at dinner with Jamie and Susan, a student who did her M.A. thesis with me at OSU and who is now studying for her Ph.D. at Chicago, I was asked about my own academic ups and downs. One of the things I talked about was the terrible letdown I felt after my Ph.D. orals when Sacks let me know that he'd have liked me to have done better. When Sacks took you on, he identified with you the way a father does with his child. And when you didn't perform up to his expectations, he was disappointed in you, and sometimes let you know it. When you performed well, you could feel his pride even before he said anything.

I never wanted to put that much pressure on my students, but watching them perform gives me new insight into how Sacks must have felt. I wonder too whether I communicate my concern in a way that makes the students feel pressure. Is it possible not to do that? Is there something in the adviser-student relationship that makes such feelings on the student's part inevitable? I suppose there is, especially when the two people care a lot about each other's work and each other's opinion. The more the adviser values the student the more he'll want the student to do well. The more the student values the adviser, the more he'll want to do well—and feel pressure to do well for himself and for the adviser.

Anyway, Jamie didn't show her nervousness, and she had some interested and enthusiastic questioners. Given what she had been saying about the problems with traditional ways of doing cultural criticism of American literature, she was asked to comment on a paper by another panelist that was putting Toni Morrison's *Song of Solomon* into a cultural context. There was a third paper (déjà lu for me) on Hemingway's *The Sun Also Rises*, and its author got drawn into that general discussion. In short, the session worked, and Jamie contributed nicely to its success.

Although Anne's session didn't click the same way, her paper went well. I thought she'd improved it since I'd read it earlier, and one of my friends commented that it made him want to read the Calvino novel that she was discussing.

I had a kind of anxiety of delivery about my own paper that I haven't experienced in a long time. Last night I fell asleep reading it, a sign of my desire to avoid having to deliver it. But I got all the way through it shortly before my session and decided it wasn't so bad. I went into the session determined to deliver it with some conviction. As I was reading I was aware that the conviction was mustered from without, not reenacted from within—I was seeking to add a conviction that I wasn't sure I really had. The trouble was not so much with the basic ideas—I do believe what I was saying about *Middlemarch*—but I had an acute sense that I wasn't doing enough with them. And I had never, in the too-short time I had devoted to the paper, found an effective way to connect what I was doing in my discussion of the plots to some other current issues in narrative theory. So I was wincing to myself at various "old-fashioned" locutions in the piece and wondering what the audience was going to make of it all. I did get some useful questions in the discussion, and a few people asked for copies, so I felt better afterwards. But I've resolved never again to give a paper under similar conditions.

Sunday, 5 April 1987

I wonder what will become of Susan, my former student, now in her second year at Chicago. She is a complicated woman, more complicated than I fully know, but one who has the ability to be a very distinguished worker in this vineyard. She is about my age, though, and still a few years away from the Ph.D. It gets harder to live in graduate student poverty the older you get, so I hope she can hang on and finish. I also sense that despite her considerable ability, she feels unsure of herself at Chicago, unsure of whether she knows enough, of whether she is smart enough to learn all she needs to know. After she told us at dinner the other night about her brief but serious writing block, I wanted just to shake her and say, "Relax, lighten up. Stop pressuring yourself so much that you feel you can't really be a student anymore, that you already have to know everything before you can write a word." But of course Susan knows all this already. Her insecurity is to some extent as natural as it is unnecessary. It is also a sign of how we socialize ourselves.

Rightly or wrongly, we have established an intellectual institution that perpetuates a Myth of Merit. The institution purports to reserve its most honored places for only the very learned, the very bright, and the very productive. If you are none of these, the institution will break you. Afterward you may be strong at the broken places, but you will never be honored. When the job market is tight there will be a special hurry to break you, to separate the truly learned, bright, and productive from the mere pretenders.

The trouble with the myth is not just that the institution doesn't make good evaluations of merit but also that nobody asks whether the same standard of merit ought to apply to us all, and nobody asks about the relation of the myth to such a central activity of the profession as teaching undergraduates. Nevertheless, once you have this myth instilled in you in graduate school, and once you are honest with yourself about your own limitations, you can end up getting in your own way. Susan, don't let that happen to you.

Of course, having tenure makes it easy for me to put Susan's anxieties in perspective, easy for me to forget my anxieties as a graduate student and my slow journey out of their seemingly unrelenting grip. It helps to remember how I felt whenever I drove on the Chicago Skyway. It helps too to think about my own relationship with the man who will be Susan's dissertation director, Wayne Booth.

Booth is the most eminent faculty member of the University of Chicago's English department: He's been president of the MLA; he's written four important books and numerous influential essays; he has developed an audience for his work among theorists, practical critics, and teachers of composition. In my second quarter of graduate school, before I knew Booth, I read his *The Rhetoric of Fiction* and was deeply impressed with both its analytical strength and its air of encyclopedic learning. It became a goal of mine to take a course with him and to do my best work in it. Finally, at the very end of my Ph.D. course work (spring 1975) I took his seminar in rhetorical criticism. The participants were all advanced students who were moving toward dissertations, and Booth let us set the syllabus, while he set the agenda. Each of us could ask the others to read one critical work relevant to our dissertation projects, and each of us prepared a paper for discussion that incorporated some work with that critical text. Our discussions focused in part on each student's larger project and in part on how he or she used the assigned text.

The class was very fine, and a very influential part of my training. Booth raised issues about my paper that proved to be very beneficial as I worked on my dissertation, and issues about how to deal with other critics that have influenced much of my work since. Still, to some extent I was disappointed with the way things went. Booth and I didn't get to know each other very well, in part, I concluded, because I wasn't able to meet his highest standard. At the same time, I felt—with how much accuracy I'm no longer sure—that he had too easily concluded that my paper distorted my chosen critical text and that he had too easily pigeonholed my project on language in the novel as a predictable reprise of the neo-Aristotelian arguments against the New Critics' view that literature was a special kind of language. My feelings about the experience were reflected in my anxious hesitation about asking him to write a letter of recommendation for me when I went on the job market. I thought he knew me well enough and that he rated my work highly enough to write a good letter, but even as I went ahead and asked I wasn't quite sure.

My next association with Booth came at the end of my time in Chicago. When I got ready to defend my dissertation during the summer before I came to OSU, my second reader, Joe Williams, was in Maine for the summer, and Sacks was recuperating from his second serious heart attack in eighteen months. Booth generously took over for Sacks and guided me through what was a very weird oral. Since there was no one from my committee there, and since the others, including Booth, were largely doing me and the department a service by even coming to the exam, I was the only person in the room who had actually read the whole dissertation. But it had been available to be read for about two weeks, and I had the sense that we were to observe the fiction that at least some of the examiners had actually read the document and not just the abstract I had written. When I was asked questions, I did not know what I should presuppose—or even pretend to presuppose—about the extent of the questioner's knowledge of the document. So I stumbled some as I tried to decide what I could repeat from the dissertation itself and what I needed to say beyond what I'd said there. Booth's own questions were astute, and he was kind throughout. Afterwards he told me that I had been awarded honors, though the exam committee felt the oral left something to be desired: "You got a bit tangled in your own spaghetti." So there I was again with Booth, feeling that I had met one standard and missed another.

Two years later Booth came to OSU to give a lecture, and we talked about the progress I was making on turning the dissertation into a book. Two months before, Sacks had had his third and fatal heart attack. One of the many consequences of that event was that Booth, who shared many ideas with Sacks, took on most of his dissertation students. Perhaps in part out of the same sense of duty and generosity, he offered to ensure that the manuscript would get a reading from the University of Chicago Press when I finished it. I sent the manuscript to Booth in early September, thinking that he would take it over to the press, and the editors would take it from there. His understanding was that he had offered to read it before he sent it over. He was, however, snowed under with work and couldn't get to it. The fall dragged on and I fretted more and more. Finally, he wrote me in December to say that he hadn't forgotten the manuscript and looked forward to reading it soon. In January, when I had to go to Chicago for another reason, I took courage and suggested that we get together and talk about the manuscript—as well as his recently published book on pluralism. From things Booth said during our talk, I inferred that he had finished reading the manuscript only the night before our meeting.

I can still easily conjure up the anxiety with which I walked up to his house on that cold, gray, Chicago-in-January Sunday. Perhaps melodramatically, I looked upon the coming moments as a critical point in my career—the shape of my future in the profession could be hanging on the outcome of the next hour. And since I couldn't *do* anything at that point, I had no outlet for my anxiety. The verdict, fortunately, was both swift and sweet: "Your book is even better than I expected it to be, and I expected it to be very good indeed." Anxiety became exhilaration while I did my best to remain outwardly calm. Booth not only recommended the book to the press, but then later, at the request of the editor, also wrote a very enthusiastic reader's report. I had finally met his standard. Yet even in that flattering report, which I know by heart though I have not had a copy of it for over five years, there was a (natural) allusion to my intellectual youth: "This is one of the best books by a humanist of Phelan's age that I have ever read." At times I loved that sentence, but at others I felt, with all the impatience of youth, that it was utterly spoiled by the reference to my age.

Two years later Booth asked if I would be willing to update the bibliography for his planned second edition of *The Rhetoric of Fiction*. I was grateful he asked—*The Rhetoric of Fiction* is good company—but again, while the request indicated that Booth placed considerable trust and confidence in my work, it also indicated that he regarded me as what I was, a decidedly younger scholar. When he invited me to take the job, he said that he felt it required somebody who was beyond graduate school. I supplied the inference about my academic age.

Since then we've had numerous talks in Chicago and at conferences, he's read and heard more of my work—including a few pieces directly about his own stuff, each of which mixes objections with praise. At lunch last fall after he came to hear a paper I gave at the Midwest MLA meeting, I felt that we'd finally moved into a new phase of the relationship. Both from what he said (some nice praise) and the way he expressed himself (familiarly, frankly), Booth made me feel that he had stopped thinking of me as a junior faculty member and had begun thinking of me as a friend and colleague. When I talk to him now, I no longer feel that there's still some standard to meet. I've grown up—in his eyes at least.

Thursday, 9 *April* 1987

In Edinburg, Texas, tonight. I flew into San Antonio late Tuesday, where I was picked up at the airport by Josué Cruz from OSU's Office of Minority Affairs. Josué, a native of San Antonio and a veteran of these trips, is recruiting for the whole graduate school, and serving as my guide. We spent yesterday at two schools in his home town, Our Lady of the Lake and St. Mary's, and then drove to Corpus Christi last night. This morning we went to Corpus Christi State, and from there on to Texas A & I this afternoon. Now we're here, ready for our last stop tomorrow at Pan American University. To save the university's money on airfare, however, we're going to stay until early Sunday morning. After we finish at Pan Am tomorrow, we're heading over the border to Mexico for a short visit and then to San Padre Island for a day of R & R.

The basic drill at all the places is the same. Josué and I are set up in a room with our catalogues and our applications and our prepared little speeches about the graduate school and the fellowship programs, and the students come and talk with us about their backgrounds and interests. At some point during our visit, I go and give a half-hour presentation of my research (I've been able to adapt material from the character book for all but one of the talks) to whatever students and faculty can be dragooned into attending. Sometimes the talk produces more business.

Regardless of what this trip yields in our recruiting of minority students, it is giving me a new perspective on my situation at OSU. Kristina, my host at Corpus Christi State, is one of only three faculty members in the English department. She teaches four courses a semester, and usually at least one of them is at night. Today, for example, she was to teach at 9:30 A.M., 12:30 P.M., and 8:30 P.M. Trained as a Renaissance scholar, she has to take almost all of British literature as her province. In addition, CCSU is in bad financial shape, so nobody got a raise this year, and the faculty are facing the prospect of a pay cut for next year. To make conditions more difficult, Kristina is a single parent of children who are eight and five. Given her low salary, she has to work every summer to make ends meet. She has no free time, very little money, and endless responsibilities to students, conditions which make it virtually impossible for her to publish. She would like to move, but it's hard for me to see how she will be able to. She appears to be a wonderful teacher—diligent, hard-working, able to push and encourage her students—but she also appears to be a prime candidate for burnout. Our conversation made me feel that my job is a sinecure.

Saturday, 11 April 1987

Yesterday's visit to Pan Am was the best stop on our trip. I met one of the students who will be coming to our program in the fall as well as a few good prospects for the following year. The faculty made a good effort to get the students out for my talk, and I had far and away my biggest audience. The talk, a synthesis of different parts of my book, seemed to be well received; I had good questions and some nice compliments. But about halfway through, a good portion of the audience got up and left. I carried on as best I could, though I could barely refrain from shouting, "Hey, don't leave yet! I haven't gotten to the best part. I still have to tell you about Lizzy Bennet!" Only later was I told that those people had to get to classes.

Pan Am is another place where living with tenure is a lot different from what I experience at OSU. Again one faculty member showed me around and talked to me a lot about the conditions of his job. Mike is the male counterpart of Kristina, only about ten years older and thus more established. He obviously brings great energy and enthusiasm to his job, and has a very good rapport with his students. He was very kind to me, but seemed somewhat defensive about his own professional life, even as he made it clear that he attended a lot of conferences and was working on several different projects. I think the hardest part of a job like his would be to find colleagues who would be kindred spirits. Mike seemed to have one in philosophy, but none in English. I admire both him and Kristina very much, even as I'm very grateful that I am not in their shoes.

Monday, 13 *April* 1987

Our stops in Mexico and especially at San Padre Island were enjoyable, but it's good to be home again. Best of all is that I'm not going anywhere again until July. Apparently, though, Katie has caught on to the pattern of the last few weeks. Today she asked Betty, "Where does Daddy have to go this weekend?"

Tuesday, 14 *April* 1987

Just over a year ago I learned that my best friend from Chicago had committed suicide. Spenko—he always referred to himself only by his last name—and I were in a Shakespeare class together during the first quarter of our M.A. year, but until we both took Booth's seminar at the end of our course work, I thought of him as just another one of the many people in that Shakespeare class who knew a lot more about the serious study of literature than I did. Once we started talking (in the early weeks of Booth's class), the bond between us became very strong very quickly. We were both ex-jocks (Spenko had been an all-Big Ten football player at Northwestern); both interested in theory, in style, in the struggles and rewards of writing. And we were both very interested in assessing ourselves relative to our classmates—and each other. We disagreed and argued about many things—he didn't like Jane Austen!—but found more points of agreement.

Spenko took a certain pride in defying the stereotype of the ethereal

English grad student. He lifted weights, smoked stogies, went to the fights. He walked with a heavy, resolute shuffle: the man never "took a stroll" in his life. His speech fluctuated between irony and epigram. He was second to none in his passion for the writers he admired—Shakespeare, Donne, Joyce, Dickens, Faulkner, Conrad, Nabokov—and in the middle of our conversations he'd frequently start quoting from one of them. His intensity had its down side, too. He talked about getting tied up in knots trying to write out his ideas, about black periods when he was unable to work.

That quarter when we took Booth's class was a very good time for Spenko. He was sharp in the seminar. His paper, as Booth testified, represented an impressive breakthrough in his work on the significance of unconscious associative patterns in narrative discourse. He was awarded the single dissertation fellowship given in the department. Toward the end of the quarter, he started going out with a woman whom he would marry four years later. He was full of life—and though never happy-go-lucky, clearly taking pleasure in his own growth. It was a treat to share that quarter with him, to feel our bond grow stronger every week.

Over the next two years, Spenko and I talked each other through field exams, the early stages of our dissertations, and the job market. We applied for some of the same jobs and both had interviews at Berkeley and at OSU, but our friendship was such that we didn't feel threatened by each other. Had one of us gotten the offer from Berkeley, or had only one of us gotten a job, magnanimity might have been hard for the other to muster. But we were never tested in that way. Instead, while I was being hired here, he landed a job at the University of Rochester, a place that rejected me in the first stage of the hunt. We went off to central Ohio and upstate New York, proud of ourselves and each other.

In the early years of our jobs, Spenko and I stayed in close touch. Betty and I even took Katie to meet him in Rochester the summer after she was born. Spenko was happy there, delighted with and successful in his teaching, anxious to be publishing—though less successful with his first attempts. His essays were getting rejected, and he felt that he might not have enough material to turn his dissertation into a book. And he was still subject to intense periods of writer's block.

After that summer, we slowly lost touch. The affection remained, but the contact, always initiated by me, became less frequent and our bond steadily weakened. I know little more than the outward facts. He continued to love his teaching and to struggle unsuccessfully with his writing. His marriage began to unravel. He won a teaching award and was denied tenure in the same year. He started drinking heavily. He attended an MLA-sponsored course for humanities Ph.D.s pursuing nonacademic jobs and seemed outwardly upbeat about his prospects. But he didn't leave the academy, and instead took a temporary job at one of the schools in the New York state system near Rochester. He was, however, unable to land another permanent teaching job. Last spring he shot himself.

From the outside, Spenko looks like a casualty of the reward system—though that's clearly only part of his story. Had he gotten tenure at Rochester, though, I'm convinced he'd be alive today. Which isn't to say that Rochester is to blame, only to insist that someone so committed to and successful with his teaching ought to be able to find a respected place in the academy. Instead, because he doesn't write a book, he gets fired and in his subsequent unsuccessful job-hunting learns again and again that no one is going to make it possible for him to do what he most wants.

As I think these unsettled thoughts, I must also think about alternate paths for my life. What if I hadn't been able to turn my dissertation into a book? What if things went sour between Betty and me? What if I had to face full rejection on the job market? What kind of pain must the man have been feeling, as hurt piled on hurt?

Spenko's suicide also makes me think about the fragility of friendship. Is it because we're male that the differences in our fortunes became—as I felt—some kind of barrier between us? Though I felt our bond weakening, I always thought that we'd reestablish its strength. Now I feel empty. He's gone, and I can't really understand why, no matter how many times and ways I construct the few reasons I can infer or how many others I invent. I just mourn for what's lost in his death: his distinctive personal style, his passion for literature, his commitment to ideas and his combativeness in defending his favorites, his humorous assessments of other people, including his ironic attacks on me.

I don't know where to go with these unsettled thoughts and feelings. Maybe there is no place.

Wednesday, 15 *April* 1987

Since February I have been attending the monthly meetings of the Athletic Council as the liaison between that body and the Senate Steering Committee. Unlike the meetings of any other university group that I know, these are expensive affairs. Before the official meeting, the athletic department springs for drinks and dinner in the dining room of the OSU golf course for the fifteen or so members of the council as well as a number of their own personnel. Under the rules of the university, it is not the athletic director and his staff, but the faculty-dominated council that has the charge of setting policy for the department. Rick Bay, the present athletic director, obviously doesn't like this arrangement, because he sometimes makes policy and then leaves the council to react. Last summer after Len Bias's death from a cocaine overdose and all the publicity surrounding it, Bay instituted a mandatory drug testing program for OSU athletes, coaches, and athletic department staff. In the fall, the council, scrambling to reassert their proper role in such policy matters, began a review of the program. They had an all-day meeting one Saturday in February to discuss the subcommittee's preliminary report, and then met last night in regular session to review the final report and vote on what should happen.

The meeting had some of the hottest exchanges I've ever witnessed off the playground or away from the gym. The subcommittee had developed three options for the athletic department to follow. One, phase out the present system and replace it with an extensive drug education program. Two, replace the present mandatory, random testing with a system of suspicion-based testing. Or three, modify the present system in a variety of ways: take steps to ensure the confidentiality and reliability of the tests; eliminate the testing of coaches; include alcohol in the drugs tested for. The subcommittee recommended that the council approve the first option, the athletic department and some of the other council members strongly favored the third, and nobody tried to make a serious case for the second. The choice, in effect, was testing or no testing. The choice took on greater interest because President Jennings's special assistant for legal affairs, Larry Thompson, attended the meeting as an interested party (representing another interested party) and made it clear that the central administration favored testing.

During the debate, the council members clashed about everything from the substantive issues to the appropriate parliamentary procedure to be followed. Those in favor of option one argued that testing, if not a clear violation of constitutional rights, was sufficiently demeaning and distasteful to be resisted as much as possible. Those in favor of option three felt that testing had proven to be an effective deterrent at OSU, a deterrent that was beneficial to the athletes, the program, and the university. For the most part, they expressed skepticism that education could be as effective. The distressing thing about the debate was that it frequently seemed tainted by an undercurrent of disrespect between the two sides: If you weren't so bullheaded/naive/unrealistic, you'd see it my way. That tone, of course, only intensified the heat of the discussion. For a while, the substance of the comments seemed less important than the power struggle between the different members.

The issue of testing brought all this deep feeling out because it involves the council members' feelings about both some general principles of the university and some specific political issues in the council itself. On the one hand, most academics are committed to their own academic freedom and are interested in extending that sort of freedom to students. Testing is absolutely anathema to that spirit. On the other hand, the image of the athletic program is tied in a rather complicated way to the image of the whole university. Unlike some other schools with big-time programs, OSU has never had any serious problems with recruiting violations, payoffs, grading scandals, and the rest—although from time to time some of the athletes have run afoul of the law. Those in favor of testing were implying that to drop it would leave the program vulnerable to a drug scandal and put both the athletes and the good image of the whole university at risk.

As for the situation within the council, to overturn Bay's program would be to reestablish the council as the policy-making body for the athletic department. On the other hand, to go that far would be to damage seriously the relations between the council and Bay. Then there was the Jennings issue. Should the council attempt to oppose the president's wishes here? Although I doubt that anyone made Jennings's stance more than a secondary consideration, I think that some would have welcomed the opportunity to see how he would react, while others felt that the practical course was to pay attention to his views.

I was very sorry that as liaison to the council I didn't have voting rights, especially when the vote on the first option ended in a tie. I'd have voted to phase out the program without any hesitation. After the tie vote on the first option, I expected another tie on the third, but one of the student members of the council became convinced that the program should be modified rather than phased out, so we'll keep drug testing at OSU for the foreseeable future.

Friday, 17 April 1987

Our departmental meeting this morning gave me another lesson in perspective. Murray [Beja, our chair] wanted to report on the MLA-sponsored conference on the future of doctoral studies he and Andrea Lunsford, a member of the MLA Commission on Writing, attended earlier this month. Murray gave a very detailed account of the events and discussions at the conference. No consensus emerged, but discussions kept circling back to a few issues: (1) the relation between the study of literature and the study of rhetoric/composition; (2) the extent to which doctoral programs ought to offer formal training in teaching; (3) how curricula ought to reflect the relations of history, theory, and literature.

After Murray's summary, three other faculty members spoke, all at Murray's request. Andrea filled us in on how the Commission on Writing was involved in the whole process. Louie Ulman, a first-year faculty member whose specialty is rhetoric, offered some of his thoughts on how his training made him feel he fit in a department predominantly devoted to teaching literature. I talked about possible implications of the conference for our graduate program. I suggested that we address the composition/literature split by conducting some team-taught rhetoric courses where one faculty member would be someone hitherto concerned mostly with literature and the other someone hitherto concerned mostly with composition. I also suggested that we look into establishing some kind of teaching intern plan, where grad students would work as apprentices to individual teachers. The faculty member and graduate student would regularly discuss the course material, how best to teach it, what kinds of papers and exams to give, how to grade them, and so on. We'll have to take these ideas up in the committee and consider them more fully.

After the meeting, Jamie told me that she and a lot of other graduate students felt their anxiety and depression levels go up. I was surprised, and I've been wondering since if, in part, I inadvertently contributed to their response. Before I got to my specific proposals, I suggested that I didn't think any great changes in doctoral study would be forthcoming until the reformers looked hard at the connection between doctoral programs and the tenure system. Murray reported that the conferees frequently remarked that the attendance at the conference was excellent—more than three-fourths of the schools offering the Ph.D. were represented. Such remarks were also usually accompanied by some reminder that Ph.D.-granting institutions constitute only seven percent of all schools with English departments. My point was that because of the emphasis placed on publication in tenure decisions—even at many schools without grad programs—virtually all graduate programs implicitly define success as the acquisition of the skills necessary to do tenurable research. In effect, the Ph.D.-granting institutions are concerned with preparing people to teach at other Ph.D.-granting institutions even though such institutions account for only seven percent of the nation's four-year colleges and universities, and until the reward system changes any great programmatic changes are highly unlikely.

I felt that I was saying something that almost everybody already knew, but perhaps hadn't thought much about. My purpose was to point out that any serious proposal for revision of doctoral programs ought to face these institutional facts. From my perspective as a faculty member, none of this seemed threatening. But the graduate students heard me saying that they are not being prepared for the jobs they are likely to get. I think, too, that some of them saw the very fact of the conference and the lack of consensus expressed there as a sign that some change was imminent, though its precise direction is impossible to predict and therefore impossible to prepare for.

Monday, 20 **April** 1987

Anne defended her dissertation today. She's been pushing very hard on it for the last two months because she wanted to defend now: her second reader, John Muste, who retired last year and moved to Taos, was to be in Columbus for just a few days. When I first heard her plan, I was a little skeptical, not because I didn't think she could finish, but because I thought she would end up settling for less than her best. But after weighing pros and cons, we agreed to regard the manuscript she produced for the defense as one draft short of the final version. As it turned out, she produced a very good version for today. As one of the committee members said, it's a lot closer to a book than what we usually see at this stage. I should have known she'd do something like that. I'm impressed.

The defense itself was fine—no high drama or low comedy, but a good, sensible discussion of metafiction and what Anne wrote about it. Now she can work on the final version and start pointing toward her move to Louisville.

Tuesday, 21 *April* 1987

Had a conversation yesterday with some graduate students about last Friday's departmental meeting. Some students simply wanted to be filled in on what happened, and some naturally wanted to talk about what it all meant for them. A few said that they didn't think it meant much, and Jamie tried to talk about why it depressed her and many of the other people who talked with her about it. It did have a lot to do with what I and some others said about the job market and with what that means about the relation between how they're being trained and the kinds of jobs they might eventually get. I tried to argue that their training would not be irrelevant to jobs where they had heavy teaching loads, but Jamie wasn't buying it. She seemed down on the whole program tonight, down even on the work we've been doing in the graduate committee, and, to some extent, down on me. I wonder if there's something else going on.

Wednesday, 22 *April* 1987

I'm slowly—ever so slowly, it seems—working my way back to my book. I'm rereading Calvino's *If on a winter's night a traveler*, a very clever metafictional exploration of the nature of reading that will challenge the explanatory power of my hypotheses about character and progression. I won't be able to draft the section on it in just a few days.

Thursday, 23 *April* 1987

A note from Jamie, saying that she's feeling better. She said that she's been taking everything too seriously, been unable to get any perspective on things, a function of being overtired from the heavy demands of her work, which she has not had any real break from since Christmas. She's giving two papers this weekend, and the preparations for them have added to her usual heavy load. O.K., I'll stop worrying and keep looking forward to hearing the papers.

Saturday, 25 *April* 1987

Congratulations to Jamie! Her paper for the College English Association of Ohio went splendidly; the editor of *College Composition and Communication* expressed an interest in publishing it. Then she surpassed that performance today, when her paper on Hawthorne's "Minister's Black Veil" and the paradigms of the criticism of American literature was selected as the best one given in the arts and humanities division of the Graduate Student Research Forum. She wins the $500 prize, the respect of the outside judges, and publication in a volume of proceedings. Nice going.

The judges today were impressive. They dug right in and asked good questions when the twenty-minute talk was over, and they continued for another five minutes or so after the official session was up. The core of Jamie's argument is that the dominant paradigms for the criticism of American literature work by binary oppositions (innocence-experience, individual-society, etc.) that end up distorting the literature they seek to explain. Among other things, the judges asked her whether some "distortion" is always inevitable, and on what authority she could claim that her own reading of Hawthorne's story could be said to escape it. Jamie initially appealed to the "text itself," and then apparently complicated her answer in her one-on-two with the judges. I mentioned to her afterward that I thought she did a fine job, but couldn't really claim to have special access to the "text itself." She flinched a bit when I said that (perhaps I should have waited), but when we talked about how her position construed the text in a way that could claim to be both competitive with and more adequate than the ways of those whose paradigms she was reacting against, it turned out that she'd pretty much said that during the one-on-two.

I had to leave after her morning talk, but I made it back to the tail end of the awards ceremony and learned the good news. Jamie seemed outwardly cool about winning, but I detected a deep pleasure underneath it all. After all her hard work, topped off by her staying up late last night to do final revisions, it was very gratifying to see her win. Maybe there is some justice in the world.

Tuesday, 28 *April* 1987

Played in the opening round of the annual Kappa Alpha Psi basketball tournament tonight, and we won handily. This tournament, which I've played in something like seven out of my ten years here (two wins and two other appearances in the final four), typically offers the best official competition on campus. The approximately sixty-four teams entered get split into two divisions—one for dorms and frats, one for everybody else. A draw sheet is filled in, and then teams start playing. Losers are out, winners advance to the next round. Winners of each division play for the championship. We have a very good team this year, though probably not as strong as last when we won without being challenged very much. Last year's team had a fifth-year senior (ah, youth!) who had been a third-team All-State guard in high school and who could do nothing wrong in the tournament, as well as three very good inside players, some very solid all-around players, and me (who had some good streaks). This year's team has only three out of seven guys back, but the four new players are all very good. We've had some terrific workouts getting ready for tonight—games with lots of intensity and high-percentage shooting.

Tonight we clearly had more talent than the other team, but it took us awhile to put them away. We seemed to have first-game jitters, and were consequently just a step or so out of sync. But we put together a good run in the early stages of the second half and coasted from there.

I hit our first two shots and then went cold for a while, but came back in the second half and played more consistently. It's weird that after all these years of playing I still have to reacclimate myself to the game situation—the big court, the refs, the clock, etc.—but I found myself both overexcited on a few shots and too self-conscious on others. I play best when I lose myself in the game, take plays one at a time, and concentrate on each one. When I start thinking about how many shots I've taken, how many I've made, and so on, I lose that concentration and become more susceptible to aiming the ball instead of just shooting it. Well, with that one under our belts, we should be better the next time out.

Thursday, 30 April 1987

Tonight I went to hear a colleague, Chris Zacher, give what is called an Inaugural Lecture. These lectures are in a sense the last hurdles the institution forces you to jump. After you get promoted to full professor, you are required to give a lecture explaining in nonspecialized terms what it is you do and why you do it. Chris, who has written about medieval pilgrimage and medieval travel writing in general, gave his talk the resonant title "Traveling in the Middle Ages" and rang some nice changes on its meaning as he discussed his work. Probably like every other associate professor and even some of the assistants, I find myself on such occasions thinking about what I would say. I haven't gotten much beyond a title ("Practicing Theory—and Never Making It Perfect" is the current version), but given the premature nature of such planning, that's all to the good.

I sat next to Jim Leitzel, secretary of the University Senate and member ex officio of the Steering Committee, who asked me if I had decided whether I wanted to be chair of Steering next year or chair of Faculty Council (the members of the senate who are faculty). His question presumed a lot about the way the vote would go, but given the way the committee has been working this year, I too have had the sense that if I'm not careful, I'd end up next year's chair. When I told Jim that I was going to be off-duty beginning in January and was therefore unwilling to take on either job, he wasn't in despair, but did express some concern. I'm less concerned—I'm not so sure I'm cut out to be chair of Steering—but part of me regrets the missed opportunity. To do the job well—hell, even to do it poorly—I'd have to get further inside the workings of this whole complicated institution, and I'd like the education. Finally, though, I'm too jealous of the time it would take away from the rest of my education. Next year will give me an opportunity I haven't had since graduate school. I can read and think and write without being pulled in so many different directions. And it's the reading, thinking, and writing that are the ground of everything else.

Tuesday, 5 May 1987

Went back and visited Katie's school the other day. It was, thank heavens, a much more reassuring visit. The variety of work that went on was impressive. In one corner someone was doing math, while in another someone was working on some facet of their current theme—eggs— while others were meeting in small groups with the student teacher to work on something else. Katie spent a good part of the morning working on a story that she was writing, a continuation of one of the books she had read. I helped her with that, but she had a good sense of what she wanted to do and so she rejected many of my suggestions, despite their uniform brilliance.

After recess, Katie's teacher asked her to present her recently completed home project on flowers to the whole class. Katie did this project in time-honored schoolkid fashion, not telling us about what was involved and when it was due until the very last minute and then staying up past bedtime to finish it. At the same time, says proud Papa, she put a lot of good work into the project and produced something substantial. Her shyness made it painful to watch her give the presentation. She turned crimson, she barely raised her voice, and all her body language delivered the message, "I'm being tortured." But the teacher has clearly anticipated such reactions from her charges and established one way to help. After the presentation, the other kids get to ask questions or make comments. Virtually everybody was willing to speak, and everybody who got called on said something positive: "I really like the way you did X." It was clear that the teacher has established this kind of response as the norm. If you can put yourself through the anxiety of standing in front of a group, you're in for a lot of nice strokes.

Though I had lots of other evidence that what happened on my previous visit was largely uninformative about what usually happens, it was very reassuring to witness so many good things today.

Thursday, 7 May 1987

I finally got back to writing my book today. I didn't spend the whole day on it—we have a meeting about three candidates up for fourth-year review next week, so I spent part of the morning reading some of their stuff—and I didn't make all that much progress, but it was sweet to spend several uninterrupted hours thinking about it. It's been a long time.

Friday, 8 May 1987

We won our third game in the Kappa tournament tonight. Again we were just flat out more talented than our opponents. We're still playing better in our practice sessions than we have in the tournament, but we've put together some nice streaks. I'm still not losing myself in the games in the way that leads me to play my best, and that may be part of the problem with the whole team. Nobody's really stepped forward and become the team leader.

As our reward for winning tonight we get to play two games on Sunday, Mother's Day. I suppose if you're a college kid living away from home that's not such a problem. But when you're a thirty-six-year-old full-fledged member of the bourgeoisie who wants to be home with the mother of his children on Mother's Day, you can't help wincing at the schedule. And when your thirty-six-year-old eyes see further that the team you are likely to play in your second game is (a) made up of varsity football players and (b) only going to play that one game, you can't help bitching and moaning at the schedule. On the other hand, if we lose, we'll have a built-in excuse.

Monday, 11 May 1987

Time to cash in that excuse. After winning handily in the first half of our doubleheader, we lost to the football players by six. Actually, I didn't think that fatigue was a big factor—once the game started I felt fine—but some of my teammates did. We were up one at half, but had a bad streak when the second half started—settled for not-so-good shots, allowed them to get second and third shots—and fell behind by five. We righted ourselves then and got their lead back down to two, but we couldn't get any closer. Still, we played our best game, and its drama and intensity were very satisfying. I had my head in the game most of the time and so played better. Nevertheless, already becoming fixed in my memory is an image of me shooting a wide open jump shot from the corner and missing it because I was too eager. It's one of those memories I'll always associate with this tournament, just as I remember other, happier plays from past tournaments—a left-handed forward driving baseline and throwing a blind over-the-head pass to our center breaking down the middle for a layup, my sneaking inside the football players' zone and grabbing an offensive rebound for an easy putback, running the wing on the break and getting the ball for my successful jumper against the pickup all-stars in another important game.

I regret that we never put together a whole game in which we played as well as we're capable of playing. Part of it may be that we just didn't play together enough. I think I'd have played better if I hadn't waited until I got back from Texas to start playing regularly again. But that was virtually impossible. Wait till next year.

A nice by-product of the tournament is the way Katie and Michael now tease me. They enjoy repeating this description of my play by the witty announcer at one of our games: "Number 12 comes down the line. He decides to shoot. He likes to shoot." As I tell my teammates, you've got to know your role on the team.

Thursday, 14 May 1987

Aha, aha, aha! I'm excited about an idea I developed today while working on Calvino. If the idea holds up—and my intuition tells me it will, though I haven't worked out its ramifications yet—I'm going to like this chapter quite a lot. The idea will both help me explain what's going on in *If* and will cast a retrospective light on some of the earlier discussions in the book, which I'll revise as soon as I work out the details here.

Part of Calvino's cleverness comes from the way he uses a second-person point of view to make his readers self-conscious about their own activity of reading. The first sentence of the novel, for instance, is "You are about to begin reading Italo Calvino's new novel, *If on a winter's night a traveler.*" That sentence is deceptively simple. The "you" could be me, but then again maybe it's not. The novel won't always be new, and actually, in reading the sentence I am no longer about to begin the novel but have already begun it. Calvino goes on addressing "you," recounting how "you" bought the book, and then presents a chapter entitled "If on a winter's night a traveler." After letting "you" read the opening incident, the narrator then shows "you" discovering that "your" copy of the book consists of the same sixteen-page signature repeated numerous times. "You" then go back to the bookstore to get a nondefective copy of the book. As one (but perhaps not "you") might expect, the complications continue from there, but this opening situation contains the data for my possible breakthrough. When "you" discovers the repeated signatures, Calvino's actual readers don't. Instead, they read about a Reader ("you"'s name, it turns out) making the discovery. "You" becomes a character. Yet sometimes when the narrator addresses "you," the effect is that of Calvino addressing directly the actual reader (me—and you). At other times, the address to "you" is clearly marked as directed to a character distinct from the actual reader. Today I figured out a way to talk usefully about these apparently competing effects. Calvino is creating what I call a "characterized audience" and then varying the degree to which what he says to that audience is also said directly to his flesh-and-blood audience. For instance, just before "you" discovers the repeated signatures, the narrator says, "You recognize one of those virtuoso tricks of many modern authors." It turns out that "you" is wrong about the specific trick, but the address to him is important as a signal from Calvino to us about his own virtuoso trick—his splitting/nonsplitting of "you." And calling his own maneuver a "virtuoso trick" under the guise of talking about "many modern authors" is part of the playful spirit of the whole book.

Saturday, 16 May 1987

Betty and the admissions committee are wrangling with the athletic department about how the selective policy will affect recruiting. Rather reluctantly, the committee gave the department a lot of leeway this year. The committee informed the department of the new criteria in the fall but somehow (!) the word didn't get to the assistant coaches who do most of the recruiting. Next year's football recruits were announced to the press before it was clear that they were admissible, a development that of course put pressure on the committee to admit them all. Determined to avoid a similar situation next year, the committee is trying to work out a standard that acknowledges both the more demanding criteria of selectivity and the academic support available to athletes. Rick Bay thinks that the support is extensive enough for the department to be exempt from the standards that apply to everyone else. He contends that selective admissions for athletes should wait until the statistics show that too many of them aren't prepared for college. The committee sees the issue as one of faculty power. If the athletic department can proceed as if selective admissions does not apply to them, then why can't everybody else? The committee has all the good arguments on its side. Bay can't win this one.

Betty is partly annoyed and partly intrigued by their position. While she strongly believes that the athletic department should follow the rules like everyone else, she can get far enough outside the give-and-take to appreciate the way Bay makes the case about academic support. Then she'll stop and think about how telling it is that the committee is spending so much time on this one issue.

Sunday, 17 May 1987

I keep replaying last Thursday's tenure meeting. In our department an assistant professor has an annual review conducted by the department chair and the chair of the promotion and tenure committee in each of his or her first three years. Then in the spring of the fourth year, the whole senior staff meets to decide whether a person should become a candidate for tenure. If that vote is positive (it requires a three-fourths majority), the candidate has the final tenure review, again at a meeting of the whole senior staff, in the fall of the sixth year. This schedule has been changed a bit since I went through the system. I was spared the annual reviews, and both the fourth year and the final review were conducted in the spring. Instead of having seventeen or eighteen months between the two, I had only twelve. The effect was to make the fourth year review very similar to a final one. The present system eases that pressure some. Which makes the events of Thursday night even more noteworthy: the three candidates were all rejected.

Since we have a strict rule that the discussions at the meeting are confidential, I won't say anything about the specifics of the very long give-and-take that we had about each person. But let's consider how a meeting about an imaginary fourth-year case might go. Professor Vulnerable, who came to OSU right after he finished his Ph.D. at UCLA, teaches nineteenth-century fiction and linguistics, has published four articles on nineteenth-century topics, and written a book-length manuscript on the novels of George Eliot that has not yet been accepted but is currently under review at the University of Iowa Press. He has presented his work at several conferences and has written three book reviews. He has been a good citizen of the department, serving conscientiously and intelligently on several committees. And his work on general examination and dissertation committees has been gradually increasing.

Prior to the meeting, every tenured member of the department is given a packet containing Professor Vulnerable's c.v., his self-evaluation of teaching, his statement of professional goals, summaries of his teaching evaluations, reports on his teaching by colleagues who have visited his classes, and an assessment of his Eliot book by a full professor who also works in Victorian literature. Everybody comes to the meeting having read this material. Some have also read all or part of the scholarship he has left on file in the department office. The chair of the promotion and tenure committee meeting begins the discussion by reporting the results of the poll of the other assistant professors. Not surprisingly, Vulnerable's peers all favor his becoming a candidate for tenure, and several are quite enthusiastic. This data counts for something but not, finally, all that much. The assistant professors haven't done the kind of review we're undertaking, and they typically want to see each other make it, especially at the fourth year. (Perhaps unjustly, the poll would weigh more heavily in our deliberations if the other assistants thought he shouldn't make it through. The unusual nature of this result would give us considerable pause, and we'd spend time discussing the reasons Vulnerable's counterparts offered to justify their negative votes.)

After the report, the chair invites comments on Vulnerable's teaching.

"I'm a little concerned," says the first speaker. "The summaries suggest he's a good teacher, but I notice that in many cases, especially with the lower-division courses, there's a big gap between the number of students who are registered and the number who turn in evaluations."

"I think I can explain that," says one of the people who has visited his class. "He's good, but he's not everybody's cup of tea. He's well organized, knows how to move a class from one point to another, but he's a bit dry. Our undergraduates like more theatrics. So some stop coming as regularly, while the more discerning stay and really like him. Besides, the gaps aren't there in every course. True, his winter quarter '85 Intro to Fiction shows 30 evaluations and 45 registered, but his fall '86 Intro to the English Language shows 26 evaluations and 32 registered. He may never win a teaching award, but he's doing good things in the classroom."

"Notice, too," says somebody else, "that the gap isn't there at all in the graduate courses he's done and that the summaries suggest he's more successful there. That would support what Smitty just said about the strengths and limits of his style."

"O.K.," says the first voice. "I feel better. And I like the way he talks about his teaching in his statement."

"I've been on a dissertation committee with him," says a new voice, "and I was impressed. He's a careful reader, and he gives good advice. And I know the student thought so, too."

Silence. "Other comments on the teaching?" More silence. "Then let's move on to the scholarship."

"I read parts of the Eliot book and found it uneven. I'm not sure if he knows exactly what he's up to there, and so certain parts sparkle while others seem uninspired. Could someone who's read the whole book describe the project for me?"

"Well, it's a book about the development of Eliot's sense of plotting over her career. It is the kind of project that can easily be uneven. The major insights are those about the differences between Eliot's sense of plotting in *Scenes of Clerical Life* and in *Middlemarch*, the beginning and—for Professor Vulnerable at least—the end points of the evolution he is interested in. There are some important things to say about the novels in between, especially *Adam Bede* and *The Mill on the Floss*, and Vulnerable says some of them. But not surprisingly, the real excitement for him comes as he works on *Scenes* and *Middlemarch*. And what he does there is impressive. Nobody has talked about the early stuff as well as he has, and his discussion does give us a new sense of Eliot's development. The book may need some further revisions, but I'm confident that it'll be a good contribution."

Another person says, "I read it all, and I have some reservations. Of course I come at it with my own views of what plotting is, but I don't think they're controlling my reading of the manuscript. My problem is that I don't think Vulnerable makes his own conception of plotting clear. Sometimes he seems to mean how the narrator discloses information to the reader, sometimes how a theme is explored through a developing action, sometimes the trajectory of the action itself. Part of the problem for me is that he seems to be conceiving of the project as only a book on Eliot. There's a theoretical dimension here that he doesn't pay sufficient attention to."

"I had some problems with the book, too," says a fourth voice. "I agree that he tells us something new about *Scenes*, but I don't think he's saying much new about anything else. I was really looking forward to the chapter on *The Mill on the Floss*, so I was especially disappointed that it didn't tell me anything I hadn't already thought myself or read somewhere else."

The second speaker replies, "I think you're not being fair to the book. He's not trying to produce new readings but to trace one part of Eliot's development. If his account of Eliot's plotting leads to a new reading—as in *Scenes*—that's nice. If it doesn't, that shouldn't be a problem provided that the account of her development he gives is both sound and somewhat original. I don't see all the individual novels differently after reading Vulnerable's book, but I do see the career as a whole differently—and that's what he's after."

"O.K., that helps. But what would you say about the charge that he's working with an inconsistent notion of plotting?"

"I'd have to think more about that. It didn't strike me when I was reading it, but now that old Mr. Narrative has brought it up, I think there might be something to it. My suspicion is that the different notions of plotting he mentions are all connected for Vulnerable—they're all part of some larger notion of plotting—and these different parts get differently foregrounded in the different chapters. If that's so, then he'll need to revise to make that clear, but that won't mean any major changes are necessary in the manuscript."

"My point," says Mr. Narrative, "would be that he not only has to make what he's doing clear. He also has to make it defensible. And I'm not sure he can. At the very least he'll have to engage with narrative theory more than he now does. And I'd like to see him do that because it will extend the reach of the book.

"I also want to make it clear that I'm in favor of his case. I think for someone at his stage, he's pretty well along. I think we should pass him, but we should be frank about telling him that he probably has some pretty serious work still to do on the manuscript before his tenure review, even if Iowa takes it right away."

Silence. The chair then asks for comments on Vulnerable's service, which are positive but predictably brief. Everybody likes a colleague who will work well on committees or do other work for the department or university, but nobody is given or denied tenure on the basis of service. We then take a straw vote by secret ballot followed by a short break while the votes are counted. There are a few no votes, but Vulnerable already has the seventy-five percent majority he needs. We go back over the three areas, concentrating this time on what the chair should tell him at their meeting tomorrow—the concerns about the undergraduate teaching, the concerns about the book, some advice to share his work more widely among his colleagues—and then take a final vote by show of hands. This time the vote is unanimous (it's easier to vote in the minority by secret ballot). Vulnerable will be pleased—and relieved—after his meeting with the chair in the morning.

One of the telling features of Thursday night's meeting is that no one was turned down for not having done enough. The issue in each case was the quality of the research. As I review the meeting and its outcome, looking at it from various angles, I'm also comparing it to what I imagined things were like when I was on the other side of the process. I was one of five people considered in the fourth year, and one of us didn't make it. That negative decision was a surprise to me, and a devastating shock to the candidate, my then officemate. She had published more articles than any of the rest of us but had not yet placed her book manuscript. She was obviously a fine teacher and she was an active participant in the affairs of the department. And she seemed to get along well with most, if not all, of her colleagues. In other words, from all appearances, she looked like a good bet to get tenure, and a shoo-in for the fourth-year review.

   The official story was that a lot of people had strong reservations about the quality of her book manuscript, reservations so strong that they thought it impossible for her to improve it sufficiently to get tenure the following year. I believed that story, perhaps because to do otherwise would have been to call into question the grounds of the department's qualitative judgment in my own case. My officemate, for her part, never outwardly expressed any doubt about the quality of her work, the injustice of the decision, or what she took to be the reprehensible political grounds upon which it was made. Betty, who studies such matters, commented at the time that regardless of whether she was perceiving things accurately, my colleague had adopted a very effective coping strategy, one that would enable her to push forward on the market and land another job—which she managed to do by the end of the next year.

   After Thursday, I think I have a better understanding of what happened the night of our fourth-year review. This time there was no doubt that at least two of the three candidates were, in the words of Willy Loman, not just liked but well liked, and that the third was at least liked. There was also no doubt that a lot of people had strong reservations about the work. The decisions, I am pleased to say, were not motivated by self-interest, jealousy, or personal dislike. My officemate's case indicated that to some extent the candidates will be better off if they can convince themselves of such base motivations, but this year's cases also convince me finally that those motivations were not operating back when we went through.

Still, I wonder whether we made the right decisions this time. These people all seem to be doing good work in the classroom and on their committees. I agree that for now their work is not sufficient for tenure at a research university like OSU (just as I would strongly resist the idea that research is the only thing that matters, and the idea that every school should operate with our standards), but I still wonder whether one or more of these three could have produced something of substantially greater quality in the next year and a half. Meanwhile, I wonder about the personal lives of these three people. If an M.A. student has trouble recovering from having the first draft of her thesis rejected, what happens to an assistant professor who gets fired in the fourth year?

Then there are the other folks coming up through the ranks. Tenure anxiety was bad enough before. Wait until they get this news. We can tell them that nothing has changed, that the same standards that were in force when they were hired are still there, and that we decide everybody on a case-by-case basis, but they're inevitably going to feel that the ante has been raised yet again.

Tuesday, 19 May 1987

In the graduate committee this quarter, we've moved 180 degrees on a policy about graduate students retaking general examinations, and the trajectory of that movement reveals some interesting things about the way our committee works as well as the different perspectives of graduate student and faculty member. The graduate school stipulates that any student who has not completed the dissertation within five years of taking the general examinations must retake those exams to reestablish candidacy for the degree. The specific form of reexamination is left to the discretion of the individual department. During our earlier discussions about revising the generals, the question of the form of retakes came up, but we deferred it until this quarter.

During our first brief discussion at the end of a meeting early in the quarter, the graduate students remained silent as we faculty decided that a general exam ought to be a general exam and thus that a retake ought to follow the same procedures as the original. A student would be free to change fields but he or she should still do three exams. After the meeting, however, two of the three graduate students—Jamie and Cheryl— let me know that they didn't like that policy. Regardless of any official academic justification for the rule, it would, they argued, always be felt as punitive: if you're not a good little student, if you don't finish when we tell you to, we're going to make you go through the worst part of graduate school again. Consequently, the rule makes it much harder for anyone who didn't finish within the allotted five years ever to finish.

They presented their case at our last meeting and persuaded all the faculty—easily. Instead of operating by the principle that a general exam is a general exam, we're now saying that a retake is a way to help move people along. A retake *ought* to be connected to the dissertation project. Individual exam committees can have some leeway in establishing the best format for each student, but we'd normally expect the student to submit a prospectus or a dissertation chapter and then discuss it with his committee in the oral.

I suppose you could say that we're wish-washy, but I prefer to think that this is a case where the committee process worked well and where we benefited from—were saved by—having graduate students on the committee.

Thursday, 21 May 1987

I'm moving by fits and starts with Calvino. The hypothesis about the characterized audience has held up over the last week, and I've written a section explaining how that concept also helps explain some of the addresses to identified audiences in *Lord Jim*, *Tristram Shandy*, and *Vanity Fair*. I still don't feel fully inside the details of Calvino's own uses of the audience and the intricacies of his own narrative progression. I have been able to work more consistently than I did in the beginning of the quarter, so I'm hopeful I can hammer it out before the quarter is over. But I'll have to put it away for the weekend. Katie is making her first Communion, and various members of Betty's family and mine will be coming to celebrate the occasion.

Monday, 25 May 1987

The Communion festivities were surprisingly enjoyable, and the mass itself was very good. The priest had a nice way with Katie and her two friends, and they in turn gave each other good company, giggling together, blushing together, smiling together. What Katie makes of Communion as a sacrament I'm not so sure, but she was perfectly willing to regard the day as a special event.

My mother, Betty's parents, my sister and her family, Betty's sister and her family, Betty's twin brother and his son all came from New Jersey for the weekend. Although it made certain stretches very hectic, for the most part the weekend went smoothly. Everybody was willing to go with the flow. Playing "monkey-in-the-middle" with a shifting cast of kids and grown-ups for a long time Sunday afternoon, I had a sense of peace and contentment that is all too rare during such family get-togethers. I'll have good memories of Katie's special weekend.

Wednesday, 27 May 1987

One of my limits as graduate chair is my inability to muster sympathy for people who are applying at this time of year for admission in the fall, especially when they say that they can't come without financial aid. I'm tempted to institute a policy closing off applications after about March 30th. To all these late applicants I keep wanting to say, get with the program! If you can't apply by February 1st like we tell you to, don't expect anything from us. If we let you in, be grateful, but don't ask for money, too. At times I feel like a philanthropist with limited resources who is continually besieged by requests to donate to worthy causes. Since everybody has a story, and since most of the stories are good enough to elicit some sympathy, having a policy against late applications would give me a bureaucratic mechanism for saying a collective no to all these worthy but nonfundable causes without my having to feel like a scrooge when I say no to them individually.

Another tricky side of this admissions process is giving out the last ten or so T.A.s. We have only so many to give, and we get into a lot of special cases, both with applicants who are in the program and with those trying to get in. If we save these five for inside candidates and offer these seven to people from other schools, how many of the twelve will accept the offers? And so on.

This part of the job does have its lighter side, though. The other day someone who had yet to take the GREs called to ask how necessary the scores were.

"We won't act on your application until we have them."

"Can I send my twin brother's?"

Last week I phoned one of our OSU undergraduates who had informed us that he could not accept his T.A. because he wasn't going to get his B.A. by fall—he hadn't satisfied his foreign language requirement. After we talked about pros and cons of different solutions, I asked him about his schedule this quarter. "Well, I'm enrolled, but I haven't been there for a few weeks." Can't be too sorry that this one got away.

Thursday, 28 May 1987

About a week ago I went to hear this quarter's visiting writer, Alix Kates Shulman (best known for her *Memoirs of an Ex-Prom Queen*), read from her new novel, *In Every Woman's Life*. I was struck by the quality of her style— she has the gift of metaphor—and was moved to buy the novel, which I then read in a rush over the next few days. The experience—the public reading, buying the book, consuming it so quickly—has awakened my hunger for narrative. I haven't analyzed all the sources of this hunger, but when it strikes, my greatest desire is to be curled up with a novel, turning its pages one after the other, immersing myself as fully as possible in the experiences of the characters. I am open to critical reflections about what I'm reading, but I don't seek them out. It's the forward motion of the narrative I want to follow. It's the desire for what happens next that propels me on. It's the state of being in the midst of things that I find so pleasurable. In this state, I would rather read than write, read than sleep, read than eat. Since I am coordinated enough to read and eat at the same time, I find myself staying up too late, snacking too much, and reading too fast. Finally, my attempts to feed the narrative hunger will produce satiety. I'll pick up something that I don't like, decide that I should be spending my time doing other things, and then rush to finish so I can move on to those things with a sense of closure.

I'd like to think that this elemental craving for narrative is at the base of my work—something that I don't always feel when I'm working through the thickets of critical argument, but something that I can always get back in touch with. If the hunger is at the base of my work, then I know again that I'm lucky to have the job I do.

Friday, 29 May 1987

Arrgh! Hit the dense and unyielding wall of OSU bureaucracy today. The graduate committee's proposal for a dissertation seminar, approved last quarter by the graduate faculty, has been held up by the Arts and Sciences Curriculum Committee. What is wrong with these people? I can't believe that any faculty member who thought for a minute about it would oppose the course. How's that for tunnel vision? But look at the facts. Lots of students flounder at the dissertation stage. This course is going to help people get focused and moving. Who'd be against that? Those who flounder routinely get credit for seven or more hours per quarter. Those who take this course are going to have to produce something—and are only going to get three credits for it. What's to object to?

My note from the committee chair says that the members are concerned about whether there is sufficient substance to the course for it to carry three credits and for it to count as part of a faculty member's regular teaching assignment. To give them the benefit of every doubt for a minute, I can see that maybe my description isn't clear enough. I used the subjunctive rather than the indicative or imperative when I described how the students would (will) work. But finally I can't generate any sympathy for these objections. Stop using some stupid mechanical checklist for approving courses and think for a minute about the situation of dissertation students. Then approve the damn thing and go bother somebody else.

The more I think about their resistance, the more righteous I get.

Sometimes it's tough to be the guy with more wisdom than everybody else.

Saturday, 30 May 1987

The shock wave of the tenure meeting is rippling through the graduate students. Two different signs: (1) A decision by one of our very best students, who, because she is so good and because she is working in rhetoric and composition, will do very well in the job market. After hearing the results of the meeting, she has decided definitely not to go on the market this fall, when she'll still be in the early stages of her dissertation, but to wait another year, take extra time with the dissertation, and make sure that it is as good as it can be. (2) Some gallows humor. I am planning to conduct an informal seminar this summer with my students who are at various stages of the thesis or dissertation. One of them asked if it would be followed by a seminar on passing the fourth-year review.

Sunday, 31 May 1987

Had a very surprising letter the other day from Paul Smith, one of my friendly antagonists at the San Diego Hemingway conference. He liked my paper more than I thought: Paul asks me to send him a c.v. and to apply for an endowed chair that Trinity will be trying to fill next year. So here it is, a feeler from the kind of place that Betty and I thought of going to way back when. Though I'm flattered and will send him the c.v., I can't take any of it seriously, can't imagine anything will come of it. Even after I get past my concerns about whether they could also hire Betty, I have doubts about whether Trinity—or any small liberal arts college—is really where I want to be: I've grown attached to my graduate teaching. And it's very hard for me to believe that I've done enough to be appointed to an endowed chair.

Tuesday, 2 June 1987

It's crunch time for Betty. She faces the twin tasks of doing her reviews for the next meeting of the NIH Behavioral Medicine Study Section—

another mountain of material to get through—and of writing the final report of the committee on selective admissions. Meanwhile the wrangling with the athletic department over standards for their recruits continues. Betty's work on the final report is characteristic of her work on the committee all year. She finds it taxing but satisfying, so she keeps pushing on with it, staying up late, rethinking, revising, polishing. Central administration didn't know what they were getting when she was made chair of the committee. They lucked out.

Wednesday, 3 *June* 1987

Last night after I watched the Lakers take care of business against the Celtics in the first game of the NBA finals, I went back to my chapter on Calvino. After making slow progress for an hour and a half, I was getting very drowsy, so I turned the computer off and went to bed. When I called the document up today, I reread what I had said about a surprising but significant turn in the narrative. It sounded fine until I came to this sentence: "The details of that search are less important than his opponents' attempts to do him justice: four years ago when he taught in Philadelphia, he never received such a reception."

Huh? Who wrote that sentence? It looks like something that ought to make sense, but of course it doesn't. Though I have no memory of writing it, I must have done it in some state between sleep and dim consciousness. Here's my best reconstruction. The sentence emerged from bits of the Calvino (the search), my own life (taught), and a report at half-time of the game about Isaiah Thomas's remarks that if Larry Bird were black he'd be just another good ballplayer and Hubie Brown's comment that Bird has been judged to be either the MVP or the runner-up three out of the last four years by the NBA Players Association, which is 75 percent black (the respect of this opponents and the four years). "Philadelphia" I'm more puzzled by, but it may have come by association between Thomas and his coach Chuck Daly, who had been my coach for two years at Boston College, and a long-time assistant for the Philadelphia 76ers. Another surprising feature of the sentence is that it had no typos— during a first draft, I'm usually good for two or three per sentence. Could I have both written the sentence and corrected it while drifting off to sleep? If so, perhaps I should try sleeping at the keyboard some night. I might give a whole new meaning to poetry called Dreamsongs or perhaps even rival the hypothetical roomful of monkeys pecking randomly at typewriters and eventually duplicating the works of Shakespeare.

Sunday, 7 *June* 1987

I finished drafting the Calvino chapter today. Feels very good. I got to the stage this week where my thinking and writing about the book began to clarify each other, and I finally felt that I was inside the novel, understanding the principles behind the various clever turns the narrative takes and the various demands it makes on its readers. The reason why it's so delightful even as it's difficult is that it flaunts its own status as a construct and then takes up the challenge of making you read as if it had not just done that. The principles of the construction allow Calvino lots of room for his own ingenuity, and he uses most of it. His last sentence makes a wonderful bookend to go with the opening one ("You are about to begin reading the new novel by Italo Calvino, *If on a winter's night a traveler*"). The Reader, lying in bed reading, is asked by the Other Reader when he is going to turn out the light. He replies, "Just a moment, I've almost finished *If on a winter's night a traveler* by Italo Calvino." The reply is such a nice match because it calls up the opening but adds more twists and curlicues to the reader's processing of it. Has the Reader just read about himself? Will he momentarily read the sentence he just uttered? Or, has the Reader finally gotten to the end of the chapter he began so many pages (and interrupted narratives) ago? Then why did he get to read it and not us? There are no clear answers to these questions and no firm grounds for choosing between the two main options, but that is the perfect kind of closure Calvino wants here: an ambiguity that makes us contemplate the nature of reading fiction, and the shifting relations between characterized audiences and authorial audiences.

In two or three weeks, I may decide that my present satisfaction with the chapter is premature, but for now I am very grateful to be at the stage where I can indulge myself in this possibly naive satisfaction. After I catch up on some of the other work I've been letting slide, I'll move on to the Hemingway chapter.

Tuesday, 9 *June* 1987

This quarter Gwin Kolb from the University of Chicago has been a visiting professor in the department. During the winter quarter of my first year at

Chicago I took a seminar from Gwin on Dr. Johnson and his circle that turned out to be one of the bright spots of that largely gloomy year. Gwin doesn't enrapture his students, but he treats them with kindness and respect, a treatment that I very much needed at that time. The paper I wrote for Gwin, a rather standard comparison-contrast job on *The Vicar of Wakefield* and *Joseph Andrews*, was nevertheless very important for me. Working on that paper, I began to understand more fully and clearly than I ever had before what it meant to ask a question whose answer you didn't know in advance, what it meant to develop and sustain a critical argument. I still remember how that realization led me to stay up all one Saturday night, substantially revising my draft of that paper—and finding satisfaction in the task. I felt for the first time that I had some idea of what the advanced study of English was all about. Until then, my conception was that it was essentially the acquisition of a certain amount of knowledge of texts. The smart students were the ones who read the most and had the best intuitions about how to respond. I could do the reading, but I'd been given cause to doubt my intuitions. But once I sensed that the idea of graduate study had as much to do with acquiring the skills to ask genuine questions and to distinguish among possible answers, I was finally able to make the transition between college and graduate school. I don't think Gwin set out to teach me that, but his guidance in the two conferences we had while I was working on the paper combined with signals I was getting from other sources—the comments on my first quarter papers, my reading of critical articles, my various discussions with other students—to make me ready to figure it out. If I hadn't had my realization while writing that paper, I might not be here writing this journal. Not only did I need to understand what graduate school was before I knew if I wanted to stay, I also needed to get a good grade in Kolb's course to be admitted to the Ph.D. program.

I never took another course from Gwin, but we stayed in touch while I did my Ph.D. course work, and then he and his wife, Ruth, lived as resident masters in the Burton-Judson dormitories where Betty and I worked as resident heads our last two years at Chicago. We became better friends during that time, and we've stayed in touch since. Gwin is also very friendly with Jim Battersby who, like him, works on Samuel Johnson. Jim and I successfully lobbied for Gwin's visit here this spring. It's been rewarding to see him operating in our environment.

The Kolbs had a little end-of-the-quarter gathering at their apartment over the weekend during which Gwin, usually the epitome of the reserved Southern gentleman, made a jocular but revealing reference to my development since his course. Standing in a circle, he was explaining to Ed Corbett, a senior colleague of mine and a Chicago M.A., his connections to the assembled group. When Gwin came to me, he said that yes, he'd had me in that Johnson course many years ago.

"And was Jim a good student of the eighteenth century?"

"Oh, yes, very promising—until he became corrupted."

Thursday, 11 *June* 1987

Since I could feel myself moving toward the end of the Calvino chapter, I've been letting myself do some more running. Yesterday I ran my first hard speed workout in a long time—just six 700s. It felt simultaneously good and awful. The last two were very hard for me; I went into oxygen debt by about 350 yards and would just try to hang on for the second half. But there was something cleansing about the whole workout. I felt happy fatigue when it was over—tiredness but not exhaustion, a sense of something challenging completed and a desire to move onto something else.

Friday, 12 *June* 1987

Good news: Jamie was awarded the Presidential Fellowship, on this the second try. Normally, we'd have heard earlier, but when I called the graduate school on Tuesday to find out about her status, I was told that she was in a group of several people being considered for the last few slots, or one of several being considered for a few extra over the usual limit of fifteen. At first, I wasn't going to tell Jamie this inconclusive news, but once she asked me, I couldn't see any reason to keep it from her. Apparently she took it as a bad sign, because when I told her the good news today she was surprised and said that she'd prepared herself not to get it. She seemed a bit subdued by it all, but I'm sure that in a few days she'll be very happy.

She's had a helluva spring. It's been fun to watch.

Thursday, 18 *June* 1987

Betty's in Maine doing her NIH reviewing. Wish I were there with her instead of here with my silently noncompliant book and my sometimes noisily noncompliant children.

Actually when Betty's gone like this, the kids and I do fine with the day-to-day routine. It's the little extra jobs I never quite manage—at least until the day she is getting back: getting the wash folded and put away; keeping the kitchen not just usable but attractively clean; getting the rugs vacuumed. Betty seems to manage to do all this—and more—when I go away. When she goes, the three of us hang on, each in our own way, until she returns.

Friday, 19 *June* 1987

A roller-coaster day. I finished the Hemingway revision, and felt very good about that. In addition to making my case about why Hemingway's treatment of Catherine both is and is not sexist, I explained (to my own satisfaction at least) some things I had wondered about off and on for years without ever fully working through. Why could a fundamentalist like Ronnie read A *Farewell to Arms* with its belief in the malevolence of the world and be moved rather than offended by it? Because the ethical consequences of the world view as reflected in the actions of those who hold it or come to hold it—Catherine, Frederic, Count Greffi—are all positive. For Hemingway, knowing about the world does not liberate one to the special delights of despair but imposes the challenge of living by a demanding and ethically defensible code of behavior. That conclusion, though, complicates the sexism: Is that a necessary part of the code? I'm arguing no. Instead it's something Hemingway just takes for granted, something that goes so deep he doesn't even think about it. Sounds fairly obvious now, but I'd never worked it out this way before.

Having finished that revision on top of the Calvino chapter ten days or so ago, I let myself think about completion. I have revisions to do on all chapters, but my two biggest tasks didn't seem very daunting: (1) write a concluding chapter in which I discuss a few narratives in shorter compass and reflect on the claims I want to make for what I have done; (2) do an expanded analysis of the progression of *Great Expectations* and Wemmick's role in it. When I stopped writing this afternoon, I felt a terrific sense of satisfaction, and as I took a celebratory run, I revised my plan for the final chapter.

Then tonight I decided to go with my momentum and begin that final chapter. I got nowhere, so I called up the Calvino chapter for inspiration.

It seems far less wonderful than I remember. Completion suddenly seemed to recede into the unchartable future. Heady satisfaction was replaced by melancholy resignation. And I reminded myself that when I do finish, the event won't mean anything unless the manuscript finds the right readers.

So go slow, my heart. Take things as they come. You will one day finish this book, and it will one day be published. But how soon you do it is less important than how well.

SUMMER 1987

Pushing, Progressing, Mellowing

Tuesday, 23 June 1987

Back in the classroom, this time for a graduate seminar of my own devising. In essence, I'm teaching my book, but there was a time when I thought that I really ought to devote this course to the problems of critical pluralism, the project I'll take up next. After all, I had taught a class on character last summer, and why repeat? Just because you might do it better? Just because you might be better able to finish your book? So what. A real intellectual doesn't look back but ahead. A word from one of my colleagues in another department brought me to my senses. If I were trying to finish the book and work up the class on pluralism, I'd be frustrated on two fronts this summer.

I very much want this class to go well. In Intro to Grad Study, I try not to push my preferred critical theories because that is not the purpose of the course. In critical writing, I feel that I have an obligation to prepare the students for all kinds of other courses that they might take, and thus am a bit constrained in what I choose to teach and in how far I go into my own ways of reading. Here I have no such constraints. It's my syllabus we're following and my objectives we're pursuing:

> This course will develop a theory of character in narrative, a development that will also entail exploring the nature and variety of narrative progression. This theory of character arises out of my version of a neo-Aristotelian theory of literature, and since neither neo-Aristotelianism nor my version of it is, how to say, something to conjure with in contemporary

102

theory, we shall also spend some time examining the intersections and conflicts between this theory and a variety of other recent work on the interpretation of narrative. By the end of the course, students should feel at home in the theory—or comfortable with their reasons for refusing its hospitality—should have a further understanding of several significant issues in the interpretation of narrative, and should know more fully numerous significant narratives in the Anglo-American tradition, plus one Italian import.

We got off to a good start today, I think, though by the end of the two hours I began to wonder whether I'd given them too many terms and concepts to absorb in a single session. I tried to generate the terms out of our consideration of Browning's "My Last Duchess," but I still hit them with *mimetic* (character as person), *thematic* (character as idea), and *synthetic* (character as construct); with *dimensions* and *functions* (a dimension is potentiality to signify, a function the actualization of that potential); and with *instabilities* and *tensions* (an instability occurs at the level of story, typically in some uneasy relation between characters; tension occurs at the level of discourse, typically in some uneasy relation between audience and narrator). At least I spared them *local* versus *global* instabilities and *completeness* versus *closure*. We'll be using the terms and concepts all quarter, so perhaps I should have given them Jim Battersby's advice: "If you miss the bus the first time, keep standing on the corner; it'll surely come round again."

Wednesday, 24 June 1987

The admissions committee continues its work into the summer. There are special cases to consider, students asking for reconsideration, and so on, but the pace should be slower. Betty remains chair but will step down from that post in the fall and become a regular committee member. She likes this arrangement, because she's glad to yield some of the burden of the work without having to walk away from what the committee has started this year.

Meanwhile, since she is not teaching this summer and her term as director of the Sociology Research Lab is ending, Betty is turning her attention to some research on working mothers and their child-care arrangements. She and a colleague have applied for funding for this re-

search as part of a large grant that several people in the sociology department have submitted. The funding agency will be sending a team for a
site visit later this summer. We'll both be busy, but the total demands on
our time should be reduced.

Saturday, 27 June 1987

For the past few weeks Katie, Michael, and I have been spending many of
our evenings at the town pool. These trips are a combination of work, fun,
worry, and wonder. The work comes in part from my attempts to muster
my enthusiasm for the pool. The kids are always eager to go, but I'd just
as soon live the rest of my life with no nearer approach to swimming than
an occasional run in the rain. The work also comes in managing their
conflicting desires and in getting them to leave when I ask. Fortunately,
the pool schedules rest periods for the kids every hour (the other night
Michael, showing a budding gift for simile, exclaimed that these were "as
boring as church") and we can usually negotiate an agreement to leave at
one of them. The fun comes from watching them enjoy the water in their
own rather timid ways and from the various games—tag, catch, taxi,
whatever—that we improvise. As I watch Katie try to overcome her fear of
getting her face wet, I wonder if she'll ever be much of an athlete, wonder
if she'll ever want to be one. Then I worry that she'll never even learn to
swim, so that as she grows older going to the pool will be more difficult
for her as she falls further behind her peers. Should I push her here? And
what about in other situations? Michael's recklessness makes me worry
less about his reluctance to get his face wet. It's his stubbornness that
gets me these days. Will we always be negotiating things? And watching
him next to Katie I worry that he'll never be as quick a study as his sister.

   If I am conscious of time passing in my own life, I am even more
conscious of it in theirs. As my pool thoughts suggest, I frequently see
them simultaneously in the present and in the future. This natural tendency is helped along in Katie's case because, even more than Michael,
she seems to be several ages at once. This last month she has picked up a
phrase that reminds us of her approaching adolescence. The phrase is
only two words, but the tone of the delivery conveys a great deal of
affect—unfortunately, all of it negative: "Who gives?" she asks, loading
the question with all the scorn her eight-year-old voice can muster—

enough that this thirty-six-year-old finds himself inclined to supply her with the appropriate direct object.

Curiously, as I see them in the future, I do not see myself as any older. For them, I have many models—my former self, my memories of Betty, my brothers and sisters, even some of my students. For me, it seems, no model quite fits. I'm stuck with who I am now.

Sunday, 28 *June* 1987

2 A.M. Finished the draft of the concluding chapter, sans some final remarks about the whole project. It feels good, though I'm not sure the discussions in shorter compass work. After giving almost fifty pages to *If on a winter's night a traveler,* I feel odd—even guilty—about giving a half-dozen each to *The Armies of the Night, Middlemarch,* and *Mrs. Dalloway.* I am feeling provisional about the whole thing. Every time I want to say, "I'm almost done," I remind myself that I can't really be done until it's accepted.

Tuesday, 30 *June* 1987

More on the complicated things that happen between advisers and students. Here's the background. (1) In about a week Jamie and I are going to the Penn State Conference on Rhetoric and Composition to participate in a session on rhetorical approaches to literature. The third panelist is Ann Dobyns, an assistant professor here, and the moderator is Louie Ulman, also of our department. (2) A few weeks ago I had been hard on a few pages of an early version of Jamie's paper on audiences in *Huckleberry Finn.* It seemed to me that although she was making a lot of sense in what she was saying, some of it had been said before by other people. I suggested that she take up a somewhat different question that would allow her to do some more challenging analysis and still get at her main problem. (3) Just last week she gave me a very nice gift—a well-preserved old copy of *Pride and Prejudice*—along with a gracious note giving me some credit for her success this year in winning the prize at the Forum, the Fellowship, and a Graduate School Leadership Award. While thanking her, I also told her that I felt fortunate to have the opportunity to teach someone with her skill, dedication, and commitment.

Yesterday morning Jamie gave me a copy of her paper. Flush from having completed my draft the night before, I promptly sat down and read it, while still feeling the positive emotions of the last week. My judgment this time was that she was operating with a very strong reading of Twain's novel, so strong that she sometimes lost the thread of her argument about audiences. I indicated some ways in which I thought Twain's discourse was more nuanced than she was acknowledging, and I suggested that she cut some of what she was saying about the specifics of teaching the novel. Finally, I also suggested that she introduce the paper differently, and I wrote a few sentences to illustrate what I meant. I dropped the paper by her house on my way home, thinking that I had been of real service—prompt, on target, concrete, and thorough.

Wrong again.

Today before class I found a very brief note from Jamie in my mailbox, asking whether I had a few minutes to talk with her about my comments after this afternoon's meeting of the ABD group. Her first question was straightforward enough, simply asking me to clarify something I had said. When I did, she agreed. Then this: "When I came to talk with you about this paper two weeks ago, I was trying to tell you that Ann wants it to be concerned with teaching and that I had told her it would be. Now you're advising me to take out a lot of what I say about teaching. And if I follow your suggestions for the analysis itself the paper will be too long, and I'll have to cut everything else about teaching." And this: "You want me to use this first paragraph? I guess you do." And later: "I can't believe I'm giving up a week at the beach for this paper."

Being a quick-witted fellow, once she tells me again what she had tried to tell me earlier, I catch on.

If you're feeling caught between Ann's conception of the paper and mine, let me back off. But which paper do you want to write?

One that talks about teaching because Ann invited me to do that kind of a paper and because I said I'd do that kind.

Why didn't Ann tell me to do a paper about teaching?

I don't know—maybe because she and Louie just wanted to have you in the session and didn't want to tell you what to do.

But I specifically asked whether the paper should be about pedagogy when the four of us met to discuss the session and was told it didn't have to be.

But Ann's been to the conference and she says it's very oriented toward teaching.

We go on in this unproductive way for a while, then finally turn to what Jamie might do with the paper she gave me yesterday—which she now doesn't much like—and with my comments—which she also doesn't much like. We don't get very far before we both have to leave. She says that she thinks she can try to use some of my suggestions and still preserve the focus on pedagogy. Feeling lousy, I wish her luck and go.

Driving home, after some rueful reflections about the difference between the intention of my comments and their effect, I begin to wonder whether I am way out of line in not worrying about paying attention to pedagogy in my own not yet finished paper. When I get home, I call Ann, tell her about my talk with Jamie, and ask if my paper should be primarily oriented toward pedagogy. When she says no, but it shouldn't neglect pedagogy entirely, I ask her to call Jamie and tell her the same thing. Jamie calls me later and reports that Ann has altered her own paper to make it less specifically concerned with teaching. Consequently, Jamie feels less obligated to stick to her original plan and more comfortable with what she's done and what she still needs to do.

The moral this time? Take your pick: (a) always listen until you're sure you understand (why didn't I catch on to Jamie's dilemma when she first tried to tell me about it?); (b) in doing a panel like this one, be absolutely sure that everybody shares an understanding of its purpose; (c) don't rewrite somebody's prose, especially their first paragraphs; (d) all of the above.

There's something else here, though, something that counterbalances the negatives. Jamie's feeling so caught by everything is a result not just of my failure to listen and my overzealous commentary but also of the intensity she brought to the paper. And my feeling lousy is in part a result of my having invested a lot in my reading of the paper yesterday. If we're getting that involved in the work, something positive must result. Mustn't it?

In a strange way, I'm also glad that Jamie let me feel her frustration today, and not just because I think she had cause to do it. If she hadn't done that, I'd never have understood the context in which she was trying to deal with my comments, and I'd never have understood the gap between their intention and their effect.

Wednesday, 1 July 1987

Yesterday I wrote a note to the editor at the University of Chicago Press, telling him that I expect to finish the book by the end of the month. That may be optimistic, since I do want a couple of colleagues to read it before I send it off, and I still have a lot of revisions to do. But I also like the idea of having that as a goal. I've got this momentum now and I want to ride it.

Friday, 3 July 1987

Besides my regular seminar, I'm having once-a-week meetings with my graduate students who are doing generals or dissertations with me. At our first meeting last week the ten of us set up a schedule. Since we had a gap for next week, I offered to present my chapter on Hemingway. The group seemed to think that was a good idea, though I'm not sure how they'd tell me it wasn't. In any case, I was up most of the night working on it, and I finally figured out what was bothering me about the chapter. My revision and expansion still left the seams showing. My core argument had been placed within a larger framework, but it had not been sufficiently integrated with what preceded and followed it. We'll see what the students think next week.

Things are going slowly in the character course. The students there seem engaged with the issues I'm raising, but they are still struggling a bit with the theoretical framework I'm trying to teach. It's now clear that they need some time to become comfortable with all the terms and concepts I'm throwing at them. I need to be patient and give them that time.

I'm a little worried that my design for the course doesn't build in enough repetition. I'm following the basic progression of my book, a structure that purports to have each pairing of narrative and theoretical reading highlight a new, important problem for the theory of character and progression to solve. Rather than having a basic thesis that is exemplified in different ways by the different narratives, the course works by gradually tracing the multiple contours of the theory. The conclusions that we've reached so far in our analyses of Orwell and Austen won't be easily transferable to James and Fowles because their narratives represent different kinds of progression and different relationships among the components of character.

I can see now that this kind of developing argument may be better for the book than the course, especially since I'm trying to make the seminar work even more inductively than the book. I guess it's only natural that the students seem to be struggling a bit at this point. I have to trust myself, them, and the theory I'm teaching. Again, I find myself saying, go slow and easy here.

Saturday, 4 July 1987

Happy birthday, America. I was able to restrain my patriotism sufficiently to leave the parade early this morning—a grotesque affair, actually, with its celebration of things military—and put in an hour or so revising some of what I've said about *1984*. It's great to be at this stage where I've developed what's more than a first draft of the whole thing. Now when I work on pieces I feel both productive and efficient. I understand how what I say in one part of the book has implications for what I say in another. I have a clear sense of the whole argument and can plug into it at almost any point. I am no doubt blind to some of its problems, unaware of some issues that I ought to be addressing, but now the writing is coming very well—easily and confidently.

It was a year ago today that I sat down determined to take the various pieces of the book I had done as conference papers or journal articles and make them part of a grand seamless argument. Betty had gone to New Jersey to visit her parents. I had had Katie, Michael, and two of their friends all morning, and then the friends' mother took them all. I went to my office and sat at the computer for about four hours and wrote the first five pages or so of the introduction. Though the book has changed on me this year, those five pages have remained pretty much intact. They got me going, and now, a year later, I'm moving toward finishing. I like the Fourth of July.

Tuesday, 7 July 1987

At Penn State. The momentous news of the day is that I played basketball with Stanley Fish, a leading light in the world of critical theory, someone whose arguments I've tried to counter in print a few times, and someone with whom I first talked about playing ball almost six years ago. Stanley apparently plays all the time, but accuracy requires me to report that his own modest assessment of his abilities is on target: he will never be anybody's choice for all-MLA. We didn't play against each other, but were teammates in pickup games at the Penn State rec center.

For reasons I've not yet fathomed, I got myself ridiculously worked up in the second game we played, arguing with my opponents, playing with a chip on my shoulder, and generally getting into a state that I rarely enter and don't especially like. I guess it was a result of pride and anxiety. The players in the game were not very good, so I expected to win—after all, we had ME on our side. When we were struggling because we threw the ball away or left people open for uncontested layups, I got angry. When players on the other team questioned my calls, I got hostile and right-eous. We finally won the game, I scored most of the baskets and got most of the rebounds, but I left feeling regretful about my missing maturity. I may think that Fish is a weak player, but he must think I'm some kind of idiot madman on the court.

The less momentous news is that we had our session—"The Uses of Rhetoric"—today. Jamie's paper, I thought, was very good (she took *some* of my suggestions, but worked out a lot of other things herself). I gave mine, on character and progression in Ring Lardner's "Haircut," believing it this time. And Ann talked well about her strategies for encouraging and responding to disagreements in her classes. Unfortunately, however, thanks to me, Stanley came to the session and then in effect attacked Ann. She got extremely defensive, and the interchange didn't go any-where beyond Fish's explaining once again—and to some extent expand-ing upon—the position he had already explained in his keynote address this morning. Our session became his. He can teach us all a lot about the uses of rhetoric.

As I write this out, I'm starting to see that these two news items may be more related than I initially thought. Frustrated by what happened at the session and my own inability to intervene in any useful way, I may have been trying to exercise a control in the basketball game comparable to the control I saw Fish exercise earlier this afternoon. What you can do there, I can do here, Stanley. When my teammates and opponents didn't cooperate, I insisted on that control anyway. I finally got it—and then felt stupid for insisting on it.

Wednesday, 8 July 1987

Home again. During our ride to State College and back, Jamie and I talked about all kinds of things—her family, my family, Twain, Hemingway, Fish, the Graduate Student Conference to be held this fall at OSU, feminist criticism, running, her dissertation, my book. I also found myself talking to her about Sacks—how he taught, what he was working on when he died (too soon—he was only 49), what it was like to work with him, how generous he was, how complex a personality—at once self-deprecating and egotistical, full of life and seemingly haunted by a consciousness of his own mortality.

I've been thinking of Shelly a lot lately, perhaps because now that I'm nearing completion of my book, I want to know what he'd think of it, perhaps because it is the time of year when he had his second, almost fatal, heart attack. Perhaps both things are working. He had that heart attack ten years ago, a few weeks after he had approved the last chapter of my dissertation. The book calls up the dissertation, which in turn calls up Shelly, and he calls up all those things I was trying to tell Jamie—including my memory of visiting him in the hospital after his heart attack, watching him, against all apparent sense and reason, sneak cigarettes, and thus indicate that he would—could?—never really recover. In talking to Jamie about him, I suppose I have been trying to establish some link between them through me. He taught me so much, I've taught you some things. You would have liked him. He would have liked you. I would have taken pleasure in watching the two of you interact.

Thursday, 9 July 1987

My dissertation students weren't shy about disagreeing with parts of my Hemingway chapter. The main issue we focused on was the new one I had developed: the connection between Hemingway's sexism and his belief that the world is malevolent. As I mentioned earlier, the chapter argues that they are separate beliefs. The sexism isn't implied in the malevolent world view, but is rather a reflex, something that is more or less taken for granted by Hemingway. The students argued that the two beliefs were more tightly tied together. I became convinced that I need to revise a bit, to show that the two beliefs do intersect. Other students backed up what Jamie had pointed out on our ride: Hemingway's implicit ideas about a man's proper response to knowledge of the world's destructiveness are different from his ideas about a woman's response to that knowledge. A man acts independently, a woman dependently. But I decided to hang onto the main points of the argument.

More generally, I think the dialogue between me and the students should help us later in the quarter. I probably was too defensive at first, but then I caught myself at it and worked at being more open to their disagreements as the session went on. I'm hoping that after taking me on, they'll be more willing to challenge each other.

Friday, 10 July 1987

I'm worried about Mary. She has been having a lot of trouble with her dissertation, trouble that I thought was the usual kind associated with beginning a project: you have a general sense of where you want to go, but you're not sure of how you're going to get there, and it isn't until you've started the trip that your actual destination becomes clearly defined. When she wrote her chapter on *The French Lieutenant's Woman* last December, I thought she had found her direction and would be able to go fairly smoothly from there. Mary is not only very smart, she is also very industrious. She's had a Presidential Fellowship this past year, and I expected her to finish this summer. Instead, she's had to spend a lot of time and energy coping with personal problems and setbacks.

Beyond these problems, though, I'm detecting some trouble in her relation to the dissertation itself. She is investigating the causes and consequences of not being able to join an author's implied audience. It is a rich subject, one that is somewhat related to what I'm trying to do in my chapter on Hemingway, but I only scratch the surface there.

I'm concerned that Mary and I are beginning to have divergent notions of what she is doing. At the first session of our dissertation seminar, she described her project as an investigation of what happens when readers can't enter the *narrator's* implied audience. When I raised the point that such a project is actually only one part of an investigation into causes of resistance to the authorial audience, she agreed, but I suspect that there is more to the issue than her "misstating" what she is doing. I think she's beginning to feel uncomfortable with the whole rhetorical framework that I typically work in—and that her project is squarely in. Anyway, she is going to do something on the assaultive rhetoric of Burroughs's *Naked Lunch*, which I have to read for the first time between now and next week. What she does there may clear up some things.

Sunday, 12 July 1987

I just finished a set of revisions on Fowles. Though I feel like I now know how the parts of the book fit into the whole, as I work on the parts my conception of the whole keeps changing as well. Yesterday I decided to split the chapter I did back in December into two, one on "The Beast in the Jungle" and one on *The French Lieutenant's Woman*. The James chapter will have a second focus on Scholes's ideas about thematizing and the Fowles a second focus on the relations between narrative and authorial audiences. Once I made that change, I became convinced that the Fowles chapter belonged more appropriately in part 2, "Incorporating the Synthetic Function," than in part 1, "Thematizing and the Mimetic-Thematic Relationship." That decision made me realize that I really have a three-part book on my hands. The chapter on Hemingway takes up twin issues that are both different from and logically after the ones I'm considering in the other chapters: evaluation of character and resistance to entering the authorial audience. The whole progression of my argument is now significantly altered, but the specifics of what I say in each chapter are not.

I've been thinking about what I'll say in the preface and what I'll want to say by way of summary. It's been a long time coming, and I imagine that I'll still make revisions after I submit the manuscript, but now I can see the end in sight.

Thursday, 16 July 1987

I had a rush teaching my seminar this afternoon. For the first time this quarter, I felt that everybody was beginning to see both the consequences and the advantages of the kind of analysis I'm suggesting that we need to do. We were comparing what we've been doing with Scholes's arguments for a thematic criticism that seeks to uncover the broad cultural codes that texts participate in. In one sense, what Scholes's model does is replace the notion of a central theme with the notion of multiple thematic codes. His argument for the model is well written and fairly seductive. Two students presented short papers applying and evaluating the model, and one of them, who is clearly very smart, praised it. I tried to show them that because the model proceeds by dividing the text into pairs of binary oppositions it is subject to many of the same weaknesses as central-theme interpretations. We focused on a fairly short text that Scholes uses to demonstrate his case. By answering a few of my pointed questions about that text, the students could see that his method leads him to neglect parts of the text. When we looked at those parts using the concepts of character and progression that we've been discussing all along, we found that we arrived at a substantially different and more satisfying reading of the text. I heard light bulbs clicking on above the students' heads as I got more animated about the whole argument and its consequences. I'm hoping that those were long-life bulbs.

This morning in the dissertation seminar, Mary presented a draft of her chapter on *Naked Lunch*. It was provocative, but I think it showed some of her anxiety of influence as well. She tried to argue that the assaultive rhetoric of parts of the book prevented us from entering the narrator's audience, but that we could nevertheless enter the authorial audience once we saw how Burroughs's depiction of the life of a drug addict is meant to be an indictment of capitalist society as a whole. The anxiety of influence was revealed, I felt, in this second part of the argument. In previous disagreements she and I have had about her chapters on *The French Lieutenant's Woman* and *The Great Gatsby*, Mary has wanted to insist on flaws that I've maintained can be understood as functional parts of a larger purpose. Here it seemed to me that she was vitiating the force of her argument about the difficulties caused by the repulsive vision expressed in the early parts of the book. My questioning about that led to a lively discussion of how the rhetoric of the book was working and whether the end justifies the means.

Though we didn't reach a consensus, I think the session was very productive. More than anything else, it showed that Mary is onto some very rich and difficult issues. She doesn't want to argue that an author can never disturb his readers or even attack them in some ways, but she wants to hold onto the notion that certain kinds of attacks are excessive, even if the purpose behind them may be admirable. I like that argument, and based on my quick reading of Burroughs, I think that he's an excellent case to work with. We talked on the phone this afternoon about her combining the argument about *Naked Lunch* with an examination of other texts where authors (Swift, Kosinski) take adversarial roles toward readers that are finally not counterproductive the way we think Burroughs's is. I'm hopeful that Mary's back on track.

Friday, 17 July 1987

I gave copies of most of the book manuscript—everything but the Dickens chapter and the conclusion—to two colleagues, David Riede and Jim Battersby. These guys are smart, relatively tough, and kind but honest. They point out problems without making one feel like a dolt.

Jim's assessment of it is especially important to me. Trained at Cornell under an Aristotelian named W. R. Keast and having worked out his own very powerful version of the neo-Aristotelian framework and tested it in more than twenty-five years of teaching and writing, Jim understands the ins and outs of what I'm doing better than anyone else I know. Furthermore, I am intellectually and personally indebted to him. When I first came to OSU, he did a lot to make me feel welcome, feel that I belonged here. He took an interest in my work, read it with care and generosity, talked to me about it in ways that no one besides Sacks ever did—understanding what I was doing, pointing out gaps, paying attention to the successful stuff, too. During my first year, I volunteered to deliver a paper in the departmental colloquium series, and Jim not only gave me advice on an early draft that guided my revision of the paper, but he introduced me in a way that was more memorable than the paper. As I struggled with the rejections I got from journals during the first few years, Jim helped me to believe in what I was doing by letting me know that he believed in it. Over the years, we've developed a mutual respect that allows for a very healthy give-and-take. As I've been working on this book and talking to Jim about it, we've had some productive disagreements— productive because they're within a context where we share more than we dispute. I once characterized these disagreements to Gwin Kolb by saying that Jim wants to keep me an orthodox neo-Aristotelian, but that's too easy. It would be more accurate to say that he wants to revise and extend our common critical tradition differently from the way I do. Anyway, I'm eager to see what he thinks of my position as I work it out in the book.

Monday, 20 July 1989

Amazingly, David Riede has already read and returned everything I gave him on Friday. In addition to some helpful queries about local issues, David has raised some good general points that I can address in the conclusion. David also said enough reassuring things to bolster my confidence in the whole project. So far, so good.

Tuesday, 21 July 1987

So much for my light-bulb theory of last Thursday's class in the character course. After our session today, one of the students came to talk with me about how she might apply some of the concepts of our course to a paper she is writing on medieval drama. During our discussion she confessed that she felt utterly lost at the end of class last week.

Well, maybe she was the exception. The drama course is a five-week intensive one, and she seems to be giving more of her time and energy to that. She's missed at least one of our sessions. Still, I'm reminded once again of how easy it is to misjudge how one's ideas are coming across in the classroom.

Wednesday, 22 July 1987

Since I missed a seminar session to go to Penn State, we made up the session today, which means that we meet for three consecutive days this week. I'm hoping that the continuity and intensity will help pull things together. Today was a little less smooth than I'd have liked. We were looking at chapter 13 of *The French Lieutenant's Woman*, the place where Fowles, through a complicated use of his narrator, signals that his characters aren't possible people but rather his constructs. The complication comes because the signal is given through the narrator's claim that the characters are acting independently of him. When I taught the book last summer, the students quickly embraced the idea that such a claim actually undermines the illusion that the characters are independent because it foregrounds their status as characters and induces us to remember that this statement is itself planned, constructed, artificial. The narrator's audience is asked to believe the narrator, but Fowles's audience is asked to recognize the ploy—or so I claim. This time the students seemed to have trouble getting the distinction between authorial and narrative audiences and its application in this case. One in particular seemed resistant to both the interpretation of the chapter and the distinction between audiences. Normally I'd like that because working through the differences would clarify my position. Today that didn't happen. I couldn't get her to offer a solid defense of her claim that we should take the narrator at face value, and she didn't find my reasoning persuasive either.

Still, I see signs of the group beginning to jell. The discussion was lively today, and just about everybody participated. The students are beginning to sound as if they are comfortable with the basic terms and concepts of my framework for analyzing character and progression.

My resistant reader did come to me the other day and say that she finds the whole system to be too analytical, too intent on dividing up the experience of reading narrative into distinct components. I can respect that. The system is nothing if not analytical, and that's not everybody's preferred way of working. But I did ask her not to write off the whole course at this point. She agreed, and we then discussed the possibility of her writing her long paper on the limits of my approach. In the meantime, after a class like today's, I'm wishing that she were more analytical. She could see what Fowles is doing more clearly.

The confident tone of that sentence does betray my dilemma here. I really do think I'm right about Fowles, and I find her claim that we should take the narrator at face value naive. At the same time, I don't want just to impose my reading by fiat. The problem is to find our common ground and go from there. So far we haven't been able to do that.

Friday, 24 July 1987

I've finished the revisions of the Dickens chapter and of the conclusion and passed them on to Jim and David. Last night I had a dream about Battersby's reaction to the whole book, a sign not only of my anxiety but also of how much I value his opinion. The dream also has me thinking more sympathetically about Mary's anxiety of influence.

In the dream, Jim and I were talking about the book. Not only did he think it too heterodox, he thought it was poorly argued. He thought it was so weak, in fact, that his reading it had eroded the respect he had been giving me for the past ten years. I was no heroic figure in this dream. I did not stand up and say, I believe in this book and you should, too, regardless of how much we might disagree about it. Instead, I became convinced he was right. I haven't been so happy to wake up in the morning in a long time.

Saturday, 25 July 1987

I did a mid-quarter evaluation of the seminar the other day by distributing a form which asked the students to complete two sentences: "In these last five weeks, I hope that this course/instructor will continue to . . .", "Before this quarter is over, I hope that this course/instructor will begin to. . . ." The results are encouraging. Several people completed the first sentence with "do as he is doing." One ironic soul wrote "make lots and lots of distinctions each with a new term." There were no recurrent themes in the completions of the second sentence, though one student had this to say about our terms: "Sometimes we get bogged down in the semantics and mechanics of formidable abstract terminology. I don't think there is a cure for this. From repeated exposure I am beginning to understand the terms. They provide no aesthetic thrill in themselves; I'm confident that they will enhance my reading ability and enjoyment."

On balance, the students seem more satisfied with the class than I am, and on reflection, I suppose that's the way it ought to be.

Monday, 27 July 1987

Betty and I took the day off and drove down to the Hocking Hills, one of the more interesting topographical areas in largely flat central Ohio. The trip was planned rather than spontaneous, but it had its romantic overtones nonetheless. The main plan was to get away and be together. It worked wonderfully. We had good weather and an easy ride down. We found a quiet place for our picnic lunch and then walked through the hills. Through it all we talked—about our past, our present, our future, our children, our feeling that we've been lucky to have had so many things work out well for us. Our conversation was unstructured, and that too was part of its pleasure. One of us would strike one direction and we'd follow that for a while, then veer off to pursue something else. We succeeded in stepping off the normal work-driven track of our week-days, the (frequently) children-and-house-driven track of our weekends. It was a day of renewal, one that recalled more carefree days of summers in college when we would hitchhike from Boston to Ipswich to go to Crane's Beach. We took more baggage of all kinds with us today, and our mood was more mellow than exuberant, but it was no less satisfying.

I must confess, however, that once we got back to Columbus around 4:00 and Betty agreed to pick up the kids, I felt compelled to step back on the track again. I headed for the office, thinking that Jim might have finished reading my book manuscript. He hadn't, so I went for a run and started to think about tomorrow's class.

Tuesday, 28 July 1987

Jim returned the manuscript today. Fortunately, my nightmare of last week was not a premonition. He liked it, but as always, he's said some insightful things that I need to address. Nothing that's going to require a major overhaul, though. I called him to thank him and ask about a few things, and stressed again the positive side of his remarks. He sees a possible problem with the last chapter but thinks it works well enough. David had more reservations about that, so I'll see what kind of expansions I can make without getting myself into the task of writing forty pages on each novel. The most gratifying thing Jim said is that his theoretical disagreements melt away when I turn to analyze the narratives.

Better get to work.

Thursday, 30 July 1987

I'm exhausted, and I've got to catch a plane for New Jersey in about two hours with packing and otherwise getting organized still in front of me.

I'm so tired that I nodded off momentarily while a student was talking to me in my office hours after my seminar this afternoon (I'm not sure she noticed). But in spite of my fatigue, I want to note that today I sent "Character, Progression, and the Interpretation of Narrative" from my desk to the desk of the editor at the University of Chicago Press.

The final push: I worked into the wee hours of Wednesday morning and then all day yesterday doing revisions. Last night at about ten I went to the library to get some bibliographical information to finish a few footnotes, then when the library closed at midnight I went to my office to add that info, do some final editing, and print out the whole thing. The editing went smoothly enough, but the printing turned out to be more exciting than I would have liked. I had minor problems with the layout of a few chapters and had to redo them, but the big excitement came around 3 A.M. The printer started feeding itself the sheets it had just printed, thereby stuffing itself and gumming up its teeth until, satiated, it finally quit.

Unable to floss or otherwise free it sufficiently to get it working again, I took the liberty of borrowing David Riede's printer, a liberty he had recently authorized, though not exactly in the way I took it. For complicated technical reasons, I couldn't just switch to his system but had to take his printer from his office and hook it up to my system. I had to walk through the darkened hallways to the main office to get the passkey, then up the dark stairway to David's office where I fumbled around disconnecting his printer, and then back through the dark to my office with the printer in tow. Connecting his printer to my computer was complicated because I had to use my printer cable rather than his, and attaching it proved to be a rather tricky business for one as handy as I. On top of that, the electric cord from his machine is shorter than mine and, until I rearranged the furniture, wouldn't reach the one outlet I have in the office. Finally, however, at about 4:30 A.M., feeling like a cross between a cat burglar and a very 1980s scholar-adventurer, I was printing again, and all went smoothly to completion at about 6:30. I liked leaving the office as the sun was coming up (never did that before), even though I had to be back at nine for the dissertation seminar.

So, it's done, it's done, it's done. Finally. In a few hours, I can slip into carefree sleep.

Tuesday, 4 August 1987

Had a good weekend with our families in NJ. With the book gone, I let myself relax, unwind, let go. Since I now await a verdict, my peace is already uneasy, but it's still nice to be at this stage.

Last Thursday morning we had what is to date our most successful session of the dissertation seminar. Dennis, a student who has been floundering since passing his generals about two years ago, had drafted a prospectus to do a study of the novels of Robert Stone (author of *The Dog Soldiers* and *A Flag for Sunrise* among others). It seemed to me, going in, that Dennis's purpose was not entirely clear, though he wanted in some way to make a case for Stone as an important contemporary novelist. The group was smaller than usual, but we dug in very well. As I tried to get Dennis to say more about his purpose, he began to talk about Alisdair Macintyre's *After Virtue*, a book I haven't read but that another student had. From what they were saying about Macintyre's notion of "having a practice," i.e., of acting in the world in a certain way for a certain good, I thought that perhaps Dennis might recontextualize his project around the idea of rhetoric as a practice, a project in which Stone would be one of several examples. As Dennis responded to our questions, however, it became clear that he was committed to the idea of working primarily on Stone. So we started trying to get him to clarify the kind of case he wanted to make for Stone's importance. In the prospectus, Dennis draws a lot on the ideas of Christopher Lasch about the way our society works and on those of Gerald Graff about the potential effects of literature in society. Building on those parts of the prospectus, Dennis began to see that he could develop a system for evaluating the political power of literature and then exemplify the system through his analysis of Stone. The project would be focused on Stone, but its claims to significance would rest on more than what Dennis would say about Stone's novels.

Dennis seemed pleased: at our first meeting this quarter, he indicated that he was trying to decide among several possibilities, none of which was very well worked out. He now has a defined project. If the momentum generated for him by the session carries him through to a prospectus and on to the dissertation, I'll feel that the seminar has been a success regardless of what else happens.

Wednesday, 5 *August* 1987

Five days later, my dark night of the printer seems a bit insane, the actions of a man who's lost his perspective. The difference to the editor at Chicago between my sending the book, say, next week or the week after, and my sending it last week must be practically nonexistent. I knew that, but it didn't matter. I wanted it off my desk before I went to NJ, before July had given way to August. It was as if I were riding a wave that began back in May with the Calvino chapter and that grew and gathered speed through June and July as I took up the conclusion, the revisions of the Hemingway chapter, and splitting of the James and Fowles, the reworking of the Dickens, and the final revisions prompted by David's and Jim's comments. I had generated the wave, but since I finished the Calvino, it's as if it has been carrying me. By last week, I was fighting to stay with it and not wipe out. I sensed it getting ready to break, and I felt compelled to hang on. So I had to finish when I did—by the end of July as I had told the editor, before I went to NJ so I could tell everybody that I was finally done. I rode like a man possessed. Now, exorcised and standing on terra firma, I look back at what seems to be a calm sea, and wonder how and why it—and I—got so roiled up.

When I signed the contract for my first book in April of 1980, I agreed to do some revisions and deliver the final copy of the manuscript by the end of June. As that date approached and I still had more to do, I got more and more antsy. At one point Betty said that she had expected I'd be more relaxed once I signed the contract, but I was, if anything, more anxious. The reason then, I think, was that the contract wasn't enough. I hadn't published anything but a commissioned book review, and I had the sneaking feeling that, despite the contract, the book would never come out. I also was struck by how long it was going to take from my initially finishing the manuscript (summer 1979) to the publication of the book (spring 1981). I was anxious to finish the revisions so that I could move the process along, so that I'd have done everything possible at my end to make the book a reality.

The feeling this time is different. I have more evidence and thus more confidence that things I write can eventually end up in print. My pressing on here has more to do with my desire to collar an audience and talk at them. I've become the ancient mariner of narrative theory. I've finally figured out my story, now I feel compelled to tell you about it. I know that even if all goes well with the review process at the press, it will probably take another two years before it comes out—so let's get started. I want to be a two-book man; here, world, is that second book. Come, read, and respond.

Thursday, 6 *August* 1987

My feelings about the seminar continue to vacillate. I've been bolstered by the evaluations, but I still have the sense that by this point the students should be carrying the discussion more. In doing *Great Expectations* the other day, I felt that in order to get where I wanted, I had to take over and deliver a mini-lecture. Despite my preference for mutual give-and-take, I don't mind doing an impromptu lecture from time to time. Indeed, if used judiciously I think it can be an important part of my teaching. The discussion can take us so far, and I can build on that to take us further. Then we can move on from there together once again in our question-answer mode. My uneasy feeling this time is that I'm not always judicious about picking my spots. I worry that it's becoming more and more my course, less and less our course. Part of that no doubt is inevitable: the ancient mariner was not exactly Socrates redivivus. But part of it too, I think, goes back to what I said earlier about the design of the course. Though each unit is related to the others, the very thing that makes each new narrative significant—its challenge to what we've done so far—also makes things difficult for them. And we're moving through challenges of increasing difficulty.

Saturday, 8 *August* 1987

I haven't put the book away yet, haven't let go of it emotionally. In thinking back over its evolution, I'm struck by how much of the actual writing I did in the last year. Though I had pieces of the introduction and of chapters 1, 2, 6, and 7 in the form of conference papers or journal articles, the total didn't amount to more than about ninety-five pages. Some of that material remained intact, but more of it was transformed as I also wrote another three hundred or so manuscript pages. If I could do that much this year, why'd it take me six years to write the thing? Well, there are lots of reasons, but one of the chief is that it took me that long to get all the way inside my own project and to proceed with confidence and conviction about it. Ripeness is all.

The other day Jamie surprised me by asking, "Do you like your book?" Since I thought that there was no graceful way to answer without sounding either alienated from the work or egotistical about it, I later told her that the first question I'll ask at her final oral is whether she likes her dissertation. But I did answer her—at first cautiously and modestly:
"Parts of it."
"Parts of it?" she said quizzically.
All right, all right, I'll come clean. "I love it all." I had to laugh—both at the question and my two answers. My feelings may change, of course, as the manuscript gets read and evaluated and the book tries to make its way in the world. But for now I do feel good about it all, from its major conclusions to the very texture of many of its sentences. I brought the book into being and crafted it to tell my story in a way that I could be satisfied with. It can be a sign that I am good at what I do, a sign that I can and should make my living with my brain, that I have been right to decide to devote my life to teaching and writing about literature.
I am painfully aware that there may be nothing in the book for anyone else to praise or love, that for some readers it may be a sign that I've made a lot of bad choices, but that doesn't matter yet. I'm feeling that I've done what I set out to do, and for now that's enough.

Tuesday, 11 *August* 1987

Started Hemingway in the seminar and encountered some troubling opposition from my resistant reader. Part of my line on A *Farewell to Arms* is that Hemingway uses Frederic Henry as a narrator who tells us more than he realizes, especially in the opening chapters. Hemingway uses the narration to let us know about the destructiveness of the war and the rain and about Henry's obliviousness to these elements of his existence. I try to develop these points through some rather detailed questioning of many parts of the opening chapters. Later we'll look at the progress of Frederic from this point to one where he knows what Hemingway—and Catherine (and the audience)—have known from the beginning.

As we were working on this view of the opening, my resister countered quite reasonably by saying that our conclusions were making things too complicated, that Frederic was more mature and knowledgeable than I was suggesting. We then turned to other parts of the narrative—Frederic's argument with Passini in which he maintains that defeat is worse than war, while the Italian driver claims nothing is worse—and found, I thought, greater support for our hypothesis. Hemingway has Passini "win" the argument and then has him killed in the shelling that follows almost immediately after. Later in the narrative, Hemingway has Frederic articulate a position that is almost identical to Passini's. The student was willing to concede these points individually but didn't want to accept the conclusion that I was drawing from them, even though she admitted that she didn't have an alternative conclusion to propose. Her resistance became more troubling for me after class, when she wanted to move away from the analysis we had just done and put our differences on some other level. Coolly and dismissively, she said, "I just don't read the way you do."

I felt exasperated. I know that there are lots of ways to read, and I know that there are lots of other questions to ask about texts than the ones we're asking in this course. But I'm confident this student was sharing our question: How are we supposed to take Frederic Henry? What conclusions can we draw about his character based on his relation to the war at the outset of the narrative? I know that sharing the question doesn't entail sharing the answer—not by a long shot—but it does mean that we ought to be able to explore our differences in some productive way. When she nodded at the evidence I was giving her but refused either to accept the conclusions I drew from it or to offer evidence for her alternative view of Frederic, I felt that something fundamental had gone wrong. Her saying, "I just don't read like you do," seemed to be an easy way out for her, a way to keep her mind closed—not only to this reading of this text but to a lot of what I'm after in the rest of the course as well.

As I get a little distance on our exchange I wonder whether I'm over-reacting. I like the fact that this student is not afraid to disagree, and I can't expect her to have worked out a reading of the novel as detailed as one I've come to over many readings of it. Maybe all she meant was that she's detected something she can't quite put her finger on that makes her believe the Frederic of the early chapters is more mature and knowledgeable than I claim. But as I go back over it, I keep getting stuck on my conviction that she just doesn't want to engage with the issues I'm bringing up. As a result, I feel less sympathetic to her struggle with the general theory.

Saturday, 15 *August* 1987

One of the features of my life that I'm still getting used to is the fluctuations in my relationships with students. We work together on something for a year or more, we become good friends, and then, well, all kinds of things happen, but one not infrequent pattern is that they—and I—move on to other things and our relationship changes. Anne is one example of that, Ronnie an even more complicated one.

As I mentioned earlier, Ronnie had a class with me each of her four years as an undergraduate, and she asked me to direct her thesis. Since she has been in the M.A. program she has taken Intro to Grad Study with me, and she is now taking the character seminar. We hit it off right from the start in the Masterpieces of American Lit course she took as a freshman, but it was in the three subsequent courses that our friendship and intellectual relationship developed the most. The next two courses were honors seminars in the novel, one focusing on point of view, the other on plot and progression; the third was a critical theory course on the relation between language and literature. In the two honors courses, Ronnie became very excited about and very proficient in the kind of rhetorical analysis of fictional technique that I was teaching. In the critical theory course she began to see how that practice was connected to much larger issues about the nature of literature and criticism. In watching her learn, indeed, in preparing to teach so that I'd be ready for her insights and questions, I found great satisfaction. By the fall of her senior year, when she was taking the theory course and reading theory for her thesis on narrative technique in Fielding, Dickens, and Woolf, she was very intrigued by what she was learning and by the way she was learning it. She was being seduced by the life of the mind. We'd developed a fairly extensive shared history and could talk readily and easily about all kinds of matters intellectual. Both of us drew sustenance from our relationship.

As Ronnie thought about life beyond the B.A., she envisioned herself as a high school teacher, in the manner of a woman who had inspired her at Chardon High. She could imagine going to graduate school, but certainly not right away. And she was very involved in her fundamentalist church—so much so that any decisions she would make about her future would be largely dictated by that involvement. She wouldn't, for example, go to any graduate school where there was no branch of her religious community. Another wrinkle of that involvement affected the way she thought about a Ph.D. Following the model for women in her religious community, she wanted most to get married and have a family. If she did that, she'd of course stay home with the children while her husband worked. So what would she do with a Ph.D.? Given all that, I never pushed her to apply to graduate school. In addition to being wary of presuming that I knew better than she what was good for her, I also wanted to resist easy judgments about the relative value of high school versus college teaching.

In the spring of her senior year, however, two strange things happened—strange only because they happened together. First, Ronnie had a hell of a time writing up the thesis. She had become perfectionistic, and so either couldn't produce anything or could produce only material she judged to be unsatisfactory. Writing the final version was a torture for her, but she endured and produced a very fine piece of work. It would, I think, have benefited from one more draft, but I wasn't about to suggest that she put herself through any more pain, especially since I suspected that a good part of her problem was the reader over her shoulder. The second event was Ronnie's coming to me for advice about going to graduate school that fall. It was late in the year—May 15th or so—and though she probably could still have gotten a T.A., I advised against it. Get away from the torture of writing for a while, do what you've been planning to do for six years, and then come back. You'll have a good chance for a fellowship and then you can go to graduate school under optimal conditions.

She took my advice, she did get a teaching job, she did get a fellowship, she has not had any major writing blocks—and she has not been as good a graduate student as she was an undergraduate. The reason, I think, is that somewhere between that theory course and this year, the life of the mind lost its appeal for her. I've detected a kind of distance between herself and her work in English that was never present before. As an undergraduate she always had a tendency to work hardest at what she most liked and to let her native intelligence carry her through her other courses. That worked fine for her undergraduate education requirements, but it doesn't quite carry the day in graduate school. I'm convinced that the reason she gives in to that tendency here is that she never really committed herself to this program, never decided that this was going to be the most important thing in her life. In that respect, I sometimes think that she gave up the life of the mind for her church. When the trajectory of her intellectual development was broken by her year of teaching people who didn't want to be taught, her connection to the larger issues she'd been thinking about was also broken—and I gather her connection to the church solidified even further. She came back to graduate school not with any deep hunger to learn more and more about literature and criticism, but with a hope that she could take some courses she would like and fit the greater demands of a graduate program into the rest of her life.

Ronnie's participation in the course this summer has been complicated by her engagement this spring and by her getting mononucleosis earlier in the quarter. Once Ronnie became engaged to Bob (or Rob-Bob, as Katie and Michael call him) she became even less committed to school. She started to think about how soon she could get the M.A., not what she still wanted to learn but what she still had to do before she could leave. She has enough pride to want to do well, but in a sense she has become a lame duck. She is not preparing for anything, not really building toward anything, just finishing something before moving on to more important things. Her getting mono has unavoidably contributed to her disengagement. She has had to miss class, she has not had energy to read, she has fallen behind and is only now catching up. Rather than functioning in the seminar as the intellectual leader, she is just trying to hold her own. My affection for Ronnie hasn't diminished, but I simply don't feel involved with her in the old way. The main link between us is a lot weaker. I have the sense that we're just playing out the string too—We certainly don't seem to be building toward anything.

Many of these thoughts crystallized for me just recently, after an incident that occurred on the Thursday after I was up all night printing my book manuscript. Ronnie called sometime before class to say that over the past day and a half she had gotten caught up in some activities with her roommates and now was feeling so fatigued from the mono that she thought she'd miss our session that afternoon. I thought that was crazy but didn't say so right away. I just said that since she had already missed several classes she ought to come this afternoon and then go to sleep. She half-jokingly resisted, "If I get in trouble with my doctor, I'll blame it on you." This was too much for me, even as a jest, and perhaps as a result of my own fatigue, I dropped my politeness and said with some steel in my voice, "No. You'll blame it on the blueberry picking and the pie baking." Her tone became colder after that, but she said that she'd come.

Her demeanor in class proclaimed that though I might require her presence, I couldn't require her involvement. She was the picture of alienation—didn't make eye contact with me (or anyone else as far as I could tell), didn't say anything, and spent a lot of time looking off into space. I was annoyed but didn't challenge her. Then, while in NJ, I began to think more sympathetically about her still feeling the effects of mono. So when I got back, I called her to see how she was and to find out if she was still angry with me. She was much better, and she seemed to hold no grudge. She did say that she didn't get much out of the class, but I resisted the temptation to comment on what she put into it, and asked her instead if I were on her enemies list. "No, you could never be there." So we achieved a rapprochement. But the whole incident wouldn't have happened two years ago. She wouldn't have wanted to miss, wouldn't have thought of the class as optional, as less important than the things she did with her roommates.

Though some part of me wishes she had chosen differently, I don't mean to blame Ronnie for her choices. I certainly don't think that the interests of my life ought to be the interests of everybody's life. She seems very happy about getting married and, as always, very firm in her faith. It's just that, in a selfish way, I miss the old Ronnie and the intellectual excitement we shared.

Anne represents a different pattern of fluctuation. I only had her in one course—Intro to Grad Study way back in 1981—but I later served on her general exam committee, and after that she indicated that she would like me to direct her dissertation. Before she really got started, I had to ask someone to help me organize the narrative poetics conference; impressed by her intelligence and independence, I asked Anne and she agreed. It may have been the smartest thing I did in the conference planning. She was terrific. We worked together on the conference for one, two, or three days a week for about a year. In addition to the details of the planning, we talked a lot about narrative, the work of the people who were coming, her work on the dissertation, and my piecemeal work on my book. It was free and easy and comfortable. We developed a good bond. After the conference ended, I naturally saw her less, but of course we stayed in close touch as she worked on the dissertation and made her way through the job market. But since April, when she finished the dissertation, I haven't seen much of her, though we've talked on the phone from time to time. I went to graduation to see her get her degree, but we didn't connect there because we were both driven away before the official closing by torrential rains. After that, she was very busy getting ready to move, and then had to deal with her father's unexpected death after undergoing bypass surgery. Add to these difficult circumstances both my own preoccupation with finishing the book and the fact that of all my graduate students, Anne is the most independent, and it is not surprising that we've been in touch less and less. Still, I feel bad that she has now moved to Louisville, and I never gave her any kind of send-off, never said good-bye. Is our connection being broken? I think not, though it is redefining itself more loosely. That's O.K., because she needs to make new connections in her new job—and ours can be redefined in the future.

Tuesday, 18 August 1987

I'm feeling good about the seminar. Though I'm still sliding into impromptu lecturing, the students are carrying more of the discussions now. Their short papers are stronger than they were earlier in the quarter. They have more resources for reading and analysis than they did before. Consequently, they raise more—and better—questions about what we read. This is the way the induction is always supposed to work.

Our discussions of Hemingway turned out to be first rate, and today we had a great time with Calvino. The difference between now and earlier in the quarter, I guess, is that at this stage of the induction we finally do share a theoretical foundation for our analyses. Earlier we were trying to build the foundation and the analyses at the same time, and that required some very tricky balancing acts for both the foreman and the construction workers. Now that the foundation is in place, now that the other analytical scaffolding is also secure, we're ready for some more sophisticated building.

Wednesday, 19 *August* 1987

Yesterday Betty left for the American Sociological Association meetings in Chicago. She'll be back late Friday night, by which time my sister Betsy and her two daughters will be here.

We have occasionally gone to conferences en famille but in general find that it's better all around for just the participant to go. That way you can genuinely attend the conference, and the parent at home can keep the kids in their routines and spend all that quality time (high and low) with them.

Saturday, 22 *August* 1987

Our visit with my sister Betsy, a lawyer who lives in Denver, and her two daughters, Megan, two, and Caitlin, four and a half months (Betsy's husband had to stay in Denver to work), has been very enjoyable. We went to the Ohio State Fair yesterday and gave Megan her first introduction to midway rides. Like Katie at her age, she loved them. Last night Betty came home after the kids were in bed, but before Betsy and I were, and the three of us had a good chat about the Phelans.

Seeing Betsy manage the two little ones, however, reminds me of when Michael was born and our parenting was a lot more labor-intensive than it is now. I was off duty for nine months starting when Michael was about four months old, and I didn't write or even read nearly as much as I had planned. Two kids seemed like more than twice the work of one. Still, although my memories of that time are vivid—pushing Michael in the stroller as I tried to read criticism; Betty and I taking turns getting up with him every night that summer when he couldn't shake an ear infection and became the-thing-that-wouldn't-stay-asleep; reading at bedtime to Katie while Betty nursed Michael—it does seem to be far back in the past. I wouldn't say what so many others have said—that it goes so fast—but rather that the accumulation of so many experiences with children gives the illusion that no one stage lasts long.

Thursday, 27 *August* 1987

Our dissertation seminar came to an end this morning with Sarah's presentation of a draft of the first chapter in her study of narrator-audience relations in George Eliot. Though I had questions about some of Sarah's premises in the chapter, the session showed that she's off to a good start.

On the whole, I think that the seminar has been worthwhile. By having the structured environment in which to present their work, all the students made progress with their projects. And I think each has benefited from seeing what the others are up to. Still, it hasn't been as successful as it could have been, largely because it's been something most people have done on the side. For the most part, people were faithful about coming and engaged in what was being said, but, with the notable exception of Jamie, who may have worked harder on the seminar than the instructor, the students didn't consistently read (or reread) the texts that their colleagues were writing about. Consequently, many of the discussions became dialogues between me and the writer—or triologues when Jamie joined in. These were often productive, and I think they were somewhat useful to the other students, but they could have been more productive and more useful if more of us had had the texts in common.

I'm also not sure how successfully I addressed some of the larger issues of writing a dissertation: defining a dissertation question, developing principles for selecting what to focus on and how to approach it; how to move from the prospectus to the dissertation; how to move toward completion. But over the ten weeks the students developed a good rapport with each other and with me, and I understand that they often spent time outside the seminar talking about what went on in it. So they learned some things about their own projects, they probably learned some others about doing a dissertation, and they provided support for each other: good enough.

This afternoon's final session of the character seminar felt very comfortable. We finished investigating Calvino's high jinks, and I took some time to offer final reflections on the theory we've been developing all quarter. It felt comfortable both because I had the sense that we were bringing our induction to an appropriate conclusion and because we had over the weeks developed a healthy sense of community. We talked more and more easily with each other, even in our occasional disagreements, and we felt that we made discernible progress together. I'll have to check this judgment against their papers and their evaluations, but I'll take it for now.

Friday, 28 *August* 1987

We went to visit the new 3.5-million-dollar OSU child care center this afternoon. It's wonderful. After twelve years of renting an old church for the space, the center now has its own facility, designed in consultation with the staff. The center has been closed this week as the staff made the move, and Betty and I have juggled our schedules accordingly. Because he's liked the idea of not having to go to the center this week, Michael resisted the idea of visiting this afternoon. But once we got him there, he didn't want to leave. His room is a lot more spacious, it opens out onto a playground, it has a water fountain that the kids can reach, it has old and new toys—in short, it's a very attractive place to be. Nice going, OSU.

Seeing the place and everyone's pleasure in it reminds me of how far we've traveled since Katie was born—and makes me think of the upcoming stages of the trip. Sometimes I think that our integration of parenting and working has been a progressive series of mostly successful attempts to deal with guilt. When we first found day care for Katie, she had been alive for less than four months, a wonderful summer during which our euphoria over her birth was followed by constant wonder and delight in her growth, her acquisition of new skills, her very existence. But we knew that to survive the coming year we needed some help, so we arranged to have her in day care for three or four hours a day and to take turns spending afternoons with her. When the day came to begin our new arrangement, Betty wanted me to be the one to drop Katie off in the morning so she could be the cavalry coming to the rescue at noon. Although we knew that Katie would spend about two of those hours away from us taking a nap, we used such metaphors with only partial irony. After about eighteen months we increased Katie's time to about five hours a day, again with a sense that we were doing something that we didn't want to publicize. Katie herself effectively broke the feeling when, at the age of three, she delayed her departure from the center as long as possible. Our feelings about Michael advanced through essentially the same stages, though they were neither as intense nor as long-lasting.

Perhaps predictably, we moved him through the introductory stages of care more quickly, beginning with part-time care when he was two and a half months, and moving to six hours or so after about a year.

Even as they have grown more independent over time, they have always wanted us. Occasionally, when I look at Katie, I envision the day when she won't need—or want—us. I wonder how I'll deal with that.

Monday, 31 *August* 1987

Back in June, I bought a weight-lifting machine. About a week ago, I finished assembling it. I owe this new age-group record for protracted completion not only to my prodigious skills as a handyman but also to the cheerful incompetence of the Marcy Co., makers of the machine. The three months it took me to get the machine up and operational could form the basis of long, tedious tale, but I'll resist the impulse to mirror in the narrative the frustration of the events, and just give the facts.

Around Father's Day, Jim buys the machine. He starts assembling it. He screws up in his usual way and so has to redo three or four of the first six steps. So far, so good. He is pleased to note that as he expected the ceiling in the basement is high enough for using the machine. He is dismayed to learn that it is too low for assembling the machine. He is especially dismayed because he cannot completely dismantle the machine: it is now bolted firmly to the wall, and the bolts are practically inaccessible. He is pleased to discover an ingenious solution—a hole in the ceiling and some careful maneuvering around the joists. Congratulating himself, he presses on. He discovers that his instructions for the final crucial steps fit a different machine. He double- and triple-checks. He has Betty check. He calls Marcy's 800 number. He has the wrong part. He goes back to Herman's and sees the right part on the floor model. He asks to trade; they don't have one in the back. They promise to call the company and get him the part. They never do.

With thoughts of the Little Red Hen, Jim does it himself. The customer representative for Marcy is cheerful and accommodating. She sends the wrong part. He tries again. Different person, same cheerfulness, same result. Tries again. Not-so-instant replay. Jim considers going to a welder. Decides to try one last time. He's ready to talk part numbers. The Marcy person wants to talk colors. "You have the gray piece? You need the black piece." Jim waits with skepticism. He gets the right part—or rather a piece to make the wrong part right. He puts the machine together. It works. Sort of. He has to redo three or four more steps. It works. Fine. Nice machine. Handy guy. The accomplishment of a job well done despite significant obstacles. What to do with these leftover pieces? Wait, one of them is identical to the missing piece that solved the problem.

Life is more exciting when you're handy.

Saturday, 5 September 1987

I finished grading the papers for the character seminar today: a couple of very good ones, many in the A— range, only one or two weak ones. I was hoping for an even better set, given my sense that the course had come together so well in the last few weeks, but in light of their assignment, I suppose I ought to be satisfied. In keeping with my principle of continually adding new issues to think about and in keeping with my purpose of making the theory portable, I required them to write on some narrative that we hadn't discussed in class; they could choose from a list of about fifteen novels ranging from *Joseph Andrews* to *The Kiss of the Spider Woman*. They had to think about what kind of question they wanted to ask, what kind of narrative they had on their hands, and how the theory they'd been learning could be applied or extended to deal with their question. Again the process is as important as the product, and the actual grades assigned to the product may not fully measure the value of the paper for the student. Anyway, I think it makes sense that most of these papers are good, even as most of them also could be better.

Having finished the grading, I read the evaluations. They're very gratifying, though I'd feel even better if the papers had met my high expectations. Not every aspect of the course is praised by every student, but some of the things they've said can keep me going for a long time. And there are some interesting remarks about the limits of what we did. Not surprisingly, my resistant reader's evaluation stood out, for she mentioned the problem arising from my vested interest in the theory, but she acknowledged me as a rare "worthy opponent" and thanked me for my "patience and understanding."

Well, all right. We part in respect. It's easy for me to believe that my unavoidable vested interest did make it hard for me to listen to her objections. But I find myself struggling against her even here. We didn't, as she claimed, read other theories just to knock them down. And what about the self-image conveyed when she compliments me as a worthy opponent? My dual response to the evaluation seems oddly appropriate. As I said in the course, the end of a progression ought to reflect its beginning and middle.

Another student, after offering some praise, notes that my "enthusiasm" was both a plus and a minus, the plus for obvious reasons, the minus because it sometimes led me to dominate the sessions too much. O.K. This student is articulating in his/her own way my own ambivalence about how much impromptu lecturing I did.

Most of the evaluations indicate that the course really did accomplish what it set out to do. I'm pleased, but I wish again that their papers had been even better.

Wednesday, 9 *September* 1987

In January of 1986, I submitted a 1,000-word essay on Wayne Booth for the *Dictionary of Literary Biography*. Just last week, I got the copyedited manuscript back and was asked to return it quickly (typical of the way publishers operate; they keep it for twenty-one months, then insist that it be back in five days). The review of the manuscript sent me to the library for further information on some of the bibliographic features of the piece, and while there I began browsing around in the journals. I came across a review of two books on character (one of which I hadn't seen before!). The review got me nervous, not because these books were being acclaimed for having answered all the questions, but because the criteria being applied in the review wouldn't lead the reviewer to think very highly of my book, either. What if someone like that is passing judgment on my baby? My anxiety was exacerbated by a more general impression from my browsing that the discourse on narrative is more concerned with issues I don't take up than with those I do. I read a footnote in an article on Booth and Bakhtin citing my first book as the most comprehensive treatment of the neo-Aristotelian view of language in narrative but a treatment that didn't take up Bakhtin. Well, I still don't take him up, but my list of revisions now includes explaining why I don't do more with his work.

Thursday, 10 *September* 1987

Spent a good part of the hours between 11 P.M. and 2 A.M. working on an abstract of a paper for the international Hemingway conference to be held in Schruns, Austria, next June. Paul Smith, whom I met at the San Diego conference in the spring, has encouraged me to submit something, and I see it as a chance to take up some issues on a larger project I'd like to do on the concept of narrative voice. The trouble is that I need to make the abstract convincing before I've really done the work I need to do. Given those restrictions (besides your ignorance, are there any impediments to your success in this enterprise?), I'm not unhappy with what I produced. I'll revise it in the morning and send it off—unfortunately, not to Paul but to the program chair, whom I don't know.

Friday, 11 *September* 1987

Here we go again. Our proposal for the dissertation seminar, having finally gotten through the Arts and Sciences curriculum committee in June, has now been sent back by the graduate school. They want a clearer specification of the course content that would justify its being listed as a 900-level (advanced Ph.D.) course. Now there's the bureaucratic mind at work. What else would it be?

Saturday, 12 *September* 1987

Tomorrow is the Corporate Challenge—a giant track meet held downtown among employees of about 100 Columbus companies—and I'll find out what kind of shape I'm in. I've picked up my training in the last month, had a good time in one three-mile race I ran, but don't feel that I'm anywhere near where I was at this point last year, when I was at the high point of my marathon training.

I'm running the distance relay, an event in which three runners take turns running a loop of 1.5 miles for three hours. Team completing the most loops wins. We have a very good team. Our lead-off man will be Barry Nelson, a thirty-year-old assistant professor in industrial engineering and probably the best runner in the club (he's done a 2:36 marathon), and our anchor man will be Miller McDonald, the guy who pulled me through the first seventeen miles of last year's marathon. We'll probably do about seven laps each, so I'll be putting 10.5 hard miles on my legs. Better get to bed—now.

Sunday, 13 September 1987

I'm in decent shape, but I'm also glad I'm not running the marathon this year. We finished second, about a minute and a half behind the winners from AT&T, and considerably more than that ahead of the third-place team from Ashland Chemical. We had the lead for about the first hour and a half, then slowly lost it and couldn't come back. We ran well; they ran better. Running is pure and uncomplicated that way—at least at this level. In basketball, teams with less ability often beat teams with more. In running, the fastest and the fittest win. Our tactics could have been different—we could have started out more slowly and perhaps finished more strongly—but the outcome wouldn't have been any different. Had Barry and I been in better shape (Miller is always in good shape)—the shape we were in this time last year—we might have won today. But on this day AT&T was better.

The running itself was quite an experience. Barry had us in second at the first hand-off, I got us the lead, and Miller kept it. I felt good on that lap and better on the second, but by then AT&T had clearly established itself as our rival, and I began to worry about getting passed on my leg. This worry made it difficult for me to relax between the second and third legs, and at that point the whole event just seemed like too much—how am I gonna make two more hours of this stuff? Once I ran again I shed the anxiety and felt fine, though the hill on the back stretch was becoming noticeably more difficult. On my fifth leg we were just two strides behind AT&T, and I worked hard to stay there. I felt that their runner was faster, and I kept waiting for him to leave me, but I suppose he felt he didn't have to. In any case, by my seventh lap we were well behind and the most important thing was survival. The hill on the back stretch had become a mountain and my legs had become twin tar-babies, but they got me through.

Finishing second's not too shabby, but it would feel a lot better if we had come up from third instead of slipping down from first.

Monday, 14 *September* 1987

Although it's officially break time between summer and autumn quarters, somehow it hasn't felt like it between catching up on leftover things from summer and looking ahead to next year's narrative conference (which I'm organizing again) and more immediately to next week's orientation for new grad students. Working on the plans for the orientation, I've hit some minor snafus. My request last spring for faculty to do some advising for the incoming students did not generate enough volunteers, so I've had to draft a few folks and make a few adjustments in scheduling to accommodate some of them. Frank O'Hare, who runs the T.A. training sessions, and I scheduled something at the same time and we had to work that out. I felt embarrassed about that. It was just a matter of our not talking with each other. We worked out the conflict without any trouble, but it reminds me that I'm not cut out to be an administrator. I'm always finding that I've overlooked something that I shouldn't have. After I've done it, I'm shocked at my own lack of foresight, but the real rub for me is that I don't seem to learn from my previous oversights.

Friday, 18 *September* 1987

Now that the pool is closed, Michael, Katie, and I are spending many of our evenings and weekends at the elementary school playground, acting out imaginary Thundercat adventures. Another entry in the toy industry's sell-toys-through-television-shows campaign, the Thundercats are part human and part feline creatures who live on a planet called Third Earth. Here the six of them—Lion-O (the "hereditary lord"), Panthro, Tigra, Cheetarah, Snarf, and the teenage twins, Wilykit and Wilykat—united by their allegiance to the Thundercat code of Truth, Justice, Honor, and Loyalty, do battle against the evil forces of Mumm-Ra the Ever-Living. Mumm-Ra is an inspired, albeit repulsive, piece of schlock—a "living" mummy who, by calling on "the ancient spirits of evil," can shed his mummy wrappings and take on the body of the most powerful superhuman this side of Michael Jordan. But if he sees his own reflection, Mumm-Ra loses his power and reverts to his mummified state. Mumm-Ra covets Lion-O's sword of Omens because its hilt contains the Eye of Thundera, the source of the Thundercats' power. If Mumm-Ra captures the sword, he will be the ruler of Third Earth.

Out of the materials of this commercialized myth of the battle be-
tween good and evil, we concoct our plots of the day. I play Mumm-Ra,
while Katie and Michael become the Thunderbrats, Wilykit and Wilykat.
We match wits and strength as we struggle for control of the sword of
Omens—a plastic version of which Michael got for Christmas last year.
We continually redefine parts of the playground as different sites on Third
Earth—these swings are Cats' Lair, that slide is Mumm-Ra's pyramid.
This side of the fence is Hook Mountain, that side the River of Despair.
We negotiate the plots within the limits imposed by three basic rules:
Mumm-Ra never wins; both Kit and Kat have an opportunity for some
heroic action; nobody, not even Mumm-Ra, gets seriously hurt. Some-
times negotiating the plots takes us longer than acting them out. Katie
and Michael try to collaborate, but Katie frequently wants to revise
Michael's suggestions. I often end up as arbitrator—Mumm-Ra the Ever-
Just.

Apart from those squabbles and Michael's inability to accept any
proposal—or necessity—to end the game and head home, I enjoy our
playing very much. Betty and I sometimes worry that we've let Michael
pay too much attention to his cartoon heroes, but this game seems like a
nice by-product.

AUTUMN 1987

Loading Up, Wearing Down, Hanging On

Tuesday, 22 September 1987

Today I identified one of my problems. Apart from the book, which had its own strange pace, I'm not working leisurely on things, and I don't see my way to doing that soon. The precipitating incidents that lead me to this brilliant deduction are these: (1) Yesterday I got a somewhat scolding letter from the program chair of the Hemingway conference informing me that the call for papers asked for completed essays, not abstracts (I hadn't seen the call). I was being given a second chance, though: I need to send him a short paper—six pages or so—by the end of next week. (2) Today I got a phone call from the chair of my session at the upcoming Society for Science and Literature [SLS] conference, inquiring about my progress with that paper, which has to be delivered October 9th, and requesting that he be able to see it before then. So I have to do two papers in a week and a half (or less) and get the quarter going in the Intro to Grad Study course and keep up with grad studies business and all the rest. Somehow I didn't think things were going to work out this way.

Once the book was off my desk, I envisioned that I could turn to the Hemingway paper in an unpressured way, do some reading and thinking about voice, think about what I already can say about A Farewell to Arms in connection with what I might say about For Whom the Bell Tolls, which I would also reread, and write something that while still provisional and tentative would be substantial enough to get me space on the program. Then later, after I go off duty in January and before the conference in June,

I could revise the paper in light of further reading and thinking that I'd do in that time. During these last six weeks, too, I had hoped to work a bit on the pluralism paper for SLS, so that after I sent in the Hemingway, I could turn to that and develop something fairly substantial.

This plan of course was ridiculously naive. Once the book was off my desk, I needed to take care of some Shandies (cleaned my desk!), and I also wanted to lighten the heavy load of the character course, the dissertation seminar, the graduate committee, and the book itself. The combination of what I needed and what I wanted meant that rather than working on either project in an unpressured way, I worked on them not at all—or in the case of the Hemingway, only as necessity demanded in the eleventh hour.

As I think about the other conference papers I've written in the last year, I'm admitting another pattern and wondering whether it will be permanent. My work life now is such that I write about what I've committed myself in advance to write about and I do it when the commitment comes due. The positive side of this situation is that I'm continually forcing myself to produce new text—and presumably, at least the germs of new thoughts. The negative side is that I frequently don't feel ready to do justice to the projects I've taken on. I'm envisioning an alternative where I read and think and write without being driven by deadlines. The positive side of this alternative, I think, is that I would speak publicly only when I felt ready. The negative side is that I might never feel ready. There are always reasons not to do research, always things that get in the way of making time to write. Even when I did, the writing would suffer from not having the early drafts already exposed to the scrutiny of others in the field.

The solution, I guess, is to pick one's spots carefully, and that's what I've tried to do here. The Hemingway paper is an opportunity to launch my investigation of voice, and the SLS paper an opportunity to advance and expand some things I've already developed about pluralism. It's just that launching is hard when you haven't laid in the provisions you need, even though you know that if you can just get out of the harbor, there's a great supply store on the island not too far away.

Thursday, 24 *September* 1987

First meeting of Intro to Grad Study tonight. We have a new version—a five-credit course that does bibliography and introduces the students specifically to our program at OSU as well as allowing more time for the kind of work we did in the course last winter. One difference between doing the old version and this one is that I get the students right away— when grad school, OSU, and the English department are all still new and exciting to them. They seem ready to eat up whatever I'm going to serve, if I can place it before them with a smile and a smidgen of plausibility.

We didn't do anything earthshaking tonight, but I did try to orient them to the course by getting them to think about literary criticism as a discipline that is distinctive within the humanities because the products of the discipline are in some ways different from the objects of study. Historians study history, or at least historical documents, and write history; philosophers study philosophy and write philosophy; we study literature but write criticism. Hoping to head off some of the problems I encountered in last winter's course, I made a point of stressing that Intro to Grad Study was atypical because it was less concerned with teaching them a specific body of knowledge than with helping them develop skills of reading and thinking appropriate for English studies in general.

We're offering two sections of the course (Mac Davis is teaching the other section), so I have about half as many students as I had last year. Each section also has an advanced Ph.D. student working as a course assistant. Lois and Molly will attend class and run one of the one-hour discussion groups that we're having in addition to the Tuesday-Thursday two-hour sessions. I like this part of the plan too, and I expect that, as I do, my students will find Lois to be a great asset.

One potential trouble spot: the class meets 7:00 to 9:00 on Tuesdays and Thursdays, and Betty has her admissions committee meetings from 3:00 to 5:00 on the same days. Our plan is that I'll pick up Katie and Michael, come home and start cooking, we'll rendezvous for dinner at about 6:00, and then I'll run off and teach. If I'm prepared in advance, if Betty really can get out of the meeting at 5:00, if Katie and Michael are really ready to leave when I get them between 4:00 and 5:00, if I can cook something that doesn't take too long without too many interruptions from the kids or the phone, then the plan will work fine. Tonight the course of the two-career family did not run smooth. Betty couldn't get out of the meeting at 5:00, and she had to go back to her office, where she was waylaid by something else, so she didn't get home until 6:30. I didn't get home from the class until almost 10:00. Katie was already in bed, and

Michael was on his way. Not a big day for parenting—or sharing time with Betty.

Friday, 25 *September* 1987

Betty and I went through a sad scene with Michael this morning. Somehow earlier this week he decided that Fridays should be his day off from preschool. We discouraged this notion whenever he voiced it, but he blithely went along asserting his plan. I suspected there might be trouble this morning, but knew that a lot would depend on his mood and his memory, so didn't worry too much. Initially, we went along as if it were any other day. I made his lunch, he picked out a book he wanted to bring, and so on. Then he remembered it was Friday and made his announcement. Betty and I both explained that we had to work and he had to go to school—with the usual success. We tried to focus his attention on the good things he could do there and on plans for the weekend. No luck. He claimed a headache and a fever; we felt his forehead and pronounced him healthy. Various subterfuges failed—I'll bet I win our race into the building, Michael; whoever wins gets to keep your lunchbox—so finally we just had to pick him up and take him to the car. He grabbed the doorframe. We pried his fingers off. He wailed even louder and more plaintively as Betty went to put him in the car. She backed off for a few minutes, and then I just put him in, despite his tears. Finally, Betty suggested that after school they could try to order some new Silver Hawks sweat suit that he had seen in the Sears catalogue (how many other four-year-olds read the Sears catalogue?). This bribe of desperation (easily rationalized because we were going to get it anyway) softened him some, but he upped the ante: Could they also buy a new Silver Hawk figure? Well, we can look for it. And can you take me in instead of Daddy? I suppose, if you'll be happy. "I'm getting happier by the minute."

Betty reported later that he did cheer up on the way in, but as she tried to leave, he melted back into tears and protests. What an awful way to start the day. If we hadn't gone through so many days in which he's disappointed to have to leave the center, we'd feel even worse. Mercurial, thy name is Michael.

Katie meanwhile is becoming increasingly independent about getting out to school on her own. She sets her alarm, gets up faithfully to it, gets

dressed, comes into our room where we are frequently fighting the knowledge that it's time to start another day, announces that she's going
downstairs, goes down, fixes herself something simple for breakfast, and
then reads until it's time to leave for school. She still wants one of us to
make her lunch and walk with her to the front door, but otherwise she
seems intent on announcing her maturity with this behavior. We'd prefer
it if she were more interested in interacting with the rest of us over
breakfast, but in light of what Michael pulled this morning, I'm not going
to complain.

Saturday, 26 *September* 1987

Ran my first race since the Corporate Challenge last night, a five-miler
through downtown Columbus called Night Moves. I surprised myself by
running the race in just over 28 minutes and feeling strong for the whole
race—my last mile was my fastest. Another nice surprise: in that last mile
I passed the runner from the AT&T distance relay team whom I had run
stride for stride with in the fifth leg.

My time was only a second off my personal record. Was it just the
ideal weather? I'm pretty sure I haven't peaked yet. Maybe I can break 28
minutes sometime this season.

Sunday, 27 *September* 1987

After a day of despondency in which I thought that I simply wasn't ready
to write the Hemingway paper, I rallied and completed it in two days this
weekend. In one sense I was right. I am not ready to write the paper I want
to write, but once I accepted that, I was able to write a draft that sketched
some ideas I'll want to pursue later.

One down, one to go. Tomorrow I'll begin working on how to say no to
another critic's interpretation and still be a genuine pluralist, i.e., someone who believes that there are multiple valid interpretations of any one
work and multiple valid critical systems.

The SLS conference is in Worcester, Mass., which gives me a chance to
visit my brother Joe, who lives just one town away. My mother is planning
to drive up from New Jersey and so are three of my sisters. When I was

talking with my mother today about all these plans, I mentioned that I still hadn't written the paper.

"You haven't written it yet? You better get going."

"Hey, I'm gonna write it this week. Get off my back, will you?"

Some kids never grow up.

Tuesday, 29 *September* 1987

As I began to work on the pluralism paper today, I read through the correspondence I've had with the moderator about it and discovered, much to my dismay, that he wanted a copy of the paper by September 1 so he could write a comment on the whole session. It's right there in black and white in a letter dated July 6th. Now I understand why he called me last week asking about the paper. I feel like such a jerk. Read the text, read the text, read the text!

I've written a fairly full abstract—two single-spaced pages—and he does have a copy of that, but there are lots of gaps to fill. I made some headway today, and I'm determined to finish a draft and send it Express Mail tomorrow. I am going to take a chance, though, and go to sleep tonight. I'll be a wreck the rest of the week if I don't, and I'm optimistic that I can still finish by 4:30 tomorrow afternoon.

Wednesday, 30 *September* 1987

Well, I finished the draft and got it in the mail. Though naturally I wish I had more time to work on it, I like what I've come up with and was surprised at how smoothly the writing went today. By contrast with the Hemingway paper, I have thought about this one a lot and, I guess, I've got something to say. I'll rework the piece some before I give it next Friday, but at least the moderator will have some time to incorporate my paper into his response.

Friday, 2 *October* 1987

Yesterday was Betty's 38th birthday, but because I had to teach last night we did most of our celebrating today. Betty has always liked celebrating her birthday, and the kids (and their father) have picked up her enthusiasm, so the four of us had a good time with the presents and the cake and the choruses of " Happy Birthday to You." Tonight Betty and I went out to dinner and just relaxed, just enjoyed our unhurried and uninterrupted togetherness. Happy mellow birthday.

Sunday, 4 *October* 1987

Talking to Jamie the other day about friends of mine from Chicago who never finished their degrees and about some students we both know here who seem to be floundering, I began to wax philosophical. For some people the humanities are a trap. They enter graduate school because they like to read and think, but then they get hung up by all the requirements, by all the anxiety of being continually evaluated and constantly worried about future employment. Many of them finally find some safe place to exist—the world of ABD—but it's a place they can't get out of for the longest time. Some plod on but often end up without employment. Both groups often just drift into something else, often with disappointment, sometimes with bitterness, about how they've spent an important part of their lives.

As I was holding forth like this, I thought that Jamie would recognize that I was also implicitly telling her that she wouldn't be trapped, that she wasn't someone I worried about—otherwise I wouldn't talk this way to her. But she didn't see it that way. My disquisition raised her anxiety about her own future. I tried to reassure her.

You'll be all right. Even if Hemingway is right and the world is out to get us, even if there is no justice and you don't get a job, you're tough enough to land on your feet and find something else you like.

Gee, thanks. Why don't I feel better?

All right, all right. I think I'm beginning to understand.

We laughed about the turn the conversation had taken, but while laughing, she also told me that I should never talk to her like that again.

I sure as hell wish the job market were better.

Monday, 5 *October* 1987

Anxious thoughts of an author waiting to hear from his press as he sees others enter the marketplace. My colleague, Mac Davis, heard this week that Wisconsin was going to publish his book on the question of the subject and contemporary criticism. A friend of mine at another school had his book hit the bookstores this week. I've watched Mac struggling with the writing of the book and with some ups and downs of getting it accepted. Now that the good news is here, I feel happy for him in a straightforward and uncomplicated way. With my other friend, my feelings are less pure. I am pleased to see the book appear and I'm looking forward to reading it, but I'm more aware of a selfish tug that wants to withhold my sharing in his satisfaction until I learn the fate of my manuscript. I guess I'm just jealous that his book is at the stage where I want mine to be. Why I'm jealous of him and not Mac I don't especially want to inquire into. Just let it be noted that struggling with this, alas, too genuine, ignoble feeling is part of my waiting process.

Tuesday, 6 *October* 1987

Today begins about a ten-day period of craziness. This evening I'll leave to teach Intro to Grad Study around 6:30 and will return somewhere between 9:30 and 10:00. By the time I get home, Betty will have turned Katie and Michael over to a baby-sitter and left for Washington, where she'll be evaluating proposals for NIH until Friday afternoon. On Friday morning I'll leave for Worcester, where I'll give the pluralism paper in the afternoon. I'll stay with my brother until Monday, when I'll drive back toward Boston, see some former teachers from Boston College, and then spend the night with old friends from Chicago who now live in Needham. I'll come back early Tuesday morning, get ready for my class that night, and have some kind of a reunion with Betty, Katie, and Michael. Then next Thursday the Graduate Student Conference will begin and Richard Ohmann, one of the invited speakers, will be staying with us until Sunday. After that, the rest of the quarter will be a breeze.

Knowing each other for as long as we have, Betty and I typically can get on each other's wavelength from a look, a gesture, an intonation. This morning, however, it was clear that under the pressure of our different demands over the next several days, we're already operating at different frequencies. At breakfast, I checked with Betty about her schedule next Tuesday. Looking at her calendar I noticed that she's booked for a meeting at 9 and a meeting at 3, so I asked if she could get home between meetings.

"Why would I want to do that?"

Pause.

No light dawns. I guess I have to say it.

"To see me!"

We both broke up, a laugh enjoyed the more because it signaled that we were back on the same wavelength.

Thursday, 8 *October* 1987

I'm worried about Mary again. She's had a rough summer and fall— illness, a death in the family, other problems. Currently, she is preparing—with great anxiety—to go on the market. Her anxiety, though clearly visible and counterproductive, is nevertheless an improvement over her state a couple of weeks ago when she was talking about quitting because she couldn't afford to live on her T.A. salary. She wanted, I'm sure, to be talked out of that plan, and I was glad to oblige.

What's especially worrisome to me about Mary's situation is that she seems to have regressed in self-confidence and intellectual maturity. When she took my courses, she was vigorously independent, willing to buck the tide if she thought she had good reason to. Because she is also smart, she always kept me on my toes. But instead of growing in independence and conviction as she's worked on the dissertation, Mary has been beset by more and more doubts. Part of what's happening may just be that she isn't psychologically ready to launch out on her own. Part of it may be that, as I've worried about before, she has lost her intellectual belief in some of the assumptions underlying her dissertation. In any case, I'm not sure how to help her. My strategy now is just to focus on the immediate tasks. We're working on her letter of application. I'm making suggestions on her writing samples. I'm writing her a good letter of recommendation. If she could have success on the market, the problems with the dissertation might be solved. If she isn't successful, then I don't know. Whatever happens, I really want her to finish. It would be a waste if she left after working as much and as well and as hard as she has—and being so close.

Friday, 9 *October* 1987

It's about 1:30 A.M. I have to leave for the airport in less than five hours, and I have to finish folding the wash before I go to sleep. But I don't feel frazzled. I had a pretty good Intro to Grad Study class tonight; I reworked my paper; I packed. I feel that I'm running my life, not that it's running me, something I haven't been feeling since I was faced with the task of writing the two papers in such a short time. I'm still behind on work for next spring's narrative conference and on a few things with the graduate committee, but I feel like I can catch up on all those things. So I'm looking forward to this weekend in New England—and looking forward to coming back and rolling the sleeves up once again.

Tuesday, 13 *October* 1987

It was a good weekend. My paper went well, and I had good visits with lots of people—especially Joe and his family, my three sisters, and mother.

I liked the way the paper went because it provoked some interesting discussion and helped me believe that what I was saying about pluralism, critical politics, and testing critical modes is worth pursuing. Sometimes you give a paper and get little or no feedback, while at others you get a lot. And the amount of discussion of your work is not always correlated with its quality. I think the paper I gave at Penn State was better than the one I gave in Worcester, yet I got more response this time. I felt energized by the session, and I'm looking forward to developing what I said into something longer and more fully considered.

One reason I got so much attention is that I focused my discussion on the work of some feminist critics. I object to the way one feminist says no to some others. In effect, she claims to be more feminist. Then I develop an alternative way of saying no—or more accurately, yes, but—that involves a careful look at the execution of their mode of criticism.

The first response I got was from a woman who objected not to my analysis itself but to my choice of feminist criticism as my example. "Of all the criticism that you could say no to, it bothers me that you picked feminist criticism." It was a good and natural point, and I tried to turn it back on her. The comment recognizes my claims about the politics of criticism and seems to say that I ought not to be able to question feminism. I chose the example not because I'm hostile to feminist criticism—on the contrary—but because it seemed the most fruitful way to explore the problem of saying no in a qualified way. She made a face but didn't pursue the argument, perhaps because she concluded I was hopeless. In any case her comment got the discussion rolling, and it went on for a good long time.

Notwithstanding the invigorating quality of the session and the pleasure of seeing family and old friends, the emotional high point of my trip was the forty minutes or so I spent walking around the campus of what is now the Boston College law school and was once Newton College of the Sacred Heart, Betty's alma mater. Walking around BC didn't make me nearly as nostalgic—perhaps because it has changed more than Newton, perhaps because over time, memory has retained BC as a complicated place where I tasted all kinds of experiences, positive, indifferent, and negative. By contrast, time and memory have simplified and purified my experiences at Newton, clustering them all around the wonder of friendship turning into love. Every place I walked by called up a scene of our shared past. Our three years of educating each other on the Newton campus became telescoped into my forty-minute sentimental journey. On this lawn outside her sophomore dorm, Betty and I sat and talked for over four hours on my first visit in September of my freshman year. On this playing field down by the Quonset hut, one Saturday a few weeks later, she and I worked the clock at the sophomore-senior football game (won by the sophomores without any chicanery from the timekeepers), and one Friday evening that next spring fell gently and for the first time into each other's arms. In that old classroom in Stuart we studied for fall semester exams the next year, frequently interrupting each other to talk about our work, our hopes, our future. In this small, friendly library we were almost locked in for the night a few weeks later. On these steps of her senior dorm, we would linger past curfew whenever we could get away with it.

I now know something new about the intoxication of nostalgia.

Wednesday, 14 *October* 1987

In Intro to Grad Study now we're going over some of the same territory we explored in the course last winter: analyzing some practical criticism of

Wuthering Heights. I always like these discussions. I like to get inside somebody else's argument and look around at the foundation and the fur-
nishings. What's weak, what's strong? What has substance, what's just
a facade? How does this way of looking at *Wuthering Heights* square with
the text?

Teaching how to get inside the argument and how to examine it fairly
is no easy matter, however. My strategy is to give the students a set of
questions to ask in reconstructing an essay or book—what are the critic's
question, answer, method, principles, and assumptions—and then to
work through the set with them. When the discussion clicks, it's wonderful. You can see comprehension descending upon the class. But it doesn't
always work. Discussion typically presents us with many rabbit holes to
dive down, and some lead not to wonderland but to nowhere. The trouble
is that I can't always tell in advance which kind I've got, and sometimes
have to climb back out of the hole. Still, I feel very alive in managing one
of these discussions, challenged and invigorated by the demands of paying attention to the specifics of the article, the overall progression and
clarity of the discussion, and the larger purpose of showing that this is
how one can effectively read criticism. So far I'm pleased with the class.
They're very sharp and very engaged. I hope I don't lose them in the
realms of abstraction.

Friday, 16 *October* 1987

About 1 A.M. At the opening session of the Graduate Student Conference
earlier tonight, we got into some sticky issues about graduate training.
Phyllis Franklin, executive secretary of the MLA; Jerry Graff, of Northwestern; and Ohmann, of Wesleyan (Conn.) each gave strong presentations, to which Pat Sullivan, one of our Ph.D. students, responded—or
rather, partially responded, as she also discussed what it's like to be a
graduate student these days. She identified four problems: the privileging of literature, especially its study in the traditional historical periods;
extensive testing, which creates the sense that graduate school is one
continual winnowing process; the too-frequent experience of seminars
being conducted without reference to other scholarship, and without
some sense of a common issue to be examined; and the too-frequent

experience of having to write a seminar paper for an audience of one, the professor.

The large audience seemed appreciative of all the papers, but Pat's sent the needle on the applause meter all the way to the end of the scale. I had some reservations about the way she made her case, so I asked her two questions designed to push her to sharpen her critique. How do we (she had used our program as an example) privilege literature when our requirements stipulate that only five of eighteen courses and one of three examinations must be in literature? And how does the notion of graduate education as a winnowing process mesh with the official story that we would like all our students to succeed? Pat replied that we privilege literature simply by having any requirements about it at all, when we do not have requirements about any other fields. She answered the second question by asking me one in turn: How could testing not be construed as winnowing? Trying to talk from a graduate student's perspective, I said that I had never regarded my graduate school exams as attempts to drum me out but as checkpoints on my learning and opportunities for further learning to occur. She said she'd like to hear from other graduate students. A student from another school said that in their program the qualifying exams were openly acknowledged to have the function of separating the weak from the strong. The comments that followed moved things away from that particular issue.

At the reception following the session, Pat and I talked amiably about the interchange, though she wasn't inclined to soften her criticisms. In listening to others talk, I was struck yet again by the gap between graduate students and faculty. No faculty member agreed with Pat; many, but not all, graduate students did.

Sunday, 18 October 1987

The conference has been a great success. There were students from about twenty schools and well over one hundred people registered. Although the quality of the papers has not been uniformly high, the quality of the discussions has. Franklin had to go back to New York on MLA business, but Graff and Ohmann stayed around and went to sessions, asked questions, and participated very actively.

Last night there was a closing session to discuss conference-generated issues. We didn't go back to Pat's paper directly, but Jamie, who was moderating, raised the question of whether an occasion like the conference, which provides a sanctioned opportunity for graduate students to voice complaints, could become a way for students to be co-opted. Other students did talk about the demands that the profession in general makes on your life. Produce, produce, produce! is the command heard from the early days of graduate school on. I tried to suggest that one of the things about the profession that many people overlook is that it does offer you a lot of ways of being in it. You can dedicate yourself to its standards and try to achieve success by them, or you can reject those standards and adopt your own, provided that those are good enough to earn you tenure someplace. Perhaps rightly, this point seemed to offer little solace.

There were other telling moments. One of my current students asked how well what she is learning in Intro to Grad Study would be articulated with the rest of the graduate curriculum. I finessed the answer a bit by saying that some instructors would build on what happened in the course, while others wouldn't pay any attention to it, but that Intro to Grad Study itself was designed to enable students to profit from both kinds of courses.

Commenting on the demands that the profession can make on people, Dick Ohmann did say that he felt somewhat bent out of shape by having to work so hard for so many years. But he went on to talk about the satisfactions of a life devoted to books and students.

The conference, I think, has energized a lot of us. It's been a very impressive affair, one that Jamie, Pat, Cheryl, Amy and the others who put it together should be very proud of. My counterparts and I at Chicago would never have even dreamed of doing anything like this. The conference's success has inspired some students at Wisconsin-Milwaukee to commit themselves to organizing something similar next year.

Tuesday, 20 October 1987

In the course of some informal discussions at the conference, I talked to two of my ABD students about their experiences in Intro to Grad Study. One of them told me that taking the course made her decide to stay away from theory later on because it seemed too hard. Now she regrets her decision. The other said that the course made her realize for the first time that she had never learned how to think, and she liked it because it helped her learn. So often you don't know how you're affecting your students. I was very surprised by what both of them told me.

Sunday, 25 October 1987

Had a great family outing today. Looking ahead to a drive to NJ in December for a Christmas visit, Betty suggested that we go to the store and buy a replacement for our broken tape recorder so we could play our tapes on the trip. At first, neither Katie nor Michael wanted to go, so Betty was just going to go by herself. Fair enough. Then Katie decided that she wanted to go with Betty, which in turn prompted Michael to conclude that this was a good idea after all. O.K., we'll all go.

Let's walk, says Michael.

That's not such a good idea. The store is too far away, and I'll end up carrying you—let's take the car.

No, no, no. I wanna walk!

Half an hour later with his tears dried, Michael picks out the recorder he thinks we should get—a pink one. Not to be outdone, Katie picks out a purple one. Mom and Dad prefer one less ugly, but try to sell it on the basis of its sound. The ensuing fruitless debate lasts for another half hour. Finally, Michael agrees that the purple is better than the pink, and Mom and Dad concede that its sound is not significantly different from their more sedate black model. But as luck would have it, Providence is on our side and the purple one is out of stock, so we "settle" for Mom and Dad's choice.

After a vigorous, though blessedly brief, argument about walking vs. riding home, we return, mission accomplished. What a team.

Tuesday, 27 October 1987

Mixed feelings about our discussion of pluralism tonight. On the one hand, I liked what I got said, liked their questions, and felt that I was able to pull together a lot of what we'd been doing in our different sessions on the practical criticism of *Wuthering Heights*. On the other hand, I'm worried that as I talked about the different ways in which we developed our evaluations of the criticism, the discussion got too abstract for many of the students, too far away from Brontë's text.

After class, Lois and I talked a bit. She is very upbeat about the whole class, convinced that it's working quite well. I keep telling her that I'm worried that we're losing certain people, but I know I'd miss her optimism if she became more cautious in her appraisal. She also said something very telling about my pluralism.

Your greatest concern here is with method, isn't it?

Yup.

O.K., but I always want to bypass the method and get at the substantive issues raised by somebody else's criticism.

Fine, but you can't separate the substantive issues from the method in which they're pursued.

All right, but let's not talk only about method.

Fair enough, but let's talk about it first.

Teaching at night has turned out to be a mistake. The class is fine, I'm happy when I'm there, but Tuesdays and Thursdays from 4:00 to 7:00 are a strain on me, and from 6:00 to 10:00 are a strain on Betty. We usually do manage to have some kind of dinner together, but frequently I end up rushing through it. And often I get to the office only a few minutes before class. I don't see that much of Katie and Michael on Tuesdays and Thursdays, and a lot of what I do during our time together is to hurry them along.

In addition, because I didn't do my usual complement of graduate committee stuff during the crazy days earlier in the month, I've had that to catch up on. That feeling of being in control I had the night before I left for Worcester is now a very distant memory. One of the things I hate about feeling behind is that it influences so much else in my life. When I'm preoccupied with being behind, even the most humorous elements of something like last Sunday's trip to the appliance store can easily become the most exasperating behavior any parent in the Western Hemisphere has ever had to suffer through. While *you're* wasting all this time on such momentous issues as who sits in the back seat and who in the front, *I* could be working.

When I'm feeling this way my weekends and to some extent my evenings are infected by my restlessness. Though I don't really want to take much more time away from our family life, I do find myself wanting to say, just give me an hour or two on this, O.K.? The trouble is that two hours soon become four and the difference between a workday and a weekend day disappears. Yet sometimes we can arrange things so I (or Betty) can get a few hours for work, so when I'm feeling restless like this, I'll expend psychic energy on ways to set that up, even as I feel divided about doing it. Stress is great stuff.

Still, it could be worse. I haven't had to stop running, though I'm now doing more and more of it at night. I had a good race last Saturday—a PR for 5K, fast enough to encourage me that I can break 28 minutes for five miles. We'll see.

Thursday, 29 October 1987

Betty called me in the middle of the afternoon today.

"Guess what?"

"We have a conflict we need to work out."

"No, no, guess what?"

I got it this time. She had finished and sent off the chapter on stress that she'd been working on since the end of August. So there is one less stressor in her life now.

She has mixed feelings about having given up the chair of the admissions committee. She likes the lighter load and likes still being involved, but sometimes feels the pull to have more control, just as last year she sometimes felt the pull to act less as a chair and more as an agitating committee member.

The big grant proposal that Betty and her colleagues in sociology submitted has not received a high-priority score, but the section that she was most immediately responsible for was reviewed favorably. She and one other colleague are making plans to submit a separate proposal for their study of working mothers and their child-care arrangements. Betty has also decided to apply for a sabbatical for next year to work on this project. If she gets it, we could be off duty together next summer and fall. Wouldn't it be nice.

Sunday, 1 November 1987

To be promoted from associate professor to full professor in our department and college, you need to have written a book since your promotion from assistant professor. Since some of our current associate professors were promoted without a book, we now have some people in the associate rank whose cases for promotion hinge on a first book and some whose cases hinge on a second. This disparity, created largely by the way criteria for tenure have changed over the years, makes the step from associate to full fraught with all kinds of complications. People going up with two books are inclined to believe that they ought to make it because, after all, they've done more than some of the people who've been promoted in recent years. People going up with one book are obviously not going to look as strong as those with two. For them quality is even more important. As a result, from the outside, some of the decisions made by the full professors—and the college promotion and tenure committee— look arbitrary: he made it with one book, she didn't with two. He only had one book, but look at everything else he's done for the department and the university: how could they say no to him and yes to her who's written more but isn't the same presence in the department? Those making the decisions no doubt have their reasons, but I'm by no means always able to fathom what they are.

Unlike decisions about promotion from assistant to associate professor, which are mandated by the calendar, decisions about promotion to the full rank can come at any time, and they are set in motion in one of two ways. Either the full professors decide at their annual spring meeting that it is time to consider one of the associates, or an associate can initiate consideration by requesting it. This fall five associates were considered for promotion. All had put themselves up. Three made it. One is a poet who has published extensively and who's won many awards. From the outside his case looks open and shut. The second is Mac, whose recently accepted book is his second, so again, that looks fine. The third is a guy who was turned down a few years ago and whose credentials haven't changed all that much, though his (first) book is now out and reviewed. The two who didn't make it are in some ways the more surprising cases. One of them is a person with two books, the other somebody with one who has won a teaching award and given distinguished service to the department and the university for many, many years.

It's not my place to question the decisions. I haven't read all the relevant material, I wasn't at the meeting, and I'm not going to tempt anybody to break confidentiality by trying to find out what was said or how close the votes were. I'm more interested in the fallout from the meeting as it settles on the two people I know best. Mac, who has been having a rough time in his personal life, appears to have been buoyed enormously. He's been very, very up when I've seen him lately—maybe too much so. He's wanted this promotion for a long time, and in fact almost jeopardized his chances of ever getting it by being so angry that it hadn't come sooner. If he hadn't gotten it this time, he'd have been in a bad way. So it's good to see him bouncing down the halls these days.

The person denied with one book is very angry. That's understandable. You don't put yourself up if you don't think you're ready, and when you get rejected, you don't meekly conclude that you weren't. You get angry over the stupidity, injustice, or base motives of your senior colleagues. But there's something else in the fallout, something more dangerous because it may be more permanent. He looks deeply wounded, as if some part of his spirit's been broken. Though I expect him to heal, I also get the sense that he'll carry the scars from this decision for a long time.

The reactions of both friends reveal a lot about the whole academic ladder that they—and I—are trying to climb. The ladder has only a few rungs—grad student, assistant professor, associate professor, full professor, and (sometimes) chaired professor—and it gets narrower as it goes up. Once you've reached the third rung, you can stop climbing and just stay on the ladder. But by then you're used to the climb and you think about your life at least partly in terms of it. So making that fourth rung typically takes on a significance comparable to that of making those first three. In addition, making that rung also means that you've gained the approbation of those who are already there, and after that you don't have to look up any more. I don't want to underestimate the importance of this external approbation, but I still think that there's something not quite right here.

Making the fourth or fifth rung ought not to be such a big deal. Unlike the differences between the lives of assistant and associate professors, the differences in the lives of associate and full professors are small. Yes, you have the approbation, you make a higher salary, and your title gives you a little more clout. And yes, I want to be promoted. But I'm in no great hurry, because there is very little that I can do as a full professor that I can't do as an associate professor. To focus on what rank I have as I do that work is to misplace what's important about this life.

At the same time, because we have so few rungs on the ladder, because we're socialized to compete, because we see where we are on the ladder as a sign of how we're regarded by those on the different rungs, and because climbing up inevitably means getting ahead of, or catching up to, or falling behind someone else, we do attach this great importance to promotion to full professor. I may feel different when I'm up, but for now I think that both my friends have overreacted, albeit understandably.

Monday, 2 *November* 1987

We've been discussing Booth's *Rhetoric of Irony* in Intro to Grad Study and having some fun talking about its powers and limits. We focused some of our discussion on this short poem by Dorothy Parker called "Comment":

> Life is a glorious cycle of song
> A medley of extemporanea
> Love is a thing that can never go wrong
> And I am Marie of Rumania

Booth argues that the pleasure and power of irony comes from the special way in which it allows minds to meet. Authors invite readers to reject the literal meaning of the utterance and to stand with them on some new platform where both understand a reconstructed meaning of that utterance. That authors and readers often fail to share ironies isn't surprising. What's amazing is that the invitation to the dance of irony is so often recognized, accepted, and satisfactorily enjoyed. The Parker poem, slight as in some ways it is, works to highlight some of the distinctiveness of Booth's claims. Sure, it's ironic, but what is Parker's attitude here? Just where do we land when we reject the literal and try to stand with her on some reconstructed platform? Is she lightheartedly laughing at life and love and those who think life is glorious and love smooth? Or is she bitter about it all? Or somewhere in between? Furthermore, when do we know that the poem is ironic? In line one? Line three? Or do we have to wait until line four? How does a decision here affect the way we think about Parker's attitude? If we can't agree about these things, then how can we, like Booth, talk confidently about meeting an author's mind in ironic communication?

I of course have very compelling answers to all these questions, but I'll keep them to myself here. Suffice it to say that I think our discussion has made the students recognize the strength and difficulty of Booth's claims and thus has prepared them for our turn to Jacques Derrida and Paul de Man, who will try to undermine the confidence in understanding that is so central to Booth's work.

Wednesday, 4 *November* 1987

Went to Mac's class yesterday. He was teaching one of Derrida's early essays, one that is difficult going for new students but has become a classic of contemporary theory because it touches on many of the basic tenets of deconstruction.

He did a very good job with it, but I was struck by how different he and I are in the classroom. His approach has a lot of shtick, and a lot of it is about himself. If it's carried off well, as it was today, Mac's style can be a valuable means of relating to students, letting them see you as something more than some walking intellectual machine, letting them know that you're a whole human being whose personality, passions, philosophy, and experience in life are part of what you bring to your reading and thinking about literature and criticism. But the style brings with it a risk that my personality and philosophy of teaching impel me away from: sending the message that what matters most in this classroom is not our texts and our ways of talking about them but me. So I very rarely say anything about my life beyond the classroom and thus, I suppose, run the risk of sending the message that I am not easy to talk to about anything but ideas.

In addition to this difference in our personas, Mac and I also differ in how we work with the critical text. For Mac the text is a launch pad, while for me it's a diving pool. He looks at part of it with the students and then extracts certain concepts that he wants them to understand and work with. He leaves the specifics of the text behind as he illustrates the concept, indicates its ramifications by drawing upon his own experiences, applying it to his students' lives, or relating it to other texts or to ideas they've discussed previously. His structure leaves room for the anecdote, for philosophizing, for whatever happens to come up. Using that structure today, Mac succeeded in getting all the key concepts of the Derrida piece introduced and had started to raise questions about their relationship. A successful takeoff.

I try continually to direct the students back to the text, to see it as a structured argument, to see how any one concept is related to numerous others in the critic's discourse, to see how they all function together to make the critic's case. I'm important not as a source of experience that can be potentially illuminating but as someone who can keep asking questions about the students' understanding of what we've all read. My method can be fairly ruthless in its concern with forward progress—now that we've established that, let's see its connection to this next part of the essay—but I try not to drive a steamroller over the class. As I've said before, in trying to work with what the students give me in response to my questions, I don't always take the shortest route between two points, and sometimes, I fear, some of the group gets lost on our unplanned trip. But despite its risks, I'm committed to this way of teaching because I believe that the process of discussion can teach students a lot about what's involved in the understanding and interrogation of a critical text.

Obviously Mac's method and mine have different strengths and different limitations. He brings in a broader range of material, exposes the students to more things. I give them more on how to work with whatever they're exposed to. So while we are teaching the same syllabus, his students and mine are having two different experiences. He's training astronauts, I'm training aquanauts. Both kinds of training, I hope, will stand them in good stead in their work beyond this course.

Thursday, 5 November 1987

I've been working fitfully on my response to the talk Frank Kermode, a well-known professor of English at King's College, Cambridge, will give here in Columbus next week at the meeting of the Midwest MLA. When Murray asked me last spring if I'd like to do the response, I was glad to accept. Responding would be like working on an essay for Intro to Grad Study. It would also be a chance to have a good-sized audience. Now I'm not sure I was wise to be so eager.

Kermode's title is "Poetry and History," and he focuses his argument on three poems I'd never read: Horace's "Nunc est bibendum," an ode about Cleopatra; Marvell's "Horation Ode on Cromwell's Return from Ireland"; and Auden's "Spain 1937." Kermode's concerned with the relation between what he calls public myths about historical events and poems about those events. His claim is that good poems, which are aware of their own figurality, always complicate the public myths, sometimes to the point of presenting two opposed visions of the event without choosing between them. I think he does a nice job on the three poems, but I wonder whether they are sufficient for him to make his larger case. I may try to see what happens when I try to extend his argument to other poems—Yeats's "Easter 1916" and Robert Lowell's two poems about the 1967 march on the Pentagon.

I won't be an expert on any of the poems, but I can read them well enough to test Kermode's thesis. Or so I tell myself tonight, as I wish he'd written about Jane Austen or Henry James or narrative theory. Well, I still have a week left and I only have ten to fifteen minutes to fill next Thursday night. And I won't be the only one in the spotlight. Christine Froula of Northwestern will also respond.

Sunday, 8 November 1987

The Columbus Marathon one year later. I ran the second half with Miller, who had hoped to do a personal best of 2:50 (a 6:30 per mile pace). The weather was pretty good this year—sunny, in the sixties—but it was windy. Barry had paced Miller between the two- and the ten-mile marks and Miller was still on pace when I picked him up at thirteen. We ran a 6:33 between thirteen and fourteen but slowed down after that, so that by seventeen we were averaging about 6:38. Between seventeen and eighteen I asked Miller if he wanted to try to pick the pace up, but he said no, he was feeling pretty tired. We slipped to a 6:44 next and realized that Miller wasn't going to make his goal. We got back under 6:35 once or twice, but Miller couldn't sustain the faster pace. Still, he finished in 2:54 flat, a PR on the Columbus course, only about twenty seconds slower than his best anywhere, which, as he said, came when he was a younger man. He was justifiably pleased. The rest of us will have to put up with his gloating all winter, but he's earned the right.

Running the second half of the course brought back my experience of the marathon's difficult beauty. My goal last year was to break three hours, to qualify for Boston on my first try. Miller ran with me through seventeen, when I began to tire and told him not to wait for me. We had gone by the ten-mile mark in 68 minutes, and I went by the twenty-mile

mark in a bit under 2 hours and 16 minutes. At that point, I wasn't feeling
great, but I figured I could run a 10K in 44 minutes without too much
trouble. The weather, though, was cold and raw—cloudy, windy, in the
high thirties and low forties—and I was getting chilled. Between twenty
and twenty-one, I lost my drive, started concentrating on the rotten
weather and my rapidly increasing fatigue. By about the twenty-four mile
mark, I thought I had blown my three-hour goal, but I felt too lousy to
care. No one muscle, bone, joint, or organ was screaming with pain, but
none of them felt good, and none seemed interested in moving me
forward any longer. Meanwhile, my mind was already piling up the conso-
lations of the defeated: 3:04's not a bad time for a first marathon. At least
you'll run all the way, not like all these people walking along here. If the
weather weren't chilling you so. . . . If you hadn't had that trouble with
your legs last month. . . . Facing an uphill stretch of about a mile and a
half into the wind, I was nodding at my mind's profound wisdom.

Then at the water station near the twenty-four mile mark, another
friend, Ron Henricks, caught up to me and encouraged me to run with
him. I tried picking up the pace again, and suddenly I began to feel better,
even as we went up a hill and into the wind. I got into a zone where I knew
I was hurting but where I also knew that I was strong enough to push on
without injuring myself. Three hours seemed possible again, and I picked
up the pace just a little bit more, enough so that I was now running ahead
of Ron. The last mile and a quarter did stretch far longer than I ever
thought possible, but I was able to maintain the pace and finish—relatively—strong. My time was 2:59:25.

Immediately after stopping, though, I felt lousy again. I was extremely
fatigued, very cold, and sick to my stomach. Betty and the kids had come
to the finish line, and were waving and smiling at me for about five
minutes before I even noticed them. It took me another several minutes
to drag myself over to say hello. Betty says I've never looked worse.
People were encouraging me to change into dry clothes, but I opted for a
massage in a heated tent first. That helped, but as I lay on the table I
began to shiver. Just as I was finished there, another friend brought me
my dry clothes and I changed. After that I was okay. By that afternoon, I
felt tired but healthy, and I recovered without any problems.

My glimpse of the difficult beauty of the marathon—and its appeal,
despite its dangers—came in that last mile and a half. When Orwell's

Winston Smith first experiences physical torture, he enunciates a truth that runners know in their own way. "Of pain you could wish only one thing: that it should stop. . . . In the face of pain there are no heroes, no heroes." What the competitive marathoner learns is a modification of that truth. To bring pain—in the form of physical and mental fatigue—to the threshold of the unbearable and to hold it there while you press on until the finish is immensely satisfying. Regardless of how fast or slow you are, the physical and mental challenge of the marathon is essentially the same. You need to be strong enough to run comfortably but swiftly (whatever swiftly means for you) through about twenty miles and then still be strong enough to enter and remain in the zone where you are conscious of both your extreme fatigue and your ability to overcome it. To run in that zone for the last six miles is to experience the beauty of the event.

Despite my attraction to the experience, I decided that the price I have to pay for it in training is too high—too many hours out on the roads, too many hours in recovery, too many away from Betty and the kids and from other things I want and need to do. I love to run, but to dedicate myself to chasing the marathon's beauty would require too great a sacrifice. Like Virginia Woolf's Lily Briscoe, I have had my vision. Or perhaps better, like George Eliot's Mr. Brooke, I can say, "I went into that at one time."

Monday, 9 *November* 1987

Finally finished drafting my response to Kermode. I turned out to be pretty hard on the paper, harder than I thought I'd be after I first read it. But the more I worked on it, the weaker it seemed. If we grant Kermode's general point that poems about historical events complicate public myths about those events, what do we know about the relation between poetry and history? Not very much, because the category of public myth is highly problematic. Suppose, for example, Howard Nemerov wrote a poem about Watergate and we wanted to investigate the relation between the poem and the public myth. Which myth do we choose? The American political system works? A great president was hounded out of office by snooping reporters and self-important congressmen? A politician with no respect for the law was able to be president for six years and come within a hair's-breadth of leaving office not only undetected but also honored as one of the great leaders of this nation? Our choice would depend on how we decide which groups constitute the public. But regardless of which myth we choose, it is overmatched from the start. The myth will always be simple and straightforward; the good poem will always be more complex. Since we know this before analysis, it's hard to believe that it is the key to poetry and history.

Tuesday, 10 *November* 1987

As I walked into the office this afternoon and looked toward the mailboxes, I suddenly felt my stomach sink and my head ache. There in front of my box was a large brown envelope, just big enough to hold my manuscript comfortably. "Damn! I don't want to hear the bad news, not today." Then sweet release: the brown envelope was addressed to someone else.

Caught up in other things, I have succeeded in putting my thinking about the book on hold. Today was a reminder, physiologically and psychologically, of how much of myself I have tied up in the fate of the book. At the moment, I'll claim with some conviction that I believe in it enough to withstand an initial rejection. If Chicago says no, I'll send it somewhere else without substantial revisions. But that belief won't make me immune to the fact of rejection. If Chicago says no, I'm going to have some deep wounds to lick. Today's release was sweet, but it was not satisfying; I moved from immediate and deep distress back to distant and diffuse anxiety. I want of course to move from this anxiety to present and deep gratification. In the meantime, I'll try to put these thoughts and feelings back on hold.

I'm having only mixed success teaching Derrida and de Man—and tonight I relearned an old lesson about teaching. We tried to do some application of de Man to Browning's "Soliloquy of the Spanish Cloister," a poem that Booth analyzes in his irony book. I had prepared an application but hadn't carried it all the way out. I expected that once I got the students going they could pick up what I was doing and extend it. Not so. Instead, only some of them would buy the application I sketched, and many jumped to discuss the limits of the deconstructive approach. In retrospect I can see that the jump was premature. Not having fully seen how de Man would work on a new text, students were operating with a too limited notion of what he can do. We certainly got much further inside Booth than de Man.

Part of the trouble here was some complacency on my part. Over the years I've gotten much better at thinking on my feet than I initially was, much better at being able to flesh out in class the ideas I've sketched in preparing to teach. But I've learned that it's dangerous to rely on that skill when dealing with difficult material. I should have known that having only the sketch of the de Manian reading wouldn't be enough.

Thursday, 12 *November* 1987

Late. There was something both exhilarating and disappointing about my response to Kermode. We had a couple of hundred people in the audience, which was by far the biggest I've ever addressed. I controlled my nervousness and felt like I was making sense. But I don't know how many in the audience stayed with it. Kermode took a long time reading his paper, and I think lost many along the way. Since I was working inside his argument, if you didn't stay with him you wouldn't be that inclined to stay with me. Those that did stay seemed to like what I did. But Chris Froula's tactic seemed to work better. Chris objected to the very terms of Kermode's argument. She pointed out that Kermode's working with canonical texts and claiming for them some resistance to the official history of the public myths had the effect of keeping noncanonical resistance by women and other marginal groups in our cultural tradition from being heard. To make Kermode's case and then label it an account of the relation between poetry and history is to imply that such groups don't matter to history or to poetry.

Not surprisingly, Kermode was taken aback by what we did. With both his terms and what he did with them strongly challenged, he didn't have an easy time of it. He tried to get off Chris's hook by suggesting that arguments about the canon were becoming interminable and repetitious. He tried to get off mine by suggesting that I didn't take sufficiently into account his concern with value (good poems are aware of their own figurality), so my Watergate example doesn't work—no one is making a case for the greatness of any Watergate poems.

Finally, though, Kermode conceded a lot. I was pleased and surprised to hear him say that he thought I had pointed out the "crudity" of some of his categories. I hadn't used that word, but he had gotten the message.

I'm also glad tonight's over. Tomorrow I'll go to the conference, tomorrow night Betty will take off for Atlanta till Wednesday, and for the next four weeks, I'll focus on finishing up the quarter, on getting further into the conference planning, and on tying up things on the grad committee before I start my leave.

Saturday, 14 *November* 1987

Three striking events at the Midwest MLA:

(1) An old friend told me about her experience at an Ivy League school. She was denied tenure because, she feels, she was doing feminist criticism. The school is one that is notorious for *not* tenuring their junior people, and my friend was inclined to spare herself some pain by deciding not to let herself be considered. Some of the senior women assured her that she was one who'd make it and urged her to go ahead and put herself up. She did and got her neck chopped off. Then the senior colleagues "just weren't there." On top of all that pain, she had to deal with the trials of the job market and her fear that despite her commitment to her work, despite the sacrifices she'd made in her personal life, and despite her satisfaction in what she'd accomplished, she would be forced to give it up and find another way to make a living. She did succeed on the market and is now at a good place, but it took her awhile to land the job. And she feels burned by the whole experience.

Stories like that make me sick. The Ivy League mentality that nobody-is-good-enough-to-get-tenure-in-this-department actually makes a mockery of real standards. It distorts the idea that the heart of this life is being an intellectual who is able to contribute something substantial to the work of other intellectuals and able to communicate to students that knowledge and some enthusiasm for the life of the mind. That test can be rigorous, but to apply it in such a way that almost everybody fails is perverse.

(2) At the session on part-timers in the profession, one part-timer, who teaches composition, told of his experience trying to teach a literature course. Several students approached him about doing a course in some American writers who weren't taught in the regular offerings. Spurred on by their interest and excited about the idea of teaching a literature course again, he proposed to teach the course as a freebie. He wouldn't ask for extra money or for it to be a substitute for one of his sections of composition. The response of the full-time faculty was as-

tonishing: (a) they refused him the permission; (b) they assigned the same course to a full-time faculty member who of course did it instead of some other assignment; and (c) they passed a rule prohibiting part-timers from teaching more than two courses a semester. Stay in your place, part-timers.

I feel lucky to have landed between the Ivy League and the part-time world.

(3) Jamie was the respondent in the session on nineteenth-century American literature, devoted this year to history in American literature, a topic that led the speakers into arguments about the place of certain works in the canon. I couldn't hear Jamie speak because her session was held while I had to be at dinner with Kermode, Chris Froula, and a few others. But Jamie and I talked some about her task ahead of time, and she showed me a draft of her remarks. We disagreed some about the conclusions she was drawing, but as we argued back and forth I was struck with how far she'd come—or was it I who'd traveled further?—since I watched her deliver her first paper in Ann Arbor last April. Though I disagreed with some of her positions, I wasn't concerned about how she'd perform—as soon as I read her paper I thought it would become the focal point of the session. And I was right. Sarah said that Jamie stunned them all and had everybody responding to her response. And Jamie's satisfaction clearly came through in her own more modest account of the session.

In six months Jamie seems to have mastered the art of the twenty-minute conference paper.

Sunday, 15 November 1987

The proposal for the dissertation seminar has wended its way through the bureaucracy and is now an official course. Praise the Lord—after writing a rationale (to be submitted in triplicate) for the prayer you choose.

Monday, 16 November 1987

Thinking tonight about ambition in academia—my own. Last month I got another letter from Paul Smith, encouraging me to apply officially for the endowed chair. I did, and last Thursday I received a letter from Trinity's chair informing me that my name was now on a short list. On Friday, Betty and I had a good talk about whether it was worth pursuing their interest in me and decided that it was, at least to the point of getting more information about the job. "Don't turn down a job you haven't yet been offered," she said. We talked too about how this possibility at Trinity might affect the more remote possibility of our going to a more prestigious school with a substantial graduate program. We decided that we couldn't determine that and wouldn't worry about it, except to the extent that we don't want to move anywhere with the expectation that we'll move again soon. This part of our talk has made me think about my ambition—my feelings about going to a more prestigious school, being appointed to an endowed chair, switching places with Kermode on occasions like last Thursday night.

There are times when I strongly feel the pull of such ambitions. Living with the profession's reward system, and more generally being an upwardly mobile member of the American middle class, I have internalized these criteria of success. At the same time, I vacillate in my self-evaluations. Sometimes I feel that I'm damn lucky to have any job, and at others that OSU is damn lucky to have me. Sometimes my ambitions seem embarrassing, and at others they seem attainable. But above all I respond to the ambitious feelings by reminding myself that what really matters is the work: the teaching, writing, reading, thinking, the living in a community where those things matter. Beyond a certain minimum—decent working conditions, a salary that is not insulting, students who can be reached—external trappings like rank, institution, and income aren't all that important. At OSU now, the work is all there for me and the trappings are better than minimal. I like it here.

So while I acknowledge the ambition, I've decided that it shouldn't drive me, that it would be stupid (never mind ignoble) to make decisions on the basis of how one course of action or another would lead to my advancing up some ladder of prestige. As I think about this interest from Trinity, then, I admit that I find something ego-gratifying about the possibility of having an endowed appointment at this stage of my career, but I know that all we're really talking about are the external trappings of the job. What I need to find out is how the work itself might go there.

Tuesday, 17 *November* 1987

Suddenly, finishing up the quarter has gotten more complicated. Mac has gotten sick and I've taken over his section of Intro to Grad Study. But just how complicated this might be began to hit me yesterday at about one o'clock when I realized that in two hours I was supposed to be in two places at once: in the discussion group for Mac's class and at a meeting of the graduate students to discuss course offerings for next year. That meeting was originally scheduled for 4:00 but had to be moved to 3:00. Still unable to bilocate despite years of trying, I went to the general meeting for a while and then late to the discussion section, which seemed useful, though brief.

Though Mac and I have been doing the same syllabus, it's difficult for both his class and me to adjust in midstream like this. Mac and I are too different for me to adopt his kind of teaching successfully, and there's not enough time left to get them fully comfortable with mine. But we'll muddle through. We talked some about pluralism today, about how one could say at least a qualified yes to both Booth and the deconstructors. It wasn't a smash, but we were communicating with each other, I think.

My night section went very well. I'm becoming convinced that they are an exceptional class. It may just be that the difficult circumstances of the afternoon class make the night students look especially good by comparison, and it may just be that they look so good because they are finally used to me. But I think it's something more: there are a lot of good thinkers in the group.

Wednesday, 18 *November* 1987

Betty's back from the meetings of the National Council on Family Relations in Atlanta. She liked the convention more than she anticipated. She got away from her stress, saw some old friends, did her presentations, had many good conversations about her research and that of her colleagues at other schools. But she's feeling the pressure of reentry, which she partially relieved today by joking about why she likes conventions. "You don't cook, you don't make your bed, you don't have to hassle with your children, you don't have to do logistics with your spouse, you don't teach, you don't have to go to committee meetings. You talk to people who are interested in your work, you do lunch, you go out to dinner, you drink a little. It's amazingly artificial but it's nice."

Right. Why don't we find a convention we can both go to this weekend?

Friday, 20 *November* 1987

Today Barbara and George Perkins drove down from Ann Arbor with boxes of proposals and papers submitted for the 1988 narrative conference. They came to my house, where the three of us, two of my colleagues, and Jamie, who's agreed to be the assistant coordinator, worked all day reading and judging the submissions. We had room for about eighty papers and there were close to two hundred submitted, so there was a lot to do. We stayed at it from about 9:30 to 4:00 and finished the job. I'm sure that we made some mistakes—when you're working from abstracts you end up making some guesses—but on the whole I like what we've come up with.

Barbara has now pretty much turned the organizing of the conference over to me and Jamie. We'll send out the letters of acceptance and rejection; construct sessions out of the papers we accepted; figure out some kind of schedule for the sessions; and attend to the thousand details of hosting two hundred people for this particular academic ritual. But it seems more urgent to finish the quarter first. I'll think about the conference tomorrow.

Went to a cocktail party at John Gabel's house this evening and spent some time talking with my friend who was turned down for promotion to full professor. He had petitioned the full professors to reconsider his case, but they returned the same verdict, so he had to go through the rejection all over again. Nevertheless, he is doing better: "I'm sick of feeling sorry for myself, sick of just dwelling on myself. I'm ready to move on." And his spirits seemed much better than they've been for the last month or so. I'm heartened by his resilience.

We spent some of our time talking about the big OSU news of the week: Jennings's firing the football coach, Earle Bruce, which led to the resignation of Rick Bay. Jennings's move is clearly the worst mistake he has made since he became president in 1982. Bruce may not be the best man for the job, but firing him after he loses to Iowa on the last play of the game—and the Monday before the Michigan game—reinforces the image that Jennings and so many others want to counteract: that OSU is a place where winning football games is the highest priority. We all thought that Jennings was smarter than that. If Jennings and the Board of Trustees had decided that Bruce should not be retained after his contract ran out next year, then Jennings should have told Bay to let Bruce know that he would be wise to see what kind of offer he might turn up in the off-season. I would guess that Bruce's won-lost record is strong enough for him to get another good job, and then everybody (well, some more than others) could be happy. This way Bruce is furious, Jennings is under fire, the university looks bad, and the publicity generated by the whole thing emphasizes once again that OSU is a football school.

My favorite bit out of the whole affair is the way it's been treated by *On Campus*, the in-house weekly that comes out of the Office of University Publications. Their headline: "Jones new A.D. after Bay resigns."

Sunday, 22 *November* 1987

Feeling good: ran my last race of the season and got under 28 minutes— well under, in fact, at 27:34. The last two miles hurt a lot. When I went by the four-mile mark, I thought how nice it would be if it were the finish line; I was strongly tempted to stop and settle for a PR for that distance. But I knew that today was my chance to go under 28, so I just kept pushing. I didn't feel the same sense of power that I felt at Night Moves, but now I can see that my greater fatigue today was a sign of my greater effort throughout.

My first two road races back in 1982 were five milers, and after the second one, which I did in about 31 minutes, I decided that someday I'd like to be fit enough to run a 27:30. I'm not sure why—it was a nice round number, someone who ran that time finished up towards the front—but I really had no conception of how realistic a goal it was. When I had trouble last year going under 28 despite being in what I thought was excellent shape, I concluded that I was too big and slow to go much faster. So today seems especially sweet. This time is close enough to what I started out after five years ago. I may never get in good enough shape to run that fast again, but once is enough. In running as in writing, ripeness is all.

Though I've done fewer miles and raced a bit less than I originally planned, I'm content with my season. I've had some good hard workouts, but I've had a lot of easy days too. By running less and more easily, I've fit my workouts more comfortably into the rest of my life, and I've gotten better results when I've raced.

I've also enjoyed my running this fall because of the company I've kept during much of it. My noontime runs with Miller and Barry have more often been leisurely than strenuous, and during them we've hashed over the affairs of the university—the Jennings-Bruce affair of course, but also teaching vs. research, the role of service, the relation of faculty to administrators, and many other things. We disagree a lot—Miller is, to put it mildly, a conservative soul—and Barry, though more of a kindred spirit, is in a department (industrial and systems engineering) that functions very differently from English and that gives him a different perspective on things. Despite all our teasing of each other, we have enough mutual respect so that the conversations remain comfortable even when the disagreements mount. Though we don't set any policy or develop any proposals to change the university, I find the conversations a way to deepen my awareness of the place. Agronomist, humanist, engineer; full professor, associate professor, assistant professor: as we match strides, we knock heads over common concerns and thus broaden our understanding of each other and the issues we take up.

Sometimes when I run in the neighborhood, I find Jamie out putting in her miles, and then we'll often walk and talk together for a while. Last February when I wrote about teacher-student friendships in the aftermath of Jamie's visit to John Gabel's class, I noted that the roles of teacher and student always impose some barriers to such friendships. When Jamie and I talk about her dissertation or the conference, or what's going on in the graduate committee, the roles and the barriers are still there, but when we talk about running or our kids or the way we're reacting to things, the teacher-student roles recede and the barriers come down. One of the comfortable features of our walks is how easily we shift from talking as teacher-student to talking as friends. Though the shifts are fluid and comfortable, not all the discussions are. But Jamie's willingness to push me as well as her willingness to listen when I push back makes me like our bumpy talks almost as much as our smooth ones.

Monday, 23 *November* 1987

Finally heard something from Chicago: an apology and a promise. "For a number of reasons it has taken us much longer than we had hoped to get a formal review underway. Please accept my apologies. . . . The manuscript is now in the hands of two readers, and I expect their reports before MLA." Well, it's good to know that much. I can hang on another month. And I like the news that two people are now reading it.

I also like the sentence written in the space designated by the ellipsis: "I am in fact quite enthusiastic about the book and would like to go forward with it if possible." I'm leery of reading too much into that sentence—it's the readers' reports that will be decisive—but I take it as cause for cautious optimism.

Tuesday, 24 *November* 1987

The graduate school wants to adopt a merit-based system of pay raises for graduate associates and have it in place by January. This move strikes me as insane because it will make the graduate students feel like they're under the evaluation gun yet again, and that feeling is likely to impair rather than enhance their teaching ability. It also seems like the system would be impossible to administer well. The Council of Graduate Students passed a resolution against the plan at their meeting last Sunday, and everybody I talk to in the department is against it. So today I wrote a letter to the dean of the graduate school, Roy Koenigsknecht, supporting the resolution and explaining my "philosophical and pragmatic" objections to the plan.

I don't know if the letter will do any good, but at least we're now on record against the new system.

Wednesday, 25 *November* 1987

In the final segment of Intro to Grad Study, called "Literature, Criticism, and Cognate Disciplines: The Example of Psychoanalysis," we're focusing on Peter Brooks's attempt to use psychoanalysis as a way to talk not about authors or readers but about textual dynamics. Since I've written about Brooks in my book, I feel very comfortable in the discussions. And though Mac's class doesn't feel like home in the same way that my night section does, we're starting to get more used to each other. Every once in a while, though, someone will say something that reminds me that we don't share enough context for me to be asking the question I am in the way that I'm asking it. So I try to fill in the context and repeat the question.

Meanwhile, I continue to be impressed with my night section. There are some folks who never speak and I wonder about how they're taking it all in, but there is also a good number of people who are eager and able to carry on the discussion at a fairly advanced level.

It helps that I'm feeling satisfied with the teaching, because I'm feeling worn down by everything. Mac's class meets Tuesdays and Thursdays from 3:00 to 5:00, so the evening crunch these days is even worse. I've now assigned the last paper, and a lot of the students are seeking me out in office hours—and beyond—to discuss that. There is the normal graduate committee work, which I'm managing to keep up with, but some Shandies are developing: writing to the students I saw in Texas last spring; creating for the graduate school a description of our criteria for approving faculty to be dissertation directors; revising our handout on the M.A. thesis.

And there are Shandies forming on other fronts. I should be getting after Dennis. The momentum of the dissertation seminar didn't carry him very far—he has stalled short of the prospectus once again. I'm wondering about Sarah's progress and should probably call her. I have a small but knotty job to do for the Steering Committee that I keep putting off. My desk—surprise—is a mess.

These things may remain Shandies because I've got some other big jobs that I need and want to do. I have to finish making up next year's teaching schedule, I still have to get out the letters of acceptance and rejection for the conference, and I agreed to review a 300-page manuscript for a press. And things won't let up until January, when I finally go off duty. Once I finish teaching I have to prepare two papers for MLA plus get ready for what in effect will be two Christmases: we're going to NJ from December 18 to 23 then we'll be back here for the big day itself, then I'll go off to San Francisco for the convention. Then I'll come back and slow down.

Friday, 27 November 1987

Had a good Thanksgiving yesterday—slow and easy, away from work. I give thanks for that.

Saturday, 28 November 1987

Ronnie has passed her M.A. exams and will graduate in about two weeks, then get married the next day, and say good-bye to OSU. I've enjoyed talking with her about her plans, her work as a research assistant for a colleague, a baby-sitting job she's taken on to earn extra money for the wedding, and her preparation for my exam in the novel. Nevertheless, beneath the talk—and the teasing about the exam—I've also felt that we've been saying a slow good-bye: Jim, I've liked what we've done together; now I'm moving on. I've liked it too. Thanks, Ronnie. And good luck.

Tuesday, 1 December 1987

My last graduate committee meeting before my leave. Had a strange experience presenting the teaching schedule. The idea is for the committee to look it over, see if I've left gaps, and make suggestions for revision. The committee pointed out a few things I'd missed, which I was receptive enough to, but I found myself resisting a lot of their other questions and suggestions about the overall setup. The schedule is difficult to make up because you need to balance faculty requests, schedules, and abilities against student needs and demands while also thinking about what makes sense as a package of offerings for each of the four quarters. I think I was resisting in part because I had worked through all that and developed something that made sense to me. Almost every change causes ripples throughout the schedule, and I didn't want to deal with them all. But I think I was also resisting because of plain old egotism. What I really wanted was applause.

We also discussed the merit-based system of graduate associate pay raises and decided that we should do what we could to oppose it. Our first step was to agree to draft a resolution against the system that could perhaps be voted on by the full department at the meeting scheduled for 4:00. Then those students who were going to tonight's special meeting of the Council of Graduate Students could go armed with it. During the break in my Intro to Grad Study class, I came over to the meeting and presented the resolution, which passed unanimously:

> The English Department strongly opposes the institution of merit-based increases for Graduate Associates because we believe that the competitive atmosphere generated by such a system impairs the development of graduate students as effective teachers, because we believe that no differential increases should be made when the stipends are shamefully low, and because we believe that the system will seriously undermine the morale of our graduate students and faculty.

For the first time since I've been doing both classes, I thought that the afternoon session went better today. We were on each other's wavelength more consistently than before, and I think I got across both the value of what Brooks has done and some idea of its limits. Tonight things were more herky-jerky: we'd get one point established and then lose it as we tried to go on to something else.

I'm also experiencing the anxiety of forgetfulness. I couldn't remember what I'd said where. When my teachers used to repeat themselves unwittingly, I was always irritated: Can't you remember that you told us the same damn thing last time? Don't you care at all about what goes on in here? I resolved that if I ever got a job, I would always remember what I had said and what I hadn't. Now I remember whether I've said something or not—I just don't remember who the lucky audience was. And for some of this stuff, once is lucky, twice unfortunate, and thrice cursed. Bear with me, students, for just one more class.

Wednesday, 2 *December* 1987

It looks like our work on the resolution yesterday was wasted. Cowed (?) or convinced (?) by the dean, the Council of Graduate Students rescinded their initial resolution against the system. Jamie told me that Dean K. stressed the need for evaluation procedures for G.A.s, and his own motivation to get more total money into the pot for G.A. increases. While the dean was present, Jamie and Maria had no vocal allies, though after he left many more joined in. Not enough, though, to prevent the withdrawal

of the resolution or to muster support for a new one. The dean's arguments aren't convincing. You can have evaluation procedures and more
money in the pot without merit-based increases. But he's the dean and
they're only graduate students.

Where we go from here on the issue, I don't know. I still haven't
spoken to anybody—faculty or grad student—who thinks the dean's plan
is a good idea. But with the council capitulating, I'm not sure what we can
do. There is a senate meeting on Saturday, and Julian and some others
are encouraging Jamie to bring the issue up there. She's not sure that will
do any good, and I'm not either. But it might be worth a try.

Thursday, 3 *December* 1987

The phone rang at the beginning of my office hours today. "This is Roy
Koenigsknecht. I'd like to talk with you about the letter you wrote me last
week. Do you have any time today? I can come to your office." I suggest
tomorrow and he snaps the first available time. He also says that he has
shown the letter to the provost, who finds it "thoughtful." I'm sure he just
wants to mollify me, but I'm intrigued by this response. He doesn't have
his secretary or even one of the associate deans call, but does it himself;
he makes a point of coming to my turf; he lets me know that he's shown
the letter to the provost.

Maybe I should write more letters to administrators.

Last classes in Intro to Grad Study today. They did their evaluations, I
made some final comments on Brooks's work as just one example of how
to relate psychoanalysis and criticism, and then I tried to relate what we'd
done in the course to their future work in the program. In that segment I
talked a lot about how the course was just an introduction, a way to get
them aware of the nature of the discipline and the kind of skills they
would need to work effectively within it. I'm not sure what Mac had said at
the beginning of his section, but for my group I was closing the circle,
returning to themes I had hit in the opening session, hoping that they'd
have a greater appreciation of what I meant and a greater sense of how far
we had traveled in ten weeks.

Each session also ended on a more personal note. Mac came for the
last ten minutes or so of the afternoon class to say good-bye and let the

students know that he was O.K. Mac quickly reestablished his bond with the students and let them know that he'd been pretty ill but was doing much better now. He was up for this talk, but his fatigue and weariness were still plain to see. The students were marvelous: concerned, sensitive, solicitous, good-humored. The communication from each side of the desk was impressive.

In the night section, I told them that I often found it difficult to get there at seven, that I had felt more strain than usual the last few weeks, but that I was always happy when I was there. "You students deserve the credit for that. I've been energized by the interest and energy you've brought to the course. Thanks."

They applauded—for themselves or me, I'm not entirely sure, but I'll take it, I'll take it. It's a nice way to go into my year away from the classroom.

After class, Lois, who had done an excellent job as course assistant all quarter, and I spent some time talking about the course, what had worked, what hadn't, what a good group the students were. Not surprisingly, the students in Lois's discussion group were more open about their anxieties as beginning students—about what they didn't know, about how difficult some of the material seemed, and so on. It seems clear to me that our plan for having the advanced graduate student work in the course is a big plus—and even clearer that Lois did an excellent job.

After we talked through the course we talked about a miscellany of other things. I enjoyed the whole conversation very much, but it also made me regret that we hadn't had more talks like that during the quarter. Another price paid for teaching at night and being so harried.

Friday, 4 *December* 1987

Mary has been having some success in the early stages of the job search. She has an interview lined up already, and she has numerous dossiers and several writing samples out.

This morning I participated in her mock interview. Mary talked well about her dissertation, I thought, and on the whole came across as intelligent and well informed. She was somewhat nervous, but no more so than many other people in that situation, and not so nervous that it was a problem. Mary and I had a good talk afterward about it, and I felt that she accurately perceived how she was coming across. In general, she seems to be more on an even keel than she was earlier in the quarter, and though I'm not ready to predict that she'll get a job, I feel better about her prospects than I have in a while.

I leave Mary's interview to go to my meeting with Dean K. which is, finally, a standoff. He tells me that my "thoughtful" letter has been influential, but goes on to make his case about the value of the system as a way to see that evaluation of G.A.s takes place and as a way to get more money into the pot. He also stresses that he believes in local control: departments and colleges can work out their own systems for dividing up the money. Most important to me, he indicates that discriminations can be made between groups rather than individuals, e.g., all post-generals students can get an increase of X, while all second-year students can get an increase of Y. I keep trying to question the rationale for the whole policy, but he keeps answering by talking about how the policy can be carried out in a positive way. He wins the local debate by controlling the agenda this way, but fails to convince me about the fundamental issue. I of course make no headway with him.

Late this afternoon, during a session of letter-writing to Congress to urge the retention of the tax exemption on graduate student fee waivers, Jamie, Jeffrey Leptak (the vice-president of the Council of Graduate Students), and I decided that we would say something in the senate about the merit-based stipend increases. Jeff told us that Dean K. is concerned about what he (Jeff) might say in his report on the activities of the council, so he's going to be circumspect. Jamie told Jeff that she'd like to read the department's resolution, but he said it might be better if it came from a faculty member, so I volunteered. We'll see.

Saturday, 5 *December* 1987

We didn't make senate history, but we did register our opposition. Jeff set me up nicely. He ended his report by saying that there had been a lot of debate about the merit-based increases in the council, and that no doubt that debate would continue. He then asked if there were any questions. I got up—too nervously, I thought—to say that my remarks would be by way of continuing the debate, and then I read the department's resolution. When I was done, Jennings, who serves as presiding officer, asked if I had sent a copy of the resolution to the dean of the graduate school. I replied that we had spoken, that I appreciated the dean's response to my earlier letter, that I was pleased to learn that the system didn't require separate judgments on each individual G.A. but that finally I thought the attempt to link evaluation of performance to salary was "toxic." End of official discussion.

Afterwards, Dean K. came by to shake my hand, to say that he thought what I had said was "fair" (no hard feelings). Bernie Rosen, a colleague in the philosophy department whom I know from AAUP circles, suggested that I try to get the Faculty Council (the faculty members of the senate) together to pass a similar resolution. So perhaps we've kept the issue alive a little longer.

I had hoped I was past the point of getting nervous about speaking out in a public forum. I think that my natural shyness combined with some feeling that I was being ungrateful to Koenigsknecht for his visit to my office (there is no such thing as a free visit) to make me apprehensive about reading the resolution. Silly, but true.

Afterward I asked Jamie whether she wished she had been the one to speak.

"Well, it was probably better coming from you—but, yeah, I do."

Thought you'd say that.

Wednesday, 9 *December* 1987

I've been making good progress on the Intro to Grad Study papers, and on the whole I'm pleased. The students had two options: (1) do some practical criticism on one of four works I selected, challenge their results from the perspective of one of the frameworks we've examined this quarter, and finally reply to the challenge; (2) examine and attempt to adjudicate a dispute between the deconstructors and those who believe in the possibility of determinate meaning. To do either assignment well would require them to think through some important issues raised by the course, and it's evident that many of them have. While I'm feeling encouraged, I'd better go back to it.

Friday, 11 *December* 1987

One big task done: turned in the grades and the graduate reports. I established a PR for the reports, doing almost all of them in about four hours this morning. I was driven by the challenge of it all—could I concentrate well enough and long enough to say what I wanted about each one without spending two days?—and by some uneasiness about my progress with my jobs. I finished grading yesterday afternoon and took it easy last night. Then when I got up this morning, I felt the burden of the reports and my other unfinished work lying heavily on me, and I regretted not working last night. The session this morning worked off some of that regret.

The evaluations for Intro to Grad Study reinforce my sense that the course worked, even as they're helpful about some things that can be improved. The evaluations are also fairly consistent between the two sections, though to my surprise Mac's group on the whole is more positive than mine. The two main suggestions for improvement are to give more background in the history of modern criticism and to give more structure to the discussion sections. Though I deliberately refrained from more background because of my worry that the course would turn too much into a lecture survey in criticism, I'm now convinced that, if only for their peace of mind, I should do more. And the idea for the discussion group sounds good, though I'm not sorry we left it pretty loose this first time through.

It's a relief to find so many students in Mac's section saying that they benefited from the exposure to both of us. I wonder if we should, as some of them suggest, plan some switching between sections next time.

Some end-of-the-quarter silliness from a few of the Intro to Grad Study students. As a token of their gratitude for the course and of their esteem for my teaching they gave me a sweatshirt whose inscription alludes to what I'd called the a posteriori nature of good neo-Aristotelian crit-icism—"Neo-Aristotelians do it from behind." Although I will never wear this shirt anywhere, although I fret about its heterosexist bias, I am pleased by their gesture—I think. In my thank-you note, I played pro-fessor and said that it would be uncharacteristic if I didn't also comment on their gift as a sign of what they got out of the course. "While I *am* appreciative, I want to know why you didn't have the shirt say 'Pluralists do it in multiple positions' or perhaps, 'I want to get inside your framework.' This way I have to wonder whether the main thing you got out of the course is the knowledge that you should never turn your back on a neo-Aristotelian." And I signed it "Marie of Rumania."

Saturday, 12 *December* 1987

Before we left for Ronnie's wedding this morning, Paul Smith called to let me know that Trinity is going to interview me—either at MLA or afterwards on campus.

   While Ronnie was taking her vows, my mind kept wandering back to the phone call and its eventual consequences. Do I—we—really want to move? What would Betty do? What would it be like to go to a small private college in New England after eleven years at our large Midwestern university? What would it mean for the kids? Slow down, slow down: there are a lot more steps to this process. Where would I rather be interviewed? I said I'd be happy to do it either in San Francisco or in Hartford, but should I have expressed a preference? Amid all my questions, I felt the warm glow of the well-flattered ego—no doubt the real reason I kept replaying the phone call in my head.

   Ronnie's wedding was very sweet. She was radiantly happy—someone who believes (knows?) her dreams have come true and wants everybody to share her joy. That was great to see. But while she was exuding this powerful happiness, she was also blithely promising to be subject to her husband in all things. That left Betty and me shaking our heads.

Monday, 14 *December* 1987

Told Murray about Trinity's interest in me. He said all the things I hoped he would: "I don't want to lose you." "I think I speak for the full professors when I say that the department would do everything it could to keep you here." He also surprised me a little by saying, "Name your price." I don't know if I have a price. As I said earlier, I'd like to think that money isn't the issue here. But it's nice to be told that if I got an offer, I could expect a counteroffer.

Tuesday, 15 *December* 1987

Got the last of the letters of acceptance for the conference out today, and I've made some progress on my MLA paper on pluralism. I'm slowly getting through my various tasks.

Betty called me at the office to lighten my load. "Concentrate on getting your work done. I'll take care of the Christmas stuff."

In lightening my load, she also lifted my spirits. One of the few sources of friction between us has been that I work too much and leave her with jobs like the Christmas shopping. What she did today was done not out of exasperation but generosity. So while I'm still feeling over-worked, I'm also feeling lucky.

Thursday, 17 *December* 1987

Trinity called. They want to interview me at MLA. This is getting serious.

In an hour or so we're off for our Christmas visit to New Jersey. We'll see a lot of relatives, exchange a lot of gifts, eat a lot of fancy meals, and log a lot of miles on the Toyota. When we come back on the 23rd, the kids will still be wired, but Betty and I will probably be worn out. Then we'll have our Ohio Christmas to get through. Holidays are such a joy.

I go, however, in pretty good shape. I've been up late every night this week, but I've managed to hammer out drafts of both my papers. In the first one I'm defending pluralism against two people who are attacking it because they see it interfering with a more urgent kind of political crit-icism that they want to do. From one of the panelists I have only a few pages outlining his position; from the other I have a full paper, and I engage with his argument fairly closely and am pretty hard on it.

I'm a little worried about this trend I seem to be following of criticiz-ing everybody else. I was hard on the feminists in my paper at Worcester, hard on Kermode, and am now hard on this panelist. If I'm becoming a curmudgeon who thinks that nobody can make a sound argument, then I'm violating my own pluralist principles. But as I go back through the panelist's paper I still find the problems I point to. And now I'm being seduced by the recognition that my argument also has the advantage of showing that one can defend pluralism and still argue with other critics.

The second paper, for a session on "The New Thematics: Powers and

Limits," is coming out of the chapter in my character book on Scholes and the limits of thematizing. My task is one of adapting something to the occasion, so it has required a different kind of thinking. I'll need to do some more with it when we get back, but I'm not too worried about it. My main concern is to do something that will be up to the quality of the papers presented by the other two panelists, Peter Rabinowitz and Jerry Graff. (There, I'm not a full curmudgeon yet.)

Wednesday, 23 *December* 1987

Back from the whirlwind tour of our NJ relatives just in time to finish preparations for our own Christmas. Having hit about four different residences and received gifts at them all, Katie and Michael may have already overdosed on presents. I'm afraid that the next few times Michael walks into anybody's house, he's going to ask, "Do you have any presents for me?" But the trip went well. Even the driving wasn't too bad, though I had a brief moment of terror about 3:30 this morning when Michael awoke in the motel and announced, "I'm bored." Fortunately, he went right back to sleep.

I took the kids to practice for the Christmas pageant that they'll be in at Newman Center tomorrow. Michael is to be a shepherd, Katie an angel. Katie hooked up with some of her friends and fellow angels very easily. Michael made a new friend, a three-year-old named Neil, who decided to follow the five-year-old's every move. Since Michael was rather spacey in rehearsal today, he and Neil may end up as the lost shepherds.

Saturday, 26 *December* 1987

About 2:00 A.M. A good, peaceful day, after two rather long nights. It took me longer to rework my paper on Scholes than I thought it would, and I ended up making some further revisions to the pluralism paper as well. But now they're ready.

The Christmas pageant went off well. The angels were upset because they had one of their dances cut short, but only the most cognizant of the cognoscenti noticed. The shepherds did fine—*all* those called by the angel found their way to the stable.

Our NJ trip took only the smallest edge off the pleasure of Christmas morning for the kids. Michael now has the entire collection of Definitely Dinosaurs, and Katie enough clothes to keep her warm for the rest of her life. The Christmas season alternates between the awful and the wonderful. Today, fortunately, the pendulum swung the right way.

I just finished reading a not very well-known novel, Chester Himes's *Blind Man with a Pistol*, which Peter Rabinowitz will talk about at our session on thematics. Just before that had a nice, easy, five-mile run through a soft rain. When I was done, I felt content, peaceful, pleased with our family Christmas, ready to accept my MLA papers as they now stand, ready to deal with the craziness of the convention without getting too caught up in it. I am a bit apprehensive about what I might learn about my book manuscript, but everything else—seeing old friends, interviewing at Trinity, having my ideas challenged in the sessions, getting a sense of how far my own interests are diverging from the dominant theoretical discourse, watching the egos on parade, participating in some interviews for our prospective faculty, working on the committee on resolutions—I feel ready to take in stride. I'm also cautiously optimistic about Mary's MLA. She now has at least three interviews lined up.

In general, I feel more mellow, less anxious than I have since before I left for Worcester. It's a nice feeling, induced in part by the run but also by the easy pace of our day, by our comfortable togetherness, by a feeling that though I could still work on my papers, I've done O.K. with them. Hope the feeling lasts once I get to San Francisco tomorrow.

WINTER 1988

Searching, Waiting, Steadying

Friday, 1 January 1988

The feeling didn't last. It was an eventful convention for me, but not one
that I felt mellow about. I didn't sleep well any night, slept worst before
my biggest day, Tuesday the 29th, when I had the Trinity interview and
gave my two papers. But the story of my convention and the loss of
mellowness starts earlier. The flight out to San Francisco went smoothly,
and I had a good visit with old friends who now live out there and who
put me up on the night of the 26th. But the next day, when I had plans to
have lunch with Booth, things started to go wrong.

Booth had given me a phone number where he could be reached, and
I started calling him at 10:00 that morning. I tried again at 10:30 and then
about every fifteen minutes until noon (when I accepted the fact that
lunch was a lost cause), and then two or three times later in the day. No
one ever answered that phone. I went to his session that night and
learned that he'd become ill and had flown back to Chicago. I later found
out that he was O.K., but that miss on the first day would be repeated for
me—in different ways and with different consequences—for the rest of
the convention.

There were some comical variations on the theme. When I first put my
name tag on, I had it upside down, much to the amusement of two young
women on the elevator who had to explain their amusement and thus
saved me greater embarrassment later. (I was going to claim that there
was great symbolic significance to wearing one's name tag upside down,

but hesitated because I was afraid one of them might say, "Yeah, it symbolizes that you're a dope.") Later, at a cocktail party the first night, someone saw my now properly affixed name tag, shook my hand, and attempted to remind me that we had a mutual interest in computers and composition. No, I'm sorry, but that's not me. Then when I asked him about his work, he seemed offended and annoyed:

"So, you're working on computers."

"Obviously."

O.K., be that way.

Another time, while walking to my room, I was accosted by somebody waiting for the elevator who greeted me warmly, shook my hand, and then realized he had the wrong person. He had the grace to acknowledge his error immediately, to apologize, and to save face by claiming with nicely modulated irony that it was a great pleasure to meet me anyway. Only at the MLA.

There were more serious variations on the theme. My interview with Trinity, tentatively scheduled for Monday at 1:30, was not confirmed before I got out there. In the meantime, I had realized that I was supposed to attend the meeting of the committee on resolutions at 1:45. So after some telephone tag, we finally got the interview rescheduled for Tuesday at 11:30, which meant that I'd have that interview in the morning and the two papers in the afternoon. It also meant that I was keyed up the night before and didn't sleep very well.

The biggest missed connection was between me and my copanelists at the session on pluralism. They made their attacks, I tried to show that these attacks were on a position that I wouldn't want to defend, but that from the one I did, I could argue that they didn't make their cases very well. In a sense, I was counterattacking, but my main point was that pluralism couldn't be trashed so easily. It is a metacritical position, not one that was a full rival to the kinds of Marxist criticisms they were advocating. They came back swinging. One of the observers later described the scene as "wild." It felt like a disaster to me. They didn't hear what I was saying. I could tell that they didn't think I had heard what they were saying. A lot of their attack seemed to me to become personal. "You can accept this politics and that politics at different times and on different occasions: Who are you, man? Just an empty liberal." I simply said that I thought we were still missing each other, I acknowledged that I may not have done full justice to their case, but otherwise I wanted to get back out of the fray. I sensed it was hopeless. We weren't connecting, nor were we going to. Still, I was stung by it all and immediately thought that I had been too rough and perhaps unfair. Even now I'm still processing the event, still trying to make sense of it, still feeling the wounds.

I think my paper was both too blunt and too unclear. When I tried to show that the essay on "The Perils of Bakhtin" demonstrated "the perils of monism," I pulled only one of my three main punches. So it was natural for that panelist to swing back. If you give your shots, you ought to be ready to take them. Thinking back over the responses I've done in the last few years, I can see that I've become more bold in my saying no. Having gotten at least some acknowledgment of the validity of my polite no in the past, I may have paid more attention to the no and less to the politeness here. So I guess I asked for it in several ways. Some lessons have to be learned the hard way.

Another lesson I'm drawing from the session is that I need a term other than pluralism to talk about what I mean. It seems that no matter how many times you say pluralism isn't simply open marketplace tolerance people don't get the point. I don't know what the term should be yet—methodologism? metadisciplinism?—but I'll think of something. I've also become convinced that I need to do an even more extended treatment of the politics of pluralism—and of theory more generally—in my book. The discussion was about politics, not criticism, and though the two can't be totally separated, the political ought not be so dominant. In pushing me toward these conclusions the session was productive. But I still feel like I'm doing a salvage operation on it.

There was a much less serious missed connection at the session on thematics. Peter did a very nice job with his paper, mine seemed to be O.K., and then Jerry tried to put the whole discussion into a broader context and ended up away from thematics and on the way departments organize the curriculum. He got the few questions we had time for, and we never got back to thematics. Nevertheless, what Jerry did was justified in the sense that his discussion of thematics led him in a logical progression toward the points he wanted to make about the curriculum more broadly. Peter and I also got a few compliments after the session broke up, so I think that what we were doing was heard. And there were a lot of people at the session.

Another missed connection of sorts—potentially serious, but perhaps not—involved a friend of mine who interviewed for our senior appointment. This guy was the star of his Ph.D. class when I first began at Chicago. We got to be friends because he too played basketball, and we've stayed in touch—mostly through meeting at MLA—since he left for his first job at the end of my first year. Just last year he moved to a prestigious Eastern school where he is now a full professor. I have some doubts about whether he would be willing to leave there for the Big Ten, but his family hasn't yet moved to his new school. If we could make it attractive enough he might move them to Columbus instead. I haven't read his book, but I've always been impressed by him when we've talked about criticism, and the articles that I've read and the papers I've heard him give have always struck me as first rate. Many of the other candidates for the position have published more, but I thought that there was a good chance that he could emerge from the interview stage as our first choice.

It didn't happen that way. I think my friend expected more of a situation where we would be selling him on OSU, less of a situation where people would be pressing him with questions about his work. And he told me later that he'd been up most of the previous night with his one-year-old daughter. In any case, he was, I thought, uneven in his performance. People wanted to know about his second book of criticism, and it became clear that he wasn't very far along on it. There were times when he seemed fuzzy about what his project would entail, others when he talked about it very well. All in all, he never really took over the interview, never kept us on the territory where he was strongest, and thus didn't do himself justice.

Immediately after the interview, he got mixed reviews from the committee. Some liked him, some didn't, others thought he was uneven. What's happened since then is something I don't entirely understand, though I've seen it happen before. The interview has become mythologized among some as the terrible performance of a glib namedropper (my friend sometimes referred to other critics—his friends—by their first names) who, though a full professor at Prestige U., hasn't done much to earn that position. What's going on here? Some principle of least effort for the memory—find a tag to stick on someone and leave it at that? Some subtle competition with Prestige—we know better than you? Something about my friend that I don't recognize because I've known him longer? Perhaps all those things. In any case, something's gone awry. But Murray liked him, and no other candidate emerged as a clear favorite, so there's a good chance that we'll bring him to campus. He'll have to make up some ground, but if I'm right about his quality, then I think he can still emerge as first choice.

My interview with Trinity was blessedly not characterized by missed connections. Paul was there, but he let the others ask the questions. They started by asking me about my paper in the thematics session, and we went from there to many of the other issues in my book, and finally to some questions about teaching. I was satisfied with what I got said: though of course I've thought of several things I should have said in response to their questions, the actual number is below my usual norm. It felt like I was giving them a good sense of what I do. If they don't want that, then O.K.

For my part, I liked the five people who were there; they asked good questions and they seemed genuinely interested in my work. On the flight home, I read through the catalogue they gave me and found much in it very attractive: a required theory component for the English major; the opportunity to teach freshman seminars; a generally interesting and varied curriculum. It's clear, though, that the M.A. program is very small—it has only part-time students, and their courses typically meet at night.

One of my few fortuitous connections at the convention was running into Paul in the hotel lobby the night before the interview and going for a drink with him. He made it plain that I was his first choice. He also added some other attractions. The salary would be somewhere between sixty and seventy thousand dollars (more than I had anticipated), and the probable teaching load would be four courses over the two semesters. He also asked me whether they had a chance for me. I said there was a chance but I didn't make any commitments—and of course neither did he.

Since the interview I've been thinking about the possibility a lot and talking it over with Betty. There are a lot of unknowns. What could Betty do? What kind of schools could we find for the kids? They're loyal Ohioans. How would moving affect them? Do we want to go back to the crowded East with all those things that attract people and make it crowded? Well, we'll see. The decision may not be up to us. The chair said that they won't make decisions about whom to invite to campus until after they're back in session on January 14th.

On a not entirely unrelated matter, I talked with the editor at Chicago, who had no real news for me. He did reiterate his own support for the book ("I want to keep you as a Chicago author") and promised to hurry up the readers after he returned to the office. He'll hurry and I'll wait.

Monday, 4 *January* 1988

Winter quarter begins today—without me. Excuse me while I roll over and go back to sleep.

Wednesday, 6 *January* 1988

Talked to Mary about her interviews, but she didn't say much that was encouraging. She felt that the people at New Mexico State were unsympathetic to her dissertation, that the interview with Kentucky took a wrong turn about midway through, and that the ones with John Carroll and St. Anselm's were okay. I tried to keep her spirits up, but based on what she said, I'm not that sanguine about her chances. Still, she's had some good interviewing experience now—maybe something will still come along this year. In the meantime, let's refocus on the dissertation.

Friday, 8 *January* 1988

Except for about three hours today, when I hurriedly wrote (I thought the deadline was *next* Friday) a proposal for funds to support the graduate committee's planned teaching apprenticeship program, I've felt off duty this week. I'm doing some reading. I played ball for the first time since the great game with Fish. I resumed weight lifting with the Marcy machine. I'm sleeping more, paying more attention to Katie and Michael—in general working on restoring balance to my life. I could get used to this.

Tuesday, 12 January 1988

I spent over two hours at the optometry clinic this morning, finding out that, as I had feared, I do in fact need glasses. I hate these signs of deterioration—I'm in shape, I'm in shape, dammit, I'm in shape—but I'm working at taking this one in stride. I keep reminding myself that Betty has been wearing glasses since she was nine, that the majority of the people in the profession wear them, that glasses are actually wonderful things.

About eight or nine years ago, one of my bespectacled former colleagues was talking with Betty about how many academics wear glasses. When Betty noted that I was an exception, Susan said, "Well, Jim hasn't read much." Maybe I've finally read enough.

Wednesday, 13 January 1988

As Betty and I have been adding up the pros and cons of going to Trinity should they make me an offer, we've been getting a sum that says we're better off here. Betty would be finding something, not going to something. I'd have to give up teaching Ph.D. students. We don't finally think of Trinity as a place from which we'd never move. So I've wondered whether I should withdraw my candidacy. I don't want to use Paul—don't want to use Trinity—just to get myself a better deal here at OSU. At the same time, it doesn't feel right to close off the possibility just yet. Its attractions—good undergraduate teaching; the somewhat lighter load; the chance to be back in New England; the advantages that would come with the chair—are strong enough to make me want to keep looking further at the differences between OSU and a place like Trinity. It may be that as we get more information and include that in our adding up of things, we'll get a different sum.

This all became clearer to me this morning when I got a phone call from a friend at the University of Houston. He had told me at MLA that Houston was going to be trying to fill a chair in critical theory, and he sounded me out about the possibility of applying. I told him that I wasn't interested, but we talked further about the possibility of my going there sometime in the next few months to give a lecture and to talk more informally to faculty and students about my work. I was eager to do that.

When he called this morning, he said that he was working on getting me the invitation and that I ought to send a c.v. to the chairman. In the course of the discussion, he also raised again the possibility of my being considered a candidate for the chair. I had no hesitation in telling him that if my giving the lecture were contingent upon my being a candidate, then I ought not come at all. I don't have that kind of certainty in my thinking about Trinity; I want to find out more about it.

Thursday, 14 January 1988

I'm very much aware that today Trinity starts its second semester. If I don't make the cut, the only consequence of the whole process might be that I become dissatisfied with my salary. While I don't have visions of dollar signs dancing in my head, I have let myself imagine getting paid a lot more than I now do. I've also thought that if I left and the department tried to replace me with someone with comparable credentials, they'd have to shell out considerably more than they do for me. So I want to say, why not just give me the raise regardless of whether I get the offer? With the offer or without the offer, I'm still the same guy with the same credentials, and I'll still do all the things I've always done.

Like anybody with even a rudimentary understanding of supply and demand, I know the answer. My analysis assumes that my market value is the same as that of the person the department would bring in to replace me. The assumption is flawed because I don't have that value until the market says I do.

There is plainly something screwy about all this. Since the way to test—and increase—your value to your department is to get another offer, the reward system actually encourages you to direct your energy toward leaving rather than staying, or at least toward exploring the possibility of leaving. Capitalism in academia conveys a powerful message. Professors are all finally free agents, able to move wherever someone else would have them, able to renegotiate their contracts whenever they can produce an offer sheet from some other school. This fact in turn means that, in some fundamental way, departments—and for that matter, colleges and universities—are no more than aggregates of free agents who happen to like the deal they have or can't get a better one. The reward system encourages loyalty not to colleagues, programs, departments, or institutions but to old number one. Under the current system, institutions have little or no reason to give big raises in the absence of outside offers. Giving the departmental MVP a big raise won't necessarily ensure loyalty to the institution. It just means that the next bidding war for the MVP's services will start at a higher figure.

Of course not everybody follows the values of the reward system all the way down the line. Many in the profession are committed to the people, programs, and institutions in which they teach. But if you become deeply committed in a way that your colleagues are not, you can be burned. They're ready to leave if they get the right deal; you want to stay. If they do leave, then what are you committed to? Their replacements? And then if they leave?

At MLA this year, I was talking with someone who has moved to Duke within the past three years as part of their very visible (and very impressive) effort to establish their English department as the best in the country by hiring people at the top of the profession.

"Duke must be an exciting place to be now."

"It is. But we're trying to get people to stop saying *now* when they say things like that."

"Do you think it will stay exciting?"

"I hope so, but a lot of people are predicting that it's all going to blow up in a few years."

We didn't go into reasons why it might or might not, but it strikes me today that our whole conversation reflected the phenomenon I'm trying to identify here. Duke brings in a few key people by giving them better deals than they have at their home institutions. Once a few are there, they can attract others through the combination of the better deal and the prestigious colleagues. ("More money and a chance to play on a World Series winner: Where do I sign?") But these folks all still remain free agents, and Duke itself can be raided by other schools who will put together yet better deals for these academic MVPs.

I'd like a better model of a department. People with diverse interests and expertise who share more fundamental beliefs about education, critical discourse, and inquiry come together to put their ideals into practice. They make a commitment to each other and to their institution because they know that without it the ideals won't be realized. The institution in turn values them for that commitment, fosters their efforts to make things work, and rewards them according to the success of the whole enterprise. Of course people would leave, but they wouldn't start with the idea that it was important to let their colleagues and institution know that they could.

How close is the department at OSU to this model? How close is the one at Trinity? At Duke? Anywhere? Relative to what I hear about a lot of places, we do O.K. here, but we're a long way from my model. Trinity and Duke I could only speculate about. But my sense is that until the reward system changes, until we stop letting ourselves be defined so much as free agents, my model won't exist.

How much am I letting myself be so defined here? As I've said before, I'd be less than honest if I didn't admit that I'm attracted to Trinity in part by the possibility of the high salary and the title. And I'm also aware of what an offer from there might mean for me here. But I don't think—don't want to think—that these attractions are what's controlling me. Suppose I don't get the offer. Just as I will be the same guy with the same credentials, OSU will be the same place with the same conditions of work. If I'm satisfied with those conditions, including my salary, before Trinity calls, then I'll be satisfied after they call back and say no. I can focus on what Trinity has to offer beyond the salary and the title. If I like what's there more than here and I don't get the offer, then I will regret the missed opportunity. Or at least I can remember this way of thinking about things when I succumb, as I sometimes do, to focusing on the gratification of having my salary doubled.

My idea of a model department raises another question: apart from whether OSU or Trinity might be closer to the model, do I owe anything to my colleagues here? I'm sure they'd all say no (a sign of how far we are from my model), and perhaps for me to say anything different would only indicate my hubris. But I feel some pull to stay and see how the revisions in the graduate program work; some pull to stay and continue to build my relationships with those colleagues I care about, to give back something of what they've given me; even some slight tug to stay out of gratitude for Julian's hiring me back when the job market was so bad. And then there's the question of what I owe to my students. I can stay on their committees—would want to—but would they be comfortable with having a dissertation director who was seven hundred miles away? Jamie and Mary will finish before I'd leave, but what about the others? I want to see their projects through to completion, and I know that I could probably do that better here than there.

All these pulls to stay would have to be balanced, I now realize, not just against the conditions of the work in a narrow sense but also against my sense of what kinds of things I could build there—what kind of a department that could be, what kinds of colleagues I would have, what kinds of relations with students. The decision seems to be more complicated all the time.

Saturday, 16 January 1988

While I was at the post office this morning, Trinity called to invite me for a campus visit. When Betty gave me the message, she asked, "Are you surprised?" We both laughed when I immediately said, "No." But I didn't think I was boasting so much as interpreting. Paul had made his feelings plain, and though I didn't see him after the interview, I felt that it had gone well enough for him not to change his mind and for him to be able to convince the others that they should take my candidacy to the next step.

Now the possibility of moving—and all the consequences that would follow—suddenly seems more real. Can we really imagine doing it? I don't know, so I'm just going to keep trying to go one step at a time.

Tonight I've been working on interpreting the various things that Jim Wheatley, who will be my host, told me about the visit. I gather that he agrees with Paul about me, but that their opinion is not entirely shared by others on the faculty. He said to Betty that they want me to come and "interview" them. He said to me that he'd like to see me there next year. But he also said some things that lead me to conclude I'm not everybody's first choice. He asked me some questions about the character book that seemed to reflect problems that some of his colleagues were having with it. He also warned me to be sure to do something substantial in my presentation. One of your strengths, he said, is being able to think through the consequences of other positions that are not fully thought out, but not everybody sees the value of that. Pick something that will show you to your best advantage. I'm not sure exactly how to tailor the presentation to address these different concerns, but I appreciate getting the general message. They're bringing me in, but I still have to convince some of the doubters that I'm the best candidate. No chutzpah allowed.

Tuesday, 19 January 1988

About 2 A.M. I've been working on the presentation for Trinity. It will be one of those tricky rhetorical situations that seem to crop up all the time in this business. My immediate audience will be the students, but the more important audience will be the silent faculty who will sit and observe. My plan is to present what we might cover in the first couple of classes in a course on character. It will be substantial as far as its quantity goes. In the first part, I'll talk a little about how my questions about character fit within a broader approach to literature as communication about human action, experience, desire, possibility, then sketch some of the thinking that has led me to develop my terms and concepts for talking about character, and finally illustrate what those terms and concepts yield when we read a dramatic monologue like Browning's "My Last Duchess." Then we'll move to the wild card feature of the program, a discussion of "Haircut." I know where I want that discussion to go and how I want to relate it to what I say about Browning. As we move from the monologue to the narrative, we see how Lardner uses the progression of his narrative to actualize some potentialities of the thematic component of character. But of course I'll have less control over what happens there. Finally, I'll talk about what kinds of issues we could take up in the rest of the course. If it works, I just might "wow them," as Jim Wheatley asked me to. If it doesn't work, they'll decide that I can never talk sensibly to undergraduates, and that will be the end of my candidacy.

Wednesday, 20 January 1988

About noon. I'm leaving for Hartford in less than an hour. I wish I'd gotten more sleep the last few nights, but otherwise I feel pretty good. I'm keyed up a bit—all right, nervous—but I'm looking forward to the trip.

After I read the first part of my presentation aloud last night, I decided that it would be better not to read it, but to do it as an informal lecture without notes: it's too compressed. But talking it through informally may mean that I'll take too long with that part and will thus have to short-circuit the discussion of "Haircut." I'm willing to take that risk, because I think that in order to meet the concerns that Jim raised I should try to do everything I've planned. I have the argument firmly in my head, so I'm not too worried about performing without the net of the prepared text.

I'm a little more worried about my meetings with the individual faculty members because what they've been reading might not match what I've been reading, and I'll come across as less informed about criticism and theory than I'd like. At the same time, I'm looking forward to these meetings, since they'll give me some sense of what the whole department is like, some sense of what it would be like to have these people as colleagues.

Called Betty about an hour ago, just to check in for the last time. Her send-off had both of us laughing: "Good luck. I hope you do well—I guess."

Friday, 22 January 1988

Whatever happens next, it was an interesting trip, and I think, a good one. I liked the faculty for the most part, I liked what I heard about the department and the college, and I especially liked the students I met. What they thought of me, I'm not so sure.

The general consensus about the presentation was that I tried to do too much. My plenty may have made me poor. If I were to be invited back, I'd do things differently, but given what Jim had said about the situation, I'm satisfied with what I tried to do and, for the most part, with how it came off. I was worried at one point in my presentation of "My Last Duchess" that I wasn't explaining myself very clearly and was in danger of losing the audience. But I seemed to get them back and then felt that the talk built appropriately to the points I wanted to make about the ending of "Haircut." Some in the audience seemed to see the payoff for all the preliminary work we had done.

But as I interpret all the signs of their response that I can remember, I reach some mixed conclusions. One of the creative writers told me that he thought what I did with "Haircut" was "lovely." He seemed to dismiss the fact that I tried to do too much: "You knew that going in." Besides agreeing that I tried to do too much, Paul commented that he "was tired of fireworks." So I guess I didn't come across as a spellbinding teacher. Paul also said that he liked how much substance there was in what I said: "If you tot up the number of points you made, you'd get a pretty high total." Jim said that he understood why I did so much: "You have to give them your framework. And you've got a lot of framework." If they my-thologize the presentations of their candidates, my myth, I think, will be built around Jim's line. Whether that works to my advantage or not will depend on whether they decide I'm only a lot of framework.

For my part, I liked the time I spent talking to the faculty, both at dinner Wednesday night and during the day Thursday. Some of them, I could tell, were not fans of mine, but most of the conversations had real substance, and most of them went somewhere. How collegial the depart-ment actually is, though, I'm not so sure. Although I felt that I was able to talk productively with most people on this occasion, I have a harder time assessing how our conversations would go if I were there. How much did we succeed in moving beyond the mutual evaluations to mutual interests in each other's work? How much basis is there for a sustained conversa-tion on issues I care about? Certainly there's a good basis with Paul and Jim—and that means a lot. But I'm less clear about the others.

My meeting with the dean, whose Ph.D. is in English, was interesting because she wanted to show me that she was both a dean and an English professor. After a few pleasantries, she informed me that she disagreed with some critical position I outlined in my letter. I gave her some rea-sons for my position and she didn't pursue the issue, but moved on to another one that she had some misgivings about. And we went through that in a similar way. I assume she just wanted to get a sense of how I would talk about literature and criticism, and I suppose that strategy worked as well as a more friendly one would have. But I couldn't help feeling that the subtext of her questions was "I am the dean. I have the authority here." On the positive side, she talked about Trinity as an intellectual community, a place whose size allowed for a lot of exchange among people in different departments, and a lot of informal exchange between administration and faculty.

My interactions with the chair were finally somewhat disappointing. She was friendly enough, she asked some serious questions, she seemed interested in answering mine, but I got the sense that she wasn't all that taken with my work, that she wouldn't be someone who would want to talk a lot to me about criticism.

In general, though, I liked the place and the people and I've come back more able to imagine myself there. The breakfast with the students reminded me of how exciting good undergraduate teaching can be. They were open, interested, eager, intelligent, full of questions. Still, I don't think adding up the pros and cons gives us a substantially different sum yet. In fact, one of the most vivid experiences of the trip was on the negative side. Wednesday night as Jim was giving me a ride to the restaurant, I was looking out the window, trying to get my bearings, and generally feeling disoriented. We stopped for a red light and as I stared at some unknown building, I had this deep realization of how much I would be asking of Betty if I were to say, "I really want this job; let's move," without her also having something to move to. I'd be saying, give up what you know, give up what you've built out of your own hard work, and follow me. I don't want to do that.

When I asked the chair whether Trinity did anything for spouses, I didn't feel greatly encouraged. We'll do whatever we can informally, but we have no formal procedures for placing spouses here or anywhere else. If I get the offer, Betty and I will of course reassess everything and I'll want to see what OSU would do, but right now I don't think I'd accept it.

Nevertheless, I must admit that I still want to get the offer and that part of my desire for it is motivated by my pride and my insecurities. Even as I continue to question what it would be like for me to work there and what Betty might do there and how things would be for Katie and Michael, I also know that I'd like the reassurance, the validation that would come with the phone call that says "we picked you."

I'm the first candidate they brought in, and they have two positions to fill, so I won't hear anything until the middle of February.

Sunday, 24 January 1988

Tonight the literary criticism group discussed two chapters of my book— the introduction and the one on *Great Expectations*. It was fun. A lot of people came, a lot asked questions, a lot seemed to want to know more about what I was doing. Nobody made me think that the argument has serious problems, but there are some places I'll consider revising in light of what was said. I did get needlessly hung up on a few questions—my explanations didn't seem to work, and I couldn't think of better ones—but on the whole I thought the night went well. In any case, it's been a nice week for having people talk to me about my work. But please, folks, now let's move on to other things. Except, that is, for the two of you out there who are supposed to be reading my manuscript for the press. You two should just get on with it—and say the right things.

These two readers, I've decided, are the instruments through which the God of Patience is exacting his revenge for my unseemly haste last July. If so, his method is working very effectively.

One of the things that the department will get on with here is filling our senior position. I missed the first candidate when I was at Trinity, but tomorrow my friend is coming. I heard a lot of good things about the first candidate, so my friend has some catching up to do. I'm looking forward to it.

Tuesday, 26 January 1988

I may have enjoyed my friend's visit too much: it's going to be that much more painful if he doesn't come. He did catch up a lot, I think. His talk was very good and seemed to be well received. He fielded the questions well, too—thought on his feet, went back to the text he was analyzing, showed his lively and wide-ranging mind at work. I'd like to think that he's now going to be our first choice, but I'm not sure. The third candidate is coming in on Thursday, and the full professors will meet to decide at the beginning of next week.

I got pleasure out of watching my friend deliver his paper, but I got even more out of just talking with him about all our common interests: theory, running, basketball, the profession, teaching, parenthood, the job search at the senior level. In one way we're very different kinds of people. He's smooth, rangy, quick; I'm none of those. And because of our different specialties and different institutions, we've had different kinds of experiences in the profession. Yet I was surprised at how many perceptions we shared, at the many ways in which we justifiably assumed a common ground and went on to talk. If he were to come, he would, I sense, become my closest colleague. I'd love it to happen.

I told him about Trinity. He told me—as he had told Murray—that he wasn't sure he would accept an offer from us. We agreed to keep each other posted about our decisions—or those made for us by others.

Friday, 29 January 1988

The third candidate for the senior position was also good. I don't think he was quite in my friend's class, but if we ended up hiring this candidate, I think we'd do fine.

For reasons that I haven't entirely followed, it may be possible for us to make two appointments. The personnel committee met today to make their recommendations to the full professors and apparently reached consensus on making the first offer to the woman who was here while I was at Trinity, but could not decide between the third candidate and my friend. My sense is that the mythologized interview has come back to haunt him. His talk itself is being mythologized as old-fashioned criticism and old work. He is also, in a strange way, being hurt here by his success elsewhere. The fact that he is a full professor with only one book of criticism is being held against him. I don't like what's happening, but maybe he's won over enough of the full professors to get the offer. For the first time in my career, I sincerely wish I were already a full professor. I want to go to that meeting.

Saturday, 30 January 1988

Back to the issue of merit-based raises for G.A.s. Before today's senate meeting, I went around and collected signatures on a petition to convene the Faculty Council in order to adopt a resolution against the system. Everybody I asked signed eagerly, and many commented on how much of a problem the system was causing in their units. So I'm hopeful we can present a united front on the issue—if we can get enough people out for the meeting.

Sunday, 31 January 1988

After considerable debate with myself, I decided to lobby for my friend with the full professors by writing them a letter explaining why I think they should extend him an offer. The letter was difficult to write because a lot of my conviction that he would be good comes from an assessment of intangible things like judgment and wisdom, and I suspect that it may only carry conviction for those who don't need to be convinced. Still, I finally decided that if he didn't get the offer and I didn't make the effort, I'd always regret not having tried.

Monday, 1 *February* 1988

Dammit, they blew it. No offer for my friend—though he came in second. From the little I've heard, and I have no desire to get all the gory details, a lot of it came down to money, although some people had questions about the quality of his first book. I gather that most people wanted to go ahead and make him the offer, but some questioned whether he was worth the kind of money we'd have to pay him to match his present salary. Since consensus was needed to approve the offer, the dissenters carried the day.

Now I wonder whether I should regret writing the letter: it's not just that I now feel partially rejected too but more a question of whether the letter did more harm than good. I imagine a voice saying, "The fact that someone feels he has to make the case indicates a problem." But I also know that it's foolish to think the letter had a great impact one way or the other. Full professors are used to making up their own minds.

If the sticking point finally was the salary, then something's really gone awry here. We'd like him if he were still an associate professor making X, but now that he's a full professor at Prestige making Y, we don't want him? Doesn't figure. Come on, full professors, wake up.

All this raises another conflict for me. I believe that for the most part we have good procedures in the department and that we need to follow them in cases like this. But I don't want to accept this outcome. Yet I have to accept it as a consequence of how we do things. Ugh. Maybe I should propose new procedures: rule by philosopher-king—me.

Wednesday, 3 *February* 1988

As time goes by, the case against Trinity grows stronger. Betty had a dream the other night in which I was kissing her in bed when her mother walked in and, apparently oblivious to my presence, scolded Betty for not leaving more room in the bed for her older sister.

It's not so much that new things are emerging in our thinking (we've talked before about complications of being closer to our families in New Jersey) as that our previous reasoning is being confirmed as time goes by. It's not the right time, Trinity is not the right place. If we were to move, we should both be going to something. Again I suppose that things could look different if I had the offer in hand and some sense of how OSU would respond, but I'm feeling more and more like one issue has already been decided. One positive side effect of this development is that I'm more prepared to hear that they're not going to offer me the job, even as I recognize that part of me still wants the validation of getting the offer.

Saturday, 6 *February* 1988

My friend called today after he received the letter telling him he wasn't going to be hired. He just wanted to be filled in a little. I got the idea that he would have come if we made the offer. That opened the wound again. Why couldn't the rest of you see what I see?

Tuesday, 9 *February* 1988

Some good news: Mary called today to say that she'd been to St. Anselm's for a campus visit and that she thought it went well. By the time she left, she felt they were no longer trying to see if she was good enough for them but instead were trying to convince her that they were good enough for her. They'll be bringing in some other people, so Mary won't hear for a while, but now we have cause for some optimism.

Monday, 15 *February* 1988

No word from Trinity yet, and I am slowly admitting that that must be a bad sign. They said that they had candidates scheduled through the 9th, but that they might schedule one more beyond that. If they did, then I could still be in the running. If they didn't, they may have already chosen someone else. I looked at their catalogue this morning to see if Presidents' Day was a holiday for them and discovered that this week is their winter quarter break. They probably would have wanted to wind up the search before then. But just maybe they decided to take the break to read more of the candidates' work. Or maybe they'll meet this week and hash out their differences.

Well, I could construct scenarios for a long time, but the first one seems most plausible to me now. I may get a letter soon, or they may save me as a backup for another candidate. Though I know I'm getting closer to the time when I'll hear something, nothing's really changed. All I can do is wait.

Meanwhile, the watch for readers' reports goes on in the same torturous boredom. Every day I hope I'll hear something, and every day the mail brings no news. I hope the God of Patience is enjoying his revenge. If the eventual outcome is positive, I'll be philosophical about the delay. but if I have to wait this long only to be rejected, I fear I'll end up offending the gods of peace and hope as well.

Tuesday, 16 *February* 1988

An eventful day, the most eventful one since I went to Hartford. The Faculty Council meeting to discuss the merit-based stipend increases for graduate assistants was interesting, strange, unsatisfying, somewhat hopeful. But it was quickly overshadowed by the mail I received after it.

Yesterday's surmise about Trinity was right: "Though we greatly enjoyed your visit . . . , I am sorry to tell you that we will not be able to offer you a position."

It stings. All the summing up we've done blunts that sting, but I still feel it. All of my assessing and fretting and weighing things finally doesn't matter, because I have not done well enough to be given the choice. They chose for me, that is, against me. And I worry about whether I badly misinterpreted how I came across during my visit. Hate to be a fool as well as a reject. I'll write to Paul and see if he has anything revealing to say. But I also know that my ego has recovered from severer blows than this one. One part of my coping is to remind myself that it is good to have closure on the episode, good to resolidify our connection with OSU, and good to settle down to some serious work on my projects about pluralism and voice.

The sting of the rejection was further blunted by the letter I got from Alan Thomas of the University of Chicago Press, though before I opened it, I had some serious anxiety ("If it were good news, he'd probably have called"; "I'm not ready for two rejections today").

> I don't need to tell you that this has been an inordinately slow review process, but I'm pleased finally to send you some result. Enclosed is a very positive report on your manuscript. I hope you are as gratified by it as we are.
>
>   I will try to get our other report as quickly as possible. We may be able to take the project to the March meeting of our faculty Board. I'll be in touch again as soon as I have further news. In the meantime, thanks for your *patience* [if he only knew].

The reader strongly recommends publication, finds "nothing that needs revision," and in general praises the book from start to finish. I've already read the report at least ten times and no doubt by this time tomorrow will have committed it to memory. Let me indulge myself further by recording just the very first sentence: "This work cogently revises and amplifies the approach to the novel developed over three generations by the so-called Chicago School and illustrates its own, new, more flexible conceptions by applying them with notable point and il-lumination to a number of celebrated novels widely varied in form and technique."

I am indeed deeply gratified.

But yes, my bedeviling god, I'm already itching for the next one.

Wednesday, 17 *February* 1988

Probably the first thing to say about yesterday's meeting of the Faculty Council is that it wasn't an official meeting. There were about twenty-five of seventy-two members present—far short of a quorum (apparently no Faculty Council meeting in anyone's recent memory has had a quorum). But we went ahead anyway. I spoke briefly from my side of the issue and then invited Dean K. to offer his perspective. He came armed for battle, handing out a set of memos designed to show how carefully the system had been thought out and how widely it had been discussed. He man-aged to keep the floor for a very long time, as people either asked for more information or tried to argue with him. Despite his dominant position in the discussion, he didn't perform all that well (but given what he was trying to defend, how could he?), and I doubt that he changed anybody's mind.

Listening to Dean K. for fifty minutes was itself unsatisfying, but parts of the next half-hour were even more so, though something was salvaged in the end. Once the dean left, we had to decide what to do. I wanted to vote on the resolution, but the senate office hadn't reproduced it, and some people understandably didn't want to vote on something that they hadn't had a chance to review and think about. Others wanted to get more information about how the graduate students felt about the issue. (Dean K. had made a point of telling them that the Council of Graduate Students had rescinded its original resolution.) A few wanted to support the new system. Finally, after much debate about what was appropriate, we voted on a resolution opposing the necessary connection between evaluating the performances of G.A.s and determining their salaries. It passed nineteen to four. Where we go with this unofficial, nonbinding expression of opinion is not yet clear, but perhaps it will be something we can build on in the next round of resistance.

Thursday, 18 *February* 1988

Maybe there won't be a next round. Today Jamie and the president of the Council of Graduate Students met with the provost (at the provost's request) to discuss the merit-based system. Or rather to be told that it was going to happen and that the appropriate thing for them to do was to work on implementing it. He even proposed to Jamie that she work on a committee charged with establishing a model system in the English department. His carrot, if it can be called that, was that if she could show that such an effort wouldn't work, he'd be willing to reconsider the system. In other words, try to get your way by working for my way. There's logic for you.

I'm discouraged. If the provost wants to do it, if the council won't really oppose it, if there are many faculty who find nothing wrong with it, then we're stuck with it.

There are a few things left to try. Bernie Rosen came by today with a draft of a resolution that we could bring to the senate. If we could debate the whole thing on the floor, we might make some progress. Of course, the provost and Dean K. would be there, but if grad students and faculty could speak in the same forum we might have some success even against their combined opposition. And if we lose there, we lose. At least we'll have tried all possible avenues of resistance. In the meantime, maybe the council will reconsider its position.

Monday, 22 *February* 1988

Still coping with Trinity's rejection. I keep going back over my visit, second-guessing my choices, reinterpreting their reactions. What if I hadn't tried to do so much? What if I had avoided the specifics of my analytical framework and used one of my more general opening gambits? But finally I've decided to stop second-guessing myself. That was me they saw, not somebody else, not some debilitated version of me. I gave it a shot; they decided I missed.

Let it be.

Wednesday, 24 *February* 1988

Good news from Mary: St. Anselm's has offered her the job. She's hesitating a bit about accepting, though. It turns out that it's a three-year appointment that also carries a heavy teaching load—four courses a semester. We're going to get together tomorrow and talk about the pros and cons. My sense tonight is that she ought to take it, but I want to hear more about her reservations.

Thursday, 25 *February* 1988

Mary has decided to accept. She had been leaning that way before our talk but, like a good theorist, spent much of the talk proposing alternative interpretations of her situation, considering ways to disconfirm her preliminary conclusion: I'll have to devote so much time to teaching that I won't publish and thus won't be employable in three years. Maybe I'd be better off to stay here next year and try the market again. I tried to meet the objections. The job, by Mary's own account, could turn into a permanent one. You liked the place, the people, the kind of teaching you'll be doing. If it's too heavy a load, you can look to leave during your second year. That means that you'll need to use your breaks and especially the summer after your first year to work on publication. At that point, you'll still be competing against ABDs and new Ph.D.s. You won't be worse off. If you are liking it, if it turns into a tenurable position, you may be set for a while. Aside from that, it will do you good to leave Columbus, and it will be very nice to end your existence as a graduate student. It's not an ideal job, but on balance you'll be better off there than hanging around here for another year. Go for it.

Mary had more or less worked it through to the same conclusion yesterday, but seemed to feel better once our talking together led her to the same place.

I'm pleased. I wish the load weren't so heavy, and I wish it were a straight tenure-track job, but after her rough time this past year or so it's very gratifying to see Mary emerge from the market with at least a decent job, one that is potentially more than just decent. Nice going. Now back to that dissertation.

Monday, 29 *February* 1988

Got a letter from Paul today, which closes the Trinity episode—and leads to the reinterpretation of some of it. The department couldn't agree about who should get an offer, and so they've ended up not making one. They never agreed about the *kind* of person they were looking for.

At first this news made me take the rejection less personally, but now I'm not so sure. If I had done better maybe I could have convinced the doubters that I was the kind of person they wanted. I wonder, too, about the division in Trinity's department. It's one thing to disagree about who is the first choice, quite another to be so deadlocked that no offer is made. Has the opportunity to strengthen the department with the senior appointment actually turned into something negative?

And what about the senior search here? We too have sustained some blows in the course of it. And we too have not succeeded in filling the position: our first choice has taken a job somewhere else. How we heal will depend in part on who eventually comes.

Sunday, 6 *March* 1988

New life in the fight against merit-based stipend increases. Tonight the Council of Graduate Students voted strongly against a resolution that approved the plan. Their turnabout is due in large part to continued agitation from Jamie and Maria. Their action now makes it easier for the faculty who are opposed to the plan to make a case. We'll do something at the next senate meeting—perhaps try to pass a resolution to support the new position. We still may not win this fight, but I'm glad it's not over yet.

This week, I figure, I'll finally get the second reader's report about the book. I don't know the exact date of the March meeting of the press's board, but the material for the meeting must have to be sent out ahead of time, so if the book is going to be presented at this meeting, there can't be much time left. And given the first report, I assume that Alan will want to present the book and will therefore get after the second reader to finish the job.

Friday, 11 *March* 1988

Damn! I was wrong. Friday—and still no word. I was so sure I'd hear this week (hadn't I been right in my feelings about Trinity?) that my heartbeat accelerated as I walked to the mailbox today. It soon returned to normal, but my spirits were dashed. I'm losing my patience (quit laughing) and may call Alan Thomas next week to see what I can find out. Writing is hard work; today this period of waiting seems harder.

Monday, 14 *March* 1988

Turns out I was wrong by only one working day: the second report came in today's mail and it is . . . positive. Overwhelmingly so. Ha!

Actually, when I first got the news this afternoon, I felt a little flat—as if the end of my wait had been an anticlimax. The reader told the press to tell me who he was—David Richter of Queens College, someone I know—and once I knew it was David, I expected the report to be positive. I missed the thrill of validation from a stranger. Tonight, however, I've decided that i wasn't giving David enough credit for intellectual independence and that I wasn't paying enough attention to the specifics of the report. These rationalizations have done their job. I'm feeling very satisfied, very, very pleased. And the specifics offer much that is pleasing.

Again let me indulge myself by quoting the first sentence of the report: "It has been a long time since I have been asked to review a manuscript that I have both enjoyed and admired as thoroughly as I did this one."

Alan Thomas's accompanying letter says that it's too late to bring the project to the board for the March meeting, but that he'll present it on April 20. He also says that it "is inconceivable that the Board would not approve the manuscript" and he suggests April 28 (when the ink on the contract will not yet be dry!) as the date for delivery of the final version. So after all that waiting, we're on the move again. One of the first things to do is to rethink the title. Richter says that *Character, Progression, and the Interpretation of Narrative* is apt but somewhat awkward. He suggests I use it as a subtitle and think of something "more memorable" as a main title. Alan says he hopes we can "decide on a better title." O.K. by me, though until today I felt satisfied with what I had. In writing to Alan today, I suggested *Reading People, Reading Plots*. I'm not sure that will stick, but it is more memorable (Star Wars fans could—and no doubt would—call it R2P2).

As I get more and more used to the idea that the wait is over, that the God of Patience has been only needling me good-naturedly, that my Dark Night of the Printer has now had a kind of vindication, and in general that my hopes for the book to this stage have been realized, I feel more and more like I've begun floating on a warm, calm, and refreshing Sea of Satisfaction. Nothing will disturb me for a while as I bask in the gratifying feeling that the work in which I have invested so much has received the validation I sought for it. My pleasure is compounded by Betty's enthusiastic sharing it with me, by the kids' own wacky participation in it— hearing that I need a new title, Michael has suggested *Stories and Funnies*. This Sea of Satisfaction is a place I rarely get to. I've only been to this most beautiful part twice before, when I got the job at OSU and when I got the first book accepted, and I never get to stay as long as I'd like. But knowing that it does exist and that it is attainable is very comforting. And now while I'm here, I'm going to try to savor it.

Wednesday, 16 March 1988

In the midst of the savoring, I've begun reflecting on the events of the last few months—Mary's search for a job, my friend's application here, and especially my involvement with Trinity and my waiting for and getting the news about the book. As I've already said about my own situations, in these events someone was looking for validation by the profession, and though that may not be the whole story, it is an inescapable part of each event. Mary's search is of the most fundamental kind—a validation that allows entrance into a new stage of a career, ascension to the second rung on the ladder we climb in this profession. My friend, who is already on the highest rung, does not need validation, but by applying at all he did in part seek it, however unconsciously. In his case it was the validation that comes with being in the position to choose between two very different institutions, a validation that moves him closer to the position in which others will say of him, "He can write his own ticket." In my involvement with Trinity, I was seeking the validation of ascending to the next rung on the ladder and of being offered a huge salary increase and an endowed chair at the age of 37. In my wait for news of the book, I have been seeking the validation of having a prestigious publisher take my work on the first submission—a validation which in turn would mean that I could climb the next rung.

This much is perhaps rather obvious. What's striking, though, is the gap between the rewards and the frustrations offered by the teaching and writing that I have described in the previous sections of this journal and the rewards and the frustrations offered in these recent events. The pleasures and pains of teaching and writing derive from their nature as complex intellectual activities. Those accompanying the search for validation come from having one's ego massaged or buffeted. What's even more striking—and distressing—is the way in which the views accompanying the search for validation can and often do infect attitudes toward the fundamental work of reading, teaching, and writing. The infection starts when you apply to and enter graduate school ("I came to OSU because I couldn't get into More Elite U., but I'm going to make the best of it"). The infection spreads when you go on the job market ("What schools are you interviewing with?"—"Not bad, but too bad MEU didn't follow up their dossier request with an invitation to interview"). It grows further when you begin to publish ("Where did you say that article is going to appear?" "Who's publishing your book?"). And it becomes most dangerous in the way you are asked to think about the job search at the highest level ("X got a great job at MEU; a six-figure salary and one course a year"). In this way of talking about such searches—and in my experience we have an amazing fascination with it—we reveal how deeply and widely the infection has spread. The highest reward of the profession is defined as getting paid a lot for relocating to a prestigious school and not having to teach.

Because of the profession's concern with external validation, many of us end up defensive or arrogant, disgruntled or complacent, bitter or smug, about where we go to school, where we teach, where we publish, what our rank is, how much we make. I see now that it is the infection of this concern that I was bemoaning and trying to distance myself from in my colleague's response to his failure to be promoted. Its presence in another form may be why I instinctively knew that I wanted to oppose the imposition of a merit pay system on our G.A.s—and why our graduate students are so strongly against it. I see too that the infection operates in the Myth of Merit I wanted to tell Susan about last year in Ann Arbor. I wonder how much of the infection was behind Spenko's self-destruction. And how much of Mary's anxiety about her dissertation can be attributed to her worry about whether it was something that others would validate when she went on the market?

Is there a way to cure the infection, some professionectomy that will be effective? I don't see any simple procedures that will work, because the main virus is rampant in our culture, with its repeated message that your worth is defined by your salary and your position. The infection is one sign of the way in which our profession exists within the larger context of our capitalist culture. But we in the humanities have always prided ourselves on our role as critics of the culture, as people who could stand aside and point out its contradictions and problems as well its achievements and strengths. Surely we need to fix our gaze on the way we ourselves participate in those contradictions and problems.

And of course I need to look at the way I've been infected, especially the way the infection was operating in my involvement with Trinity. Despite my reminders to myself that it was the conditions of the job that I most cared about, despite my feeling all along that I probably was better off at OSU, I still very much wanted to get the offer. I wanted the validation for its own sake, for the ego boost it would give me. I am not aware that being rejected has had any strong negative effects on my attitudes or feelings about my situation here, but I am now asking myself how much of my willingness to see Trinity as far from the ideal department is just a defensive strategy, a way to protect myself from the sting of rejection and thus another sign of the infection.

I am also aware that it is easier to admit my being caught in the search for validation now that I have received validation from the University of Chicago Press. Suppose I had never heard about Trinity and my book had been rejected by Chicago. How would I be feeling now, and what would the consequences of those feelings be? I'm not entirely sure, but I know I'd be very depressed about the book and I imagine that the momentum of my work would be slowed. My belief in that work would be shaken. The effects on my teaching would probably be more subtle. I'd teach the same way, but not always with the same confidence and conviction. If the book were accepted on the second submission, I could probably recover without showing many ill effects from the depression, but a second rejection would be very hard to take. And a third and a fourth would be very, very painful—and no doubt very damaging. I'd like to think that I'd never stop energetically addressing the questions and answers I care about, but the reality might be that I would experience a slow erosion of care along with the loss of confidence in my work. And that would affect both my writing and my teaching negatively. I'd probably end up withdrawing from the world of publishing and trying to hang on to enough self-confidence to be a decent teacher. But my sense of participating in a larger conversation about the books and ideas I care about would be radically altered.

Some of the things that would happen in this process would be natural and understandable. Anyone who writes wants to have an audience, and being denied access to one is very hard on one's confidence. Yet to give the profession's opinion of one's work so much significance, to be so in need of a certain kind of validation that the satisfactions of teaching and writing become subordinate to that validation strikes me as a sign of the infection. I'd be letting that one kind of validation rule the way I feel about my life, and I'd be ignoring the rewards and problems that come with the intellectual activity of writing and teaching. Perhaps now that I've seen things this way, I can begin to distance myself from that need for validation. And perhaps I can more easily do it because I have had a certain amount of validation. In either case, I find myself shaking my head at my socialization, at the power the need for the external validation seems to have (had?) over me.

Thursday, 17 *March* 1988

Last entry. In anticipating this moment, I've sometimes thought it would be clever to quote Huck Finn on finishing his book: "There ain't nothing more to write about, and I am rotten glad of it, because if I'd a knowed what a trouble it was to make a book I wouldn't a tackled it and ain't agoing to no more." But clever or not, letting Huck speak for me would be putting over a "stretcher" on you. This book has been trouble, but not much more than I expected. It has also been a way to alleviate trouble, a way to work through the events of these fifteen months by engaging in the reflection that writing about them required.

I also can't end like Huck or like any of my other favorite first-person narrators, because unlike them, I have not been living—or writing—a *Bildungsroman* or any other coherent and complete narrative. The journal will stop, but the life it recounts will not, and the relation of the events reported here to the shape of that whole life is still unknown. But writing the journal has helped me understand more clearly the current trajectory of that life.

In the very first entry, I said that I wanted to explore what it was like to live in the place that Betty and I had set out to reach so many years ago. Fifteen months later I have not so much achieved that purpose as come to understand it as misstated: There is no fixed place that we inhabit. Instead, we live in a place—or better, many places—that are constantly changing, and our relations to those places also change as our experiences draw upon or develop different parts of ourselves. I have stretched and pushed at various times and in various places these past fifteen months. My life has been touched in deep and complicated ways by the events and especially by some of the people I've written about here. Though I cannot fully articulate all the differences, I know that I am not in the same place as I was fifteen months ago, and that I am not exactly the same person I was then. Yet beneath the differences, much remains the same. Despite the changes, I have not been making any watershed decisions that radically redefine myself and my relation to the rest of the world. In coming to understand more fully how the multiple activities of my life impinge on, complement, interfere with, and sustain each other, I have also been affirming the choices that led me to these activities.

As I look ahead, I expect my life beyond the tenure track to be continuous with the experiences recounted here, but I also have a new appreciation for the difference between continuity and predictability. I cannot say how my next class, my next advisee, my next writing project will change the quality and texture of my life, and I cannot know whether those changes will be superficial and temporary or deep and enduring. I do know that to grow I need to be open to change. I also know that my ability to deal with change and my capacity for growth depend upon the strength I derive from the constants in my life, from the choices that I have been affirming over the last fifteen months.

In living with tenure, then, Betty and I got what we wanted, but it wasn't what we expected. It's more complicated—and more interesting. In answering our prayers, the gods have not punished us so much as they've educated and then quizzed us: life beyond the tenure track is not just like this (autonomy, security, possibility) and this (puzzlement, wonder, progress) and this (enjoyment, satisfaction, pleasure in balancing it all), but also like that (constraint from the institution and profession, overload from the demands) and that (strain, frustration, fatigue) and that (anxiety, rejection, pain). Do you want to go on doing it?

yes i said yes i will yes